PRAISE FOR *YANKS BEHIND THE LINES*

"There is no better expert than Jeffrey B. Miller to portray the brave young Americans who joined the CRB and served the Belgian and French civilians trapped behind German lines during the First World War. He gives us the story of their daily challenging life, the dangers they faced, their inventiveness, and their interactions with the impoverished civilians as well as with the German occupying forces and the local governments. *Yanks behind the Lines* is the story—and more—of the Americans who launched the first international nongovernmental organization. The Commission for Relief in Belgium, run by the brilliant personality of Herbert Hoover, is a moment in US history to be remembered and to be proud of."
—Clotilde Druelle-Korn, University of Limoges

"Jeffrey Miller's *Yanks behind the Lines* brings to life a little-known but hugely important and absolutely inspiring story: how nearly ten million civilians in German-occupied Belgium during World War I were saved from starvation, thanks to a group of idealistic Americans, led by a young organizational genius named Herbert Hoover. This was the shining moment when the United States first stepped upon the world stage as a generous force for all humanity. A moment worth the retelling—and remembering."
—Dayton Duncan, author and filmmaker

"*Yanks behind the Lines* is a fascinating portrait of America's first world war. Exploring a vital but little-known chapter of humanitarian intervention, Miller establishes the centrality to the American war experience of saving Belgium and France from famine."
—Branden Little, Weber State University

"With *Yanks behind the Lines*, Jeff Miller reminds us of an almost forgotten chapter from the history of World War I. The war not only cost the lives of millions of soldiers. For millions of civilians, it also meant deprivation, hardship, and hunger. In the territories of Belgium and northern France that were occupied by the Germans, American and Belgium relief organizations safeguarded the survival of the civil population. With his fascinating book, Miller raises a permanent monument to this remarkable humanitarian commitment. The book commemorates today the fact that practicing humanity in time of wars and crises can save human lives."
—Jens Thiel, Humboldt-University Berlin

BREAD TO

During WWI (1914-1918), a small band of neutral Americans in the Commission for Relief in Belgium (CRB) worked with the Belgian Comité National (CN) to create the largest food relief the world had ever seen, saving nearly 10 million civilians trapped behind German lines. It's a story few have heard.

Donations/Financing
Worldwide donations;
Allied & US Govt Subsidies

Purchasing/Whses
Buy wheat & other food;
Stockpile donations

Ships from around the world to Rotterdam
30-50 CRB ships in the process each day; Goal is 80,000 tons per month

TOTALS (1914-1919)

Imported to Belgium & Northern France
Wheat & Flour.......3.3 million metric tons
Total Food & Goods.......5.2 million metric tons

Donations/Money (in WWI US dollars)
Worldwide Donations.......$52.2 million
Govt Subsidies.......$700.5 million

Ships/Cargoes
Total delivered cargoes.......2,313
Average Cargoes per month.......43

U-boat/Other Losses
Total ships attacked, torpedoed, mined or sunk.......52
Total vessels lost.......38
Cargoes lost at sea.......114,000 metric tons

Belgium Before WWI
Slightly smaller than Maryland;
Imported 75% of all food needed;
Imported 250,000 tons a month;
Most industrialized country in Europe

Population Density per sq. mile
Belgium.......652
United Kingdom.......374
Germany.......310
France.......189
United States.......31

BELGIUM

Rotterdam to Canal Barges
300-400 pulled thru extensive B. canal network

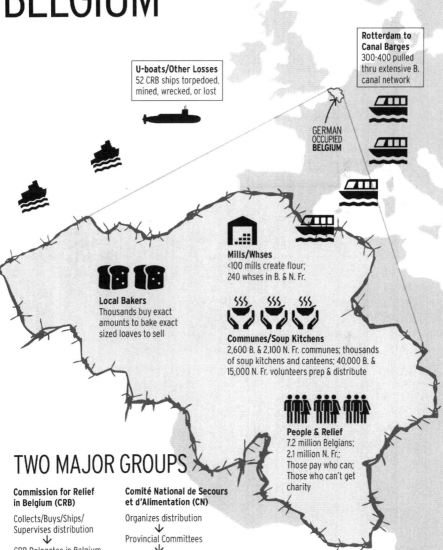

U-boats/Other Losses
52 CRB ships torpedoed, mined, wrecked, or lost

GERMAN OCCUPIED **BELGIUM**

Mills/Whses
<100 mills create flour;
240 whses in B. & N. Fr.

Local Bakers
Thousands buy exact amounts to bake exact sized loaves to sell

Communes/Soup Kitchens
2,600 B. & 2,100 N. Fr. communes; thousands of soup kitchens and canteens; 40,000 B. & 15,000 N. Fr. volunteers prep & distribute

People & Relief
7.2 million Belgians;
2.1 million N. Fr.;
Those pay who can;
Those who can't get charity

TWO MAJOR GROUPS

Commission for Relief in Belgium (CRB)

Collects/Buys/Ships/Supervises distribution
↓
CRB Delegates in Belgium (@185 men; 1 woman)
↓
Supervise agreements & distribution processes

Comité National de Secours et d'Alimentation (CN)

Organizes distribution
↓
Provincial Committees
↓
2,600 local communes
↓
40,000 volunteers prep and distribute food

Sources: CRB official statistics; *Public Relations of the Commission for Relief in Belgium*: Documents, 2 vols., George I. Gay and H. H. Fisher, Stanford University, Stanford University Press, 1929; various other books.

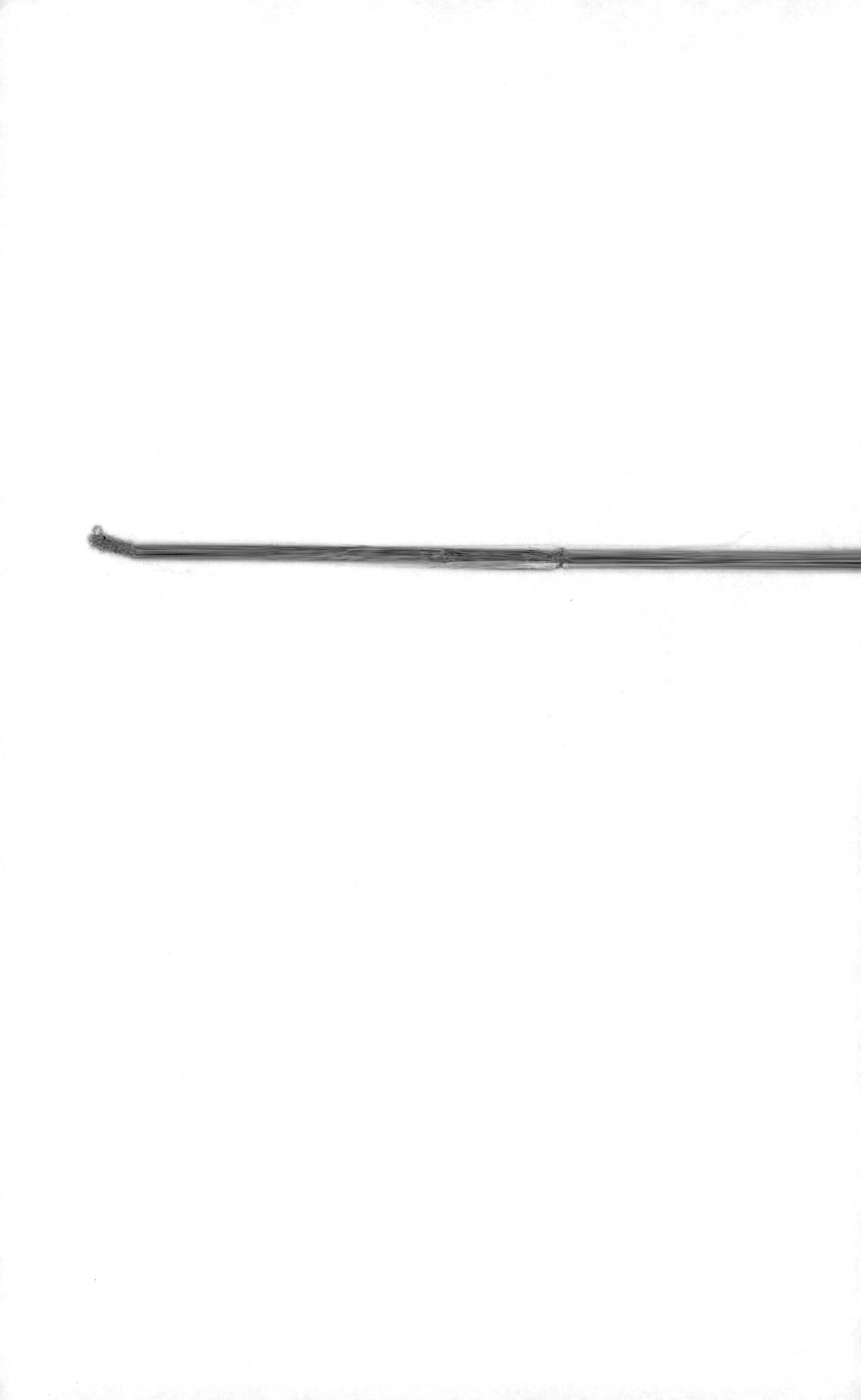

Yanks behind the Lines

By September 1914, Belgians throughout the country had no choice but to join the soup-kitchen lines as the country quickly consumed its dwindling supplies.

Public domain; Robert Withington, *In Occupied Belgium* (Boston: Cornhill Co., 1921).

Yanks behind the Lines

How the Commission for Relief in Belgium Saved Millions from Starvation during World War I

Jeffrey B. Miller

ROWMAN & LITTLEFIELD
Lanham • Boulder • New York • London

Published by Rowman & Littlefield
An imprint of The Rowman & Littlefield Publishing Group, Inc.
4501 Forbes Boulevard, Suite 200, Lanham, Maryland 20706
www.rowman.com

6 Tinworth Street, London SE11 5AL, United Kingdom

Cover photo: A German checkpoint along the electric fence that sealed off Belgium from Holland and the rest of the world. The sign, in German and Dutch, reads, "Caution, High voltage—danger of death." An electric fence powerful enough to kill was a new phenomenon that became known to many Belgians as the "dead thread." The photo was taken in 1915 near the Dutch village of Sluis in the southwest province of Zeeland. Photo courtesy of the Netherlands National Archives: Nationaal Archief/Collectie Spaarnestad/Het Leven/Fotograaf onbekend.

British Library Cataloguing in Publication Information Available

Library of Congress Cataloging-in-Publication Data

Names: Miller, Jeffrey B., 1952– author.
Title: Yanks behind the lines : how the Commission for Relief in Belgium saved millions from starvation during World War I / Jeffrey B. Miller.
Other titles: How the Commission for Relief in Belgium saved millions from starvation during World War I
Description: Lanham, Maryland : Rowman & Littlefield, [2020] | Includes bibliographical references and index.
Identifiers: LCCN 2020009563 (print) | LCCN 2020009564 (ebook) | ISBN 9781538141632 (cloth) | ISBN 9781538141649 (paperback) | ISBN 9781538141656 (epub)
Subjects: LCSH: World War, 1914–1918—Civilian relief—Belgium. | Commission for Relief in Belgium. | World War, 1914–1918—Food supply—Belgium. | World War, 1914–1918—Food supply—France, Northern. | World War, 1914–1918—Civilian relief—France, Northern. | Belgium—History—German occupation, 1914–1918.
Classification: LCC D638.B4 M553 2020 (print) | LCC D638.B4 (ebook) | DDC 940.4/7787309493—dc23
LC record available at https://lccn.loc.gov/2020009563
LC ebook record available at https://lccn.loc.gov/2020009564

™ The paper used in this publication meets the minimum requirements of American National Standard for Information Sciences—Permanence of Paper for Printed Library Materials, ANSI/NISO Z39.48-1992.

To my grandparents,
Milton M. Brown and Erica Bunge Brown,
who started it all.

To Susan Burdick—my north star,
my inspiration, my friend, my one true love.

Contents

Author's Note and Acknowledgments

I think of history in fluid terms. To me, capturing one moment in time is like capturing one moment in the bend of a river. What does the bend really look like? It all depends on your perspective. The pebble on the submerged riverbed sees it differently than the reeds on the right bank, the trees on the left, the bird gliding overhead, the fish battling upstream, or the bit of driftwood floating by.

When I was a teenager, I first heard the story of the Commission for Relief in Belgium (CRB) in tantalizing bits and pieces from my maternal grandparents, CRB delegate Milton M. Brown and Belgian dairy owner Erica Bunge. The interest that they inspired in me led to sporadic research and a long-winded, unpublished novel, *Honor Bound.* After turning to a career in nonfiction that's spanned forty years, I've spent the past ten years focusing full-time on collecting, cataloging, reading, and assimilating the documents, letters, journals, and photos of close to fifty CRB-related people. I have also studied and read about War World I and German-occupied Belgium, and I've written two nonfiction *Kirkus Reviews* Best Books of the Year (2014 and 2018) on the subject.

This book, *Yanks behind the Lines*, is the culmination and the distillation of all my work into one concise history for readers interested in learning more about one of America's finest hours in humanitarian aid. The focus is on the CRB and its Belgian counterpart, the Comité National (CN), within the context of German-occupied Belgium. I have touched only lightly on events outside the occupation because I did not want to soften my focus and I knew that numerous great books have already covered those subjects better than I could.

It is also important to note that the CRB and the CN were products of their time—women were never considered for executive positions within either organization, and only one woman, Charlotte Kellogg, was officially recognized as a CRB delegate (see chapter 6). The early 1900s was a tumultuous period of seismic upheavals in social, political, generational, ethnic, and gender norms. Even a woman's basic right to vote had not yet been secured, with success years away. The story of the CRB, CN, and German-occupied Belgium—as told by much of the historical record of letters, journals, documents, reports, and books—reflects that time and the supposedly secondary role women played in food relief. This single book cannot do full justice to the tremendous contributions of women on both sides of the Atlantic, although it does attempt to show numerous tips of the huge icebergs that lay below.

With those caveats in mind, I hope you enjoy *Yanks behind the Lines*, my tribute to the men and women of Belgium and the CRB during World War I. This book contains my vision of who those people were and what they did. It is my vision. It is my perspective of the bend in the river.

No book is a one-person project. I've been fortunate to have a team of professionals and multiple friends and family members who have helped me make this book the best possible.

In the research stage, I am grateful for the warm, welcoming, and helpful assistance of numerous individuals. At the Herbert Hoover Presidential Library Archives in West Branch, Iowa, Director Thomas F. Schwartz and his great team of Matthew T. Schaefer, outreach archivist; Spencer Howard; Craig Wright; and Lynn Smith were of tremendous help, as was independent researcher Wesley Beck.

At the Hoover Institution Archives at Stanford University, Carol A. Leadenham, assistant archivist for reference (now retired), and David Jacobs, archival specialist, guided me well. I was also aided by independent researcher and PhD candidate in history Michelle Mengsu Chang. Evelyn McMillan—a writer, researcher about World War I Belgian lace, and a librarian at Stanford University—provided information and proofed the book's sections about the Belgian lace industry.

At the National Archives at College Park, Maryland, Amy Reytar was especially helpful in navigating the State Department records.

In Belgium, I was aided in research by four men who live northeast of Antwerp and have become friends: Raymond Roelands, Roger Van den Bleeken, Marc Brans, and André De Vleeschouwer. They have studied for years the history of their area, especially during World War I. Roelands is the author of *Geschiedenis van Kasteeldomein "Oude Gracht" in Hoogboom* (*History of the Castle Domain "Oude Gracht" in Hoogboom*); Van den Bleeken and Brans are two of the authors of *Cappellen in den Grooten Oorlog* (*Cappellen in the Great War*). In Germany, I had important help regarding the German deportations from German historian Dr. Jens Thiel.

In 2011, I was fortunate to have a chance meeting at the Herbert Hoover Presidential Library Archives with Dr. Branden Little, a history professor who teaches at Weber State University in Ogden, Utah. He has been studying the CRB and many other humanitarian relief efforts for more than a decade. In the highly competitive world of academic research and writing, Dr. Little is unusual in his friendly openness in giving of his time and historical sources. I'm grateful that he has become a friend who has aided me in countless ways, big and small.

I must also thank the ever-gracious Dr. George H. Nash, scholar and biographer of Herbert Hoover. An extremely accessible and amiable man, he has been constantly supportive since I first began researching the CRB. When my efforts to find a critical document were fruitless, he was kind enough to send me a copy from his own files.

During the years that this project has been my life, I have been fortunate to come into contact with a number of descendants of CRB delegates. They were tremendously helpful and willing to share any information they had about their relatives, and they gave me permission to use that information to help tell the CRB story. They include Dr. Erskine Carmichael, nephew of delegate Oliver C. Carmichael; John P. Nelson, son of delegate David T. Nelson; Sherman (now deceased) and Prentiss Gray, son and grandson, respectively, of delegate Prentiss Gray; Margaret Hunt, granddaughter of delegate E. E. Hunt; Mariette (now deceased) and George Wickes, daughter and son, respectively, of delegate Francis Wickes; Andy Hoover and Margaret Hoover, grandson and great-granddaughter, respectively, of Herbert C. Hoover; Jim Torrey, son of delegate Clare Torrey; and Jessica Tuck, granddaughter of delegate William Hallam Tuck (who married Hilda Bunge, my great-aunt).

I am indebted to professional editor Tom Locke, who ably handled the heavy lifting of initial editing. The book's infographic was developed by professional graphic designer and friend Laurie Shields.

At Rowman & Littlefield, I will be forever grateful to my editor, Susan McEachern, who believed in me and brought my book idea to fruition. Thanks also go to Katelyn Turner, assistant editor; Alden Perkins, senior production editor; and Kim Ball Smith, copy editor, for shepherding *Yanks behind the Lines* through its various stages of production.

Overall, this book would not have been written and published without the friendship of a small group of people who have believed in me and this project beyond all reasonable expectations. The group includes Tina Miller, Leslie Miller, Gene Zimmerman, Jim Torrey, Evie Newell, David Newell, David Hiller, Mike Bren, Jessica Tuck, and Eric Karcher. Thank you all—your commitment has truly overwhelmed me.

Finally, I must thank my grandparents, who started me on this CRB journey; my parents, who taught me that passion and self-discipline can move mountains; and my wife, Susan Burdick, without whom I would never be the writer I am today. I owe her all that I am—and more.

Reader Aids

CRB—Statistical Overview

November 1, 1914 to August 31, 1919

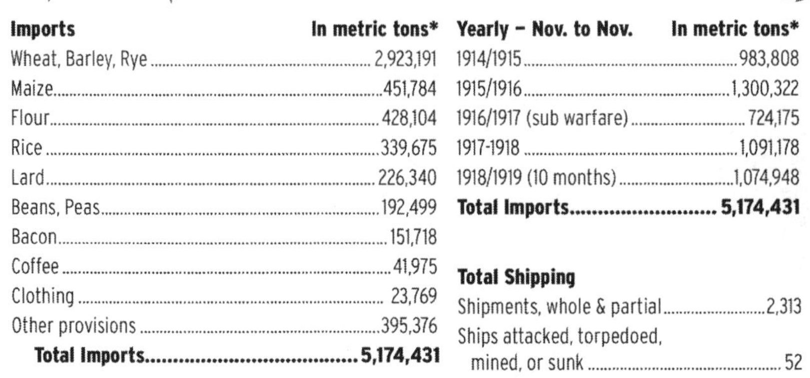

Imports	**In metric tons***
Wheat, Barley, Rye	2,923,191
Maize	451,784
Flour	428,104
Rice	339,675
Lard	226,340
Beans, Peas	192,499
Bacon	151,718
Coffee	41,975
Clothing	23,769
Other provisions	395,376
Total Imports	**5,174,431**

Yearly – Nov. to Nov.	**In metric tons***
1914/1915	983,808
1915/1916	1,300,322
1916/1917 (sub warfare)	724,175
1917-1918	1,091,178
1918/1919 (10 months)	1,074,948
Total Imports	**5,174,431**

Total Shipping

Shipments, whole & partial	2,313
Ships attacked, torpedoed, mined, or sunk	52
Of those, ships totally lost	38
Cargoes lost at sea	114,000 metric tons*

Total Funding for Relief Operations

Total American		**$421,153,287**
(US Treasury, Loans	*$386,632,260)*	
(US Charity	*$34,521,027)*	
Total British Empire		**$125,686,364**
(British Treasury, Loans	*$109,045,329)*	
(British Empire Charity	*$16,641,035)*	
French Treasury, Loans		**$204,862,854**
General Charity		**$1,128,774**
Commercial Exchange, Remittances		**$6,328,328**
Operating Surplus		**$135,637,543**
Total Funding		**$894,797,150**

American 47.1%
British Empire 14%
French Treasury, Loans 23%
Operating Surplus 15.1%
General Charity 0.1%
Commercial Exchange, Remittance 0.7%

Total Costs

Operations	$927,681,485
(Administrative	*$3,908,893)*

0.43%, or less than ½ of 1 percent;
less than 50 cents on every $100

* All tons on this page and throughout this book are metric tons.

Source: CRB official statistics: *The Commission for Relief in Belgium: Statistical Review of Relief Operations*, George I. Gay, Stanford University Press, n.d.

German-Occupied Belgium and Northern France during WWI. Three major zones were created by the Germans after the invasion: 1. The Occupation Zone (shaded) included the majority of Belgium and was controlled by the German civil government, which was ruled by Governor General Baron von Bissing. 2. Two Army Zones named Etape were controlled by each regional military authority. The French Etape contained six districts named after their major city or commune: Longwy, Charleville, Vervins, St. Quentin, Valenciennes, and Lille. The Belgian Etape had two districts: West Flanders and East Flanders. 3. Within each Etape district was a thin strip of land right behind the trenches that was called the Operations Zone (indicated by the dotted line just to the right of the trench line). Not part of the German occupation was Free Belgium, a tiny piece of land between the trenches and the French border where King Albert and his Belgian Army were stationed through the majority of the war.

PRIMARY GROUPS AND PEOPLE IN THE BOOK

The Relief Organizations

The Commission for Relief in Belgium (CRB)

Founded in London on October 22, 1914, by Herbert C. Hoover and a small group of Americans, the CRB was a nongovernmental volunteer relief organization attempting to do what had never been done before: feed an entire nation trapped in the middle of a world war. Major responsibilities included securing financial support; buying and shipping goods; warehousing, processing, and releasing those supplies to local communes; supervising operations to catch abuses by Belgians and Germans; and handling multiple government relations and guarantees necessary for relief to continue. Supervision within Belgium and northern France was conducted by a small band of American "delegates" to ensure British demands that no food was taken by the Germans. These mostly young men had to maintain strict neutrality as they watched the Belgians suffer under the harsh German rule.

The Comité National de Secours et d'Alimentation (CN)

Founded in Brussels on September 5, 1914, the CN was a Belgian organization led by financial giant Émile Francqui. The CN handled the storage, preparation, and distribution of relief supplies through ten provincial committees, 2,600 communes, and more than 40,000 Belgian workers to feed more than seven million civilians every day. It was critical that the CRB and the CN work well together, despite Hoover's and Francqui's dislike and distrust of each other.

The Comité d'Alimentation du Nord de la France (CF)

In early 1915, more than two million northern French trapped behind German lines were added to the CRB's responsibilities. The CF resembled the CN, but because the CF's territory was in the German War Zones, it was severely restricted by the German military. This meant the CF had a central committee in Brussels, although it was more of an accounting group than an executive committee. Overall coordinating control was maintained by the Brussels CRB office, while onsite supervision was handled by CRB delegates, and distribution was carried out by fifteen thousand locals at the district, regional, and communal levels.

The Comité Hispano-Hollandais

The last CRB delegates left Belgium in May 1917 because of America's April entry into the war. After negotiations, an agreement was struck that a joint committee of Spanish and Dutch, the Comité Hispano-Hollandais, would manage the relief and the new Dutch and Spanish delegates.

The Americans

Officials

James W. Gerard, US ambassador to Germany

Appointed by President Wilson in October 1913, Gerard was the person Hoover turned to whenever he needed to petition the German civilian government for critical agreements and guarantees.

Hugh Gibson, secretary to the US Legation in Brussels

Gibson was thirty-one and nearing the middle of his diplomatic career when the war broke out. He earned admiration and respect for his hard work, dedication to helping the Belgians, and unfailing sense of humor. He and Whitlock rarely saw eye to eye on issues.

Walter H. Page, US ambassador to Britain

Page became America's patron minister of relief in London and would provide critical support to Hoover and the CRB during numerous crises.

Brand Whitlock, minister of the US Legation in Brussels

When Whitlock was appointed in early 1914, he was looking forward to writing novels at the traditionally noneventful legation (a lower rank than an embassy). He would be thoroughly tested by the war and his unofficial job as major patron minister for the relief program. He would become a figure who was both respected and ridiculed, beloved and belittled. Also in Brussels were two other officials from neutral countries who were acting as relief patrons: *Spanish minister Marquis de Villalobar* and *Dutch minister Maurice van Vollenhoven.*

CRB Delegates

Herbert Clark Hoover, founder and leader of the CRB

A highly successful forty-year-old US mining engineer, Hoover was living in London before the war and searching for an entry into public service or politics. When war erupted, he organized assistance for stranded American tourists. When he heard about the potential for mass starvation in Belgium, he volunteered to help and started the CRB. Known as the Chief to the CRB delegates, Hoover would later become the thirty-first president of the United States, in part due to his humanitarian work during and after World War I.

Milton M. Brown

A 1913 Princeton graduate, Brown became a CRB delegate and entered German-occupied Belgium in early 1916. He was given the task of running the newly formed CRB clothing department. He faced continued opposition from the CN, which had developed its own extensive clothes-processing network independent of the CRB.

Prentiss Gray

After years of working in his father's steamship company, Gray was one of the few delegates who had the critical shipping experience that the CRB needed. He would become the assistant director of the CRB Brussels office and later be one of the last Americans to leave Belgium.

Joseph C. Green

A scholar who was fluent in French, Green joined the CRB in the autumn of 1915 and within a few months was accused by the Germans of being a spy for the Allies. Later, he would become the head of the CRB's Inspection and Control Department. His efforts would enrage Francqui and cause a major crisis between Hoover and Francqui.

Edward Eyre Hunt

A magazine journalist in America, E. E. Hunt became a war correspondent so he could see the war up close. When he got a clear vision of what was happening in Belgium, he joined the CRB to do something concrete for those in need. He became the CRB's chief delegate to Antwerp Province, where he helped create and develop food-relief processes.

Tracy B. Kittredge

Twenty-three-year-old Kittredge was part of the first group of ten Oxford students to enter German-occupied Belgium in December 1914. He became a well-respected delegate and recruited other notables. He took over writing the CRB's history from Joe Green and produced a fine insider's look at the relief program titled *The History of the Commission for Relief in Belgium, 1914–1917*. Hoover rejected it as the official history (probably because it detailed the relief's internal problems that Hoover hated to air publicly). It was never published for the general public, but it stands as a significant contribution to the story of the CRB.

Maurice Pate

One of the youngest CRB delegates at twenty-one, Pate was mature and level-headed as he faced multiple problems within Belgium and northern France. His experiences in the CRB would lead to a lifetime of service, most notably on behalf of children as the founding director of UNICEF after World War II.

The Belgians

Edouard Bunge and his daughter Erica

A wealthy Antwerp merchant, Bunge was vice president of the provincial relief committee, owner of Chateau Oude Gracht, and widowed father of five daughters. In early 1915, he and his twenty-three-year-old daughter, Erica, developed a dairy farm that sent milk every day to the children of Antwerp.

Émile Francqui, founder and leader of the CN

One of the most powerful financial men in Belgium before the war, Francqui ruled the Comité National like a dictator. He and Hoover had met earlier and disliked each other immensely. With his passion for his country and his domineering personality, Francqui would create continual problems for Hoover and the CRB.

The British

Sir Edward Grey, British foreign secretary

Grey was the primary official charged with resolving disputes between the CRB and British government. He became a strong supporter of the program and helped the CRB survive many crises. He appointed Lord Percy to act as liaison with the CRB.

Lord Eustace Percy, British foreign service

As the everyday liaison between the CRB and the British government, Percy's job was to smooth the way with various governmental departments. Hoover said, "His fine idealism, high intelligence, and capacity for hard work were rare in any country. . . . He knew all the paths through the red tape of government. He quickly developed a friendship for the Commission, and he never flagged in supporting us among his official colleagues."

The Germans

Baron Moritz Ferdinand von Bissing, German governor general of Belgium

A seventy-year-old Prussian military officer who had been born into the German landed gentry, von Bissing had had a distinguished military career before being appointed by the Kaiser to be governor general of Belgium. Demanding in his adherence to rules, regulations, and the hierarchy of authority, von Bissing was determined to bend Belgian citizens to his will. He also became a major stumbling block for the CRB and CN.

Baron Oscar von der Lancken, head of the German political department in Belgium

A sophisticated, multilingual diplomat, von der Lancken had spent ten years as a counselor in the German Embassy in Paris. In Brussels, von der Lancken was named head of the political department of the German civilian government and was responsible for relations with the CRB and CN. He was no great friend of Americans.

Preface

This is the true story of one of America's finest hours in humanitarian relief, a story that is unknown to most Americans. It is a tale that started more than one hundred years ago but still reverberates through our twenty-first-century world.

Today, whenever there are civilians anywhere in the world in harm's way—from a natural disaster to an armed conflict—the nearly universal response has been: "America will help." That was not the case before World War I (1914–1918). Prior to that horrific conflict—and long before US aid programs such as the Marshall Plan, the Berlin Airlift, and the Food for Peace program—America was better known as a nation of shopkeepers more interested in the bottom line than in saving strangers in need.

What helped alter that view was an American-led food relief program during World War I that began the redefinition of how the world saw America and how America perceived its role in the world. The program was founded and run by the nongovernmental Commission for Relief in Belgium (CRB) and its Belgian counterpart, the Comité National de Secours et d'Alimentation (commonly known as the Comité National, or CN). Working together, they saved from starvation nearly ten million Belgian and northern French civilians trapped behind German lines during the four years of World War I, making it the largest food relief program the world had ever seen.

The statistics are still staggering, especially given that it took place during a precomputer age devoid of technological advances such as commercial aviation, radio, or TV. More than 2,300 ship cargoes and thousands of canal barges carried more than five million metric tons of food and clothes into German-occupied territory, where 55,000 Belgians and northern French distributed it to millions of civilians every day. The operation spent nearly $1 billion in 1914 dollars (approximately $25 billion in 2020 dollars) but boasted an overhead of less than one half of 1 percent (less than fifty cents out of every $100). And the nearly ten million civilian lives saved are a sad but eloquent counterpoint to the more than nine million soldiers killed in the Great War.

It was an unparalleled feat that had never been attempted and was thought to be impossible—private citizens of a neutral country feeding an entire nation caught in the middle of a world war. The challenges were immense, from logistical obstacles and international intrigues to internal conflicts between the CRB and CN.

The humanitarian aid was necessary because after Germany's August 4, 1914, invasion of Belgium to get to its real goal, France, the Germans refused to feed civilians within Belgium and a thin strip of northern France that they occupied. Prior to the war, Belgium had been the most industrialized country in Europe and had imported more than 75 percent of its daily food. Mass starvation would begin by winter if nothing was done.

News of the impending catastrophe reached London just as a highly successful American mining engineer was wrapping up months of volunteer leadership of a group he had founded to assist the more than one hundred thousand American tourists stranded in Europe by the outbreak of war. He had turned forty on August 10 and was contemplating what to do next in his life. He was a wealthy man, but as one associate said, "He didn't want to become just richer. He wanted sincerely . . . to do public service and help people."

By late September 1914, the American was approached to help the Belgians. With little thought for his mining operations, he agreed to tackle the impossible task of feeding an entire nation. On October 22, 1914, he and a small group of Americans formed the CRB.

His name was Herbert C. Hoover, and his roles in the CRB and later as America's "food czar" and head of the governmental American Relief Administration (ARA) were, in large part, why he was later propelled into the White House as the country's thirty-first president.

Back in 1914, one of Hoover's first challenges was the British refusal to allow food through its blockade unless neutral American supervisors, or CRB "delegates," were inside Belgium to guarantee the food went only to civilians. Hoover needed US volunteers immediately but knew it would take weeks, if not months, to get them from America. Where could he find them in Britain?

He found some of the first CRB delegates at Oxford University. The school term was ending, and numerous American students (most of them Rhodes Scholars) were about to start six weeks of winter break. On Friday, December 4, 1914, the first ten Oxford students reported to the CRB office in London. They would leave the next day for neutral Rotterdam and then cross the border into war-ravaged Belgium.

Hoover took a moment from his other CRB tasks—buying tons of food, finding ships to haul it, getting all international parties to agree on conditions, securing financing for the millions he was spending every month—to speak with the young Americans.

"When this war is over," he told them solemnly, "the thing that will stand out will not be the number of dead and wounded, but the record of those efforts which went to save life."

In total, approximately 185 men and one woman (Charlotte Kellogg, wife of CRB director Vernon Kellogg) officially served as delegates in Belgium or northern France from October 1914 until May 1917, when the last Americans had to leave German-occupied territories because of America's April entry into the war.

The majority of those delegates were idealistic university students in their twenties who embodied a spirit of giving and self-sacrifice. They dropped everything in their own lives to travel thousands of miles, enter the prison that was German-occupied Belgium, tackle a job that had never been done before, and rein in their personal feelings regarding the German occupation—all to help total strangers.

Many of them did so unreservedly, with no expectation of anything in return. They did what they did simply because it was the right thing, the moral thing, to do. And in the end, the result of their labors—and the work of thousands of Belgians and northern French—was the world's largest food relief program that would set the gold standard for future humanitarian efforts.

As a result of this massive aid program, Hoover was loved worldwide and became known to many as the Great Humanitarian. And the tremendous impact the CRB had on the world would help begin the metamorphosis of the United States from a nation of self-serving shopkeepers to a world leader in humanitarian aid.

Today, Hoover's presidential fall from grace has been well-documented, while his initial rise to glory during the most horrific war the world had ever witnessed has been all but forgotten. Also neglected have been the individual stories of the young CRB delegates, who did so much to serve humanity while asking nothing in return.

Their stories deserve to be told and remembered.

Yanks behind the Lines focuses on this little-known story of massive humanitarian aid within the context of German-occupied Belgium and northern France. It does not attempt to tell the story of World War I, but it does touch on war-specific events outside of Belgium that had a significant impact on the food relief.

1

1914, Setting the Stage

"To understand Germany, you must think in centuries." While the German who said that believed he was speaking philosophically about his country alone, he was aptly describing the soul of every European power at the turn of the twentieth century. Major conflicts from the past—such as the Thirty Years' War (1618–1648), the Napoleonic Wars (1803–1815), and the Franco-Prussian War (1870–1871)—were still very much alive in the hearts, minds, and attitudes of many Europeans.

As a result, each country's collective memory was as much comforting as it was confining and controlling. By the summer of 1914, decades of European political posturing, diplomatic wrangling, treaty negotiations, and international skirmishes—inflamed by the June 28 assassination of Austria's Archduke Franz Ferdinand and his wife, Sophie—led to Tuesday morning, August 4, 1914, when the armies of German Kaiser Wilhelm II invaded neutral Belgium on the way to their ultimate goal, France.

BATTLE LINES FORGE THE WESTERN FRONT

The invading force was quickly surprised by the fierce resistance of the small Belgian Army and the sporadic acts of self-guided *franc-tireurs*, or guerrilla fighters. German soldiers' reactions to such opposition were swift and brutal—burning, looting, and mass executions in many towns and villages, including Louvain (Flemish, Leuven), Dinant, and Visé. To avoid such devastation, the Belgian capital of Brussels declared itself an open city that would not oppose the Germans as long as they marched in peacefully, which they did on August 20.

Figure 1.1. During the invasion of Belgium, German soldiers participated in burning, looting, and mass executions. The ancient university town of Louvain (Flemish, Leuven) lay in ruins after the Germans ransacked it for nearly a week, August 25–30, 1914. Public domain.

Belgium's neutrality—which had been sanctioned by all the major European powers in the 1839 Treaty of London—was a significant factor in the war. Germany's flagrant violation of Belgium's neutrality led to Britain entering the war to officially honor its commitment to that neutrality. Sides were quickly established: the Allies, or Entente Powers (Britain, France, and Russia), against the Central Powers (Germany, Austria-Hungary, and the Ottoman Empire). The United States declared its own neutrality on August 4, with President Woodrow Wilson detailing the American position in an address to Congress on August 19. The American government officially wanted nothing to do with what it saw as a strictly European dispute.

In September on the Western Front, the British and French were finally able to halt the German advance—which came within twenty-five miles (forty km) of Paris—and then push it back slightly. This success, however, came at a heavy price: in the war's initial major battles—the First Battle of the Marne and the First Battle of the Aisne—more than two million men took part, with nearly five hundred thousand killed or wounded. The stalling of the German offensive also led to months of the "Race to the Sea," in which each side swung west to outmaneuver the other until both sides had reached the coast of the North Sea.

Meanwhile, the thought-to-be-impregnable city of Antwerp, defended by a ring of fifty-four fortresses, was taken by the use of long-range artillery that simply stood miles back and blasted the forts to rubble. The city was bombed for three consecutive days before it surrendered on October 10.

In a final stand along the Yser River, Belgian King Albert and his remaining troops stood firm to save critical English Channel ports. Knowing he could not hold out forever, the king ordered the opening of sluice gates during high tide at the seaside town of Nieuport. The subsequent flooding created an impassable barrier two miles (3.2 km) wide and shoulder deep from the sea to the town of Dixmude. This watery obstacle protected a thin slice of Belgium between the Germans and the French border where the king remained with his men. The trenches dug there comprised the most western section of the Western Front and became known as the Yser Front, or the Western Flemish Front. The Belgian Army, along with parts of the French Army, manned the trenches. King Albert established his headquarters just south of the trenches and just north of the French border, near the town of Veurne.

Nearby but further inland, the little town of Ypres lent its name to one of the most massive battles of the war. The First Battle of Ypres pitted the Germans against the British in a fight that raged from October 20 until the third week of November, with hardly a movement of the line either way. Altogether, the battle took the lives of nearly a quarter of a million men.

By late November/early December, the Race to the Sea and the First Battle of Ypres were over, and both Allied and German soldiers began to dig in, establishing the four-hundred-mile front of trenches from Switzerland to the North Sea that would barely change through four years of war.

During December 1914, many of the men on both sides were sick and tired of the war and spontaneously created mini-truces and cease-fires up and down the line, culminating in the incredible Christmas Truce of 1914. Later stories told of opposing soldiers exchanging greetings, newspapers, food, and drink. Men from both sides sang songs together and reportedly even played soccer matches in the no-man's-land between the trenches.

The world would never again see such fraternization during World War I. And the bloodshed—which up to that time had shocked the world—would be equaled, and then some, in the remaining years of the war.

GERMAN OCCUPATION BEGINS

By the end of 1914, the Germans began to settle into the occupation of Belgium and a small section of northern France that lay within their domain. Even though the Germans had known their neighbor to the west for thousands of years, they seemed to have little sense of how independent, strong-willed, and resistant the Belgians would be to occupation.

Belgium was no stranger to invading armies. In fact, it was known as the cockpit of Europe, referring to the cockfighting ring where two fierce roosters would battle to exhaustion or death. In the past, Belgium had always been a region without its own country—pieces of which had belonged at times to France, Germany, Holland, Spain, and Austria. Its people were eyewitnesses to many other nations' battles across their land—most notably the Battle of Waterloo, on the outskirts of Brussels, where Napoleon suffered his final defeat in 1815.

Before the war, Belgian nationalism was thought to be nonexistent because the country had been formalized only in 1830 and because there were stark socioeconomic and linguistic divides between the Walloons, who lived primarily in the south and spoke French, and the Flemings, who lived in the north and spoke Flemish (a Dutch derivative). Few in Europe felt that such a country could possess strong nationalistic feelings.

That assumption was smashed quickly with the German invasion. According to Hugh Gibson, secretary of the US Legation (a lower rank than an embassy) in Brussels and a man who had a front-row seat to the August 1914 invasion, "Even the Belgians themselves were surprised at the depth and sincerity of the patriotism that was revealed."

The surprise was on both sides. Gibson explained, "The Germans, of course, were convinced that no real national sentiment existed and the spirited defense of the Belgians quite upset their calculations. Several German officers have spoken to me complainingly of the behavior of the Belgians as though they had in some way misled and swindled Germany by endeavoring to maintain their neutrality and independence."

Reflective of this unexpected nationalism was a Belgian story told of two "wizened city clerks" living under the German rule in occupied Brussels. As they discussed the war, one asked the other, "When and how will the Germans be beaten?" The other man shrugged his shoulders and declared solemnly, "They were beaten when they set foot for the first time in Belgium."

Before the war, Belgium, with 7.5 million residents and a landmass slightly smaller than Maryland, was the most industrialized country in Europe and the most densely populated with 652 people per square mile (the United Kingdom had 374, Germany 310, France 189, and America 31). The country imported more than 75 percent of the food it consumed and more than 78 percent of the cereals necessary for making bread, which was a vital part of every Belgian's diet.

American journalist Arthur Humphries explained: "To the Belgian, bread is not only the staff of life; it is the legs. . . . At home in America, we think of bread as something that goes with the rest of the meal; to the poorer classes of Belgians the rest of the meal goes with bread."

When the Germans invaded, suddenly Belgium's factories and coal mines were closed and thousands were out of work. Much of the harvest was destroyed, requisitioned, or left rotting in the fields for lack of workers to harvest it. And the Germans refused to provide food to the conquered Belgians. In fact, the invaders simply took food and goods wherever and whenever they wanted, despite the world's shocked reaction to their lack of responsibility. With winter only a few months away, a Belgium food crisis was coming closer every day.

But as one observer noted, "Famine sweeps over a country like a blighting wind—yesterday even its approach was unsuspected; to-day it is everywhere." By September

1914, food in Belgium was expensive and getting harder to find, but it was still in markets, restaurants, and unharvested fields that could be scavenged. Farmers retained at least some of their livestock and worked hard to produce whatever they could, no matter how small the quantity.

On the international stage, full alarm bells regarding a pending food crisis had not yet been sounded (that would happen only in October, when it became a cacophony), but within Belgium, some people and organizations had begun taking action even before the war's first shots were fired. On August 1, the Belgian government bought the entire wheat supply on the market in Antwerp and stored it for the coming need. Some began stockpiling on a local level as well.

BELGIAN EFFORTS TO BEGIN FOOD RELIEF

Overall, the country was better prepared than some for such a food crisis. It boasted numerous wealthy individuals of the upper class and merchant class who traditionally helped during tough times. The general population was ready to sacrifice and volunteer if called upon, and the country had an extensive network of canals used for mass distribution of goods. But by far the most important element to aid Belgium in this particular situation was the country's commune system of governance.

A federal government was in place, but much of everyday life and everyday affairs were handled by the more than 2,600 local communes throughout Belgium. Each hamlet, village, and town had a commune that kept track of all residents; acted to represent, protect, and adjudicate when needed; and provided charity for those who could not provide for themselves. In larger cities, there were multiple communes to handle different districts. The greater Brussels area alone had sixteen communes that dealt with its seven hundred thousand residents.

These communes worked so independently from one another and from the higher levels of government that they continued to function relatively well even after the Belgian government fled to Le Havre, France, and King Albert stayed with his troops on the Yser River.

"The whole machinery of the Belgian central government had been broken down or swept away by the invader," according to one historian. "Only the communal administrations remained fairly intact and possessed the liberty of action to permit them to meet the crisis brought on by the shortage of food and the tremendous increase in destitution. It was a happy circumstance for the Belgian population that the local government was so well organized and so relatively independent in normal times."

Because of this, the communes were the perfect vehicles for massive food distribution—if only an adequate and steady supply could be found.

The first Belgians to feel the effects of the war and therefore require assistance were the August refugees. Those who had left their homes in advance of the German armies or had been forced out by the invaders sought food, clothing, and shelter from anyone who would give it. Many headed to Brussels. Hundreds of thousands had already made it into Holland and France, but many more were still on the move because the fighting in Belgium was still fluid and would not be contained to trench warfare until November.

Communes all over Belgium attempted to deal with the coming food shortages. In Brussels, a group of wealthy individuals came together to form the nongovernmental Comité Central de Secours et d'Alimentation (Central Committee of Assistance and Provisioning, commonly known as the Comité Central) for the purpose of supplying Brussels with food. The group's elder statesman was seventy-six-year-old Ernest Solvay, the country's richest man, a distinguished and respected businessman, and a world-renowned philanthropist. The committee's president and forceful leader was fifty-one-year-old Émile Francqui, a powerhouse in the financial world and director of the Société Générale de Belgique, arguably the most important financial institution in Belgium.

Somewhat surprisingly, in the organizational meeting of the Comité Central, there were three Americans: two businessmen living in Brussels, Dannie Heineman and William Hulse, and diplomat Hugh Gibson. According to one historian, they

Figure 1.2. Émile Francqui was a major force in the Belgian financial world and a man who disliked Hoover. Francqui became the president and driving force of the Comité National, which was the Belgian counterpart of Hoover's CRB.

Public domain; CRB portrait book, Herbert Hoover Presidential Library Archives, West Branch, Iowa.

were there because forty-one-year-old Heineman had "suggested to Francqui and others that it would be of great utility to the proposed [Comité Central] to invite the [neutral] American and Spanish Ministers . . . to act as patrons; in this way the committee would be given a neutral character and protection against requisition of its stocks of supplies might be assured."

Francqui, ever the pragmatist, liked the idea and knew that in this case Belgian self-reliance could not achieve all that was needed. As a result, Brussels-based US minister Brand Whitlock and Spanish minister Marquis de Villalobar y O'Neill became patrons of the Comité Central. The first official meeting of the committee took place on Saturday, September 5. It was established that four major jobs had to be accomplished before food could arrive in Brussels:

1. The Germans had to agree to allow the food in and to not requisition it.
2. The English had to allow food through the blockade that it was establishing to cut off Germany from world trade.
3. Processes had to be developed for purchasing, shipping, transportation, and distribution.
4. Some entity had to be found to pay for such a giant undertaking.

It was a daunting task, but the stakes were too high not to try. Those in positions of prominence began using their contacts and special avenues of influence to apply pressure to the governor general of Belgium, Field Marshal Baron Wilhelm Leopold Colmar von der Goltz, to formally guarantee that the Germans would not requisition any imported food.

The task was a little easier than some would have imagined. At this stage of the war, the German thought process was straightforward: they would not feed the Belgians; there was little left to take from Belgium; they needed every man at the front; peaceful Belgians did not require many soldiers to control; and Belgians would remain peaceful if they were fed.

This logic dictated that a neutral effort to bring food to the Belgians would serve German interests. On September 17, a letter from von der Goltz to Whitlock gave a hands-off guarantee. The German agreed "not to requisition the shipments of wheat and flour destined for the alimentation [the provision of nourishment] of the Belgian civil population." However, he also stated that he and his civil government would decide on and supervise distribution. While that stipulation was totally unacceptable to Francqui and the Comité Central, it was felt that that battle could be waged later if all other hurdles of food importation had been overcome.

HERBERT HOOVER TACKLES BELGIUM RELIEF

The Comité Central gave the task of finding and securing food for importation to Millard K. Shaler, an American mining engineer living in Brussels. Armed with travel permits and permissions from the Germans, Shaler reached Holland but found no available food for purchase, so he went on to Britain. There he was able to buy 2,500 tons of wheat, rice, and beans but could not secure permission to export the food to Belgium.

The reason was clear—he was a private citizen representing a Brussels citizen group that had no formal diplomatic backing. That did not get him far in cutting through the red tape of British rules and regulations. He tried to speak with the Belgian minister in London to obtain official Belgian government support; he never got past the reception desk. Shaler sat stymied in London for the rest of September and into October, telling anyone who would listen that the Belgians needed help right away.

Meanwhile, another mining engineer, Herbert Hoover, who had been living in London before the war, was wrapping up months of volunteer service as the head of a group he had founded to assist the 100,000 to 150,000 American tourists stranded by the war (an accurate count was never made).

Born in West Branch, Iowa, to Quaker parents, Hoover had been orphaned at nine and sent to live with his uncle's family in Newburg, Oregon. There he fully developed into a quiet, intelligent, headstrong boy who became an earnest young man in the first class of Stanford University. On campus, he was initially shy but soon showed himself to be a natural-born leader. In his senior year, he met fellow classmate and love of his life, Lou Henry. Graduating with a mining degree in 1895, Hoover set off to begin making his fortune in mining operations around the world, most notably in Australia, China, and Russia. After a promotion, he returned to America, married Lou Henry on February 10, 1899, then they both left to continue his international mining. Lou Henry had graduated in 1898 from Stanford University with a B.A. in geology. At that time, she had been the only geology major at Stanford. She became Herbert's lifelong friend, business confidante, and greatest supporter.

Long before the start of World War I, Hoover had become a millionaire mining engineer. He was a no-nonsense, ambitious, roll-up-your-sleeves-and-get-it-done kind of American who was highly skilled at tackling complex problems and organizing massive operations. He also had little patience for trivial things, such as fashionable clothes, as evidenced by one colleague's dry remark that "his dress never varies—he merely writes to his tailor, 'Send me another suit,' and seldom gives himself the bother of a try-on."

Photos of Hoover at the time show a man with dark hair parted nearly down the middle, a high forehead, a strong jaw, and a downward-turned, set mouth. It could be seen as a fighter's face that had so far successfully avoided many a punch. There is also a feeling of restlessness and impatience within the strong gaze and solid pose, as if the moment the camera was clicked, the man would bound away to tackle important issues.

In August 1914, he and Lou were living in London with their two young sons, Herbert Jr., eleven, whose birthday fell on August 4 (the day Germany invaded

Figure 1.3. At the start of the war, Herbert C. Hoover was a forty-year-old successful mining engineer looking to get into public service or politics. He would go on to organize and build the Commission for Relief in Belgium (CRB), which would become the largest food relief program the world had ever seen.

Public domain; Herbert Hoover Presidential Library Archives, West Branch, Iowa.

Belgium), and Allan, seven. Besides managing his worldwide mining operations, Hoover was in London trying to secure European nations' participation in the upcoming Panama-Pacific International Exposition to be held in San Francisco in 1915. He and Lou both realized their mission was stillborn the moment the war started.

Additionally, though, Hoover, who had celebrated his fortieth birthday on August 10, was contemplating what he should do in his next stage of life. He was restless and not content to sit back and manage his mining operations. Having been raised as a Quaker, he was instilled with a "Quaker conscience" of morality that led to a strong desire to serve humanity, but he was unsure how to do so.

Options included the presidency of Stanford University and the purchase of a California newspaper as different pathways into public service and politics—two areas that deeply interested him. He wanted to help people, but as one associate later wrote, he wanted to do so "in a wholesale way. I don't think he was terribly sympathetic to the fellow selling lead pencils on the corner, but I think he was very desirous to create a society where that fellow wouldn't be selling lead pencils on the corner."

Within days of the war's start and hearing of stranded American tourists, Hoover had organized the Committee of American Residents (also known as the Relief Committee or Residents' Committee) to help his fellow Americans. By late September/early October, he was winding down the work when he was approached by his closest friend and confidant, Edgar Rickard, who was also a mining engineer and editor of a mining magazine. Rickard suggested Hoover meet Shaler.

Hoover was instantly impressed with Shaler and how serious the problem was in Belgium. Hoover took the next few days to work the project over in his head while also consulting many of his close associates who were still part of the Residents' Committee. They included Rickard, Colonel Millard Hunsiker, Clarence Graff, and John Beaver White, all of whom agreed that something had to be done to help the Belgians avert a major crisis.

While Hoover was determining what he would do, Gibson arrived in London from Brussels with dispatches from his boss Whitlock and to personally brief the US ambassador to Britain, Walter H. Page, on the critical food situation in Belgium. Shaler quickly enlisted Gibson's aid to help contact the so-far-unreachable Belgian minister in London. In short order, Shaler, with Gibson's aid, had the official backing of the Belgian government in his request to the British government to allow the food shipment through.

During this time, it became apparent to most of those involved that the coming food crisis would impact not only Brussels but the entire country and that food relief was not a temporary issue but one that would last as long as the war. While most of the general public felt the war would be over soon, there were enough unknown factors that those working on the Belgian problem began seeing it in a longer time frame than first imagined. Overall, the scope, magnitude, and duration of the project began to grow with every conversation and every day.

Regardless of the relief's ultimate size and how long the war might last, the first hurdle to overcome was the approval from Britain to ship what Shaler had already bought.

It was no small task. Arguments about the shipment were raging at the highest levels of Britain's government. To some British officials, Shaler's request of one ship of food was seen as a worthwhile humanitarian endeavor that seemed to be of limited scope. To other officials, that same shipment was seen as aiding the enemy and setting a dangerous precedent for more shipment requests.

An added element was legitimacy. A few days earlier, the shipping request had been a query from an individual representing the nongovernmental Comité Central. After Gibson's intercession, however, Shaler's request was backed by an official representing the Belgian government—the same government whose soldiers had stood and fought the Germans and in so doing had given the British and French time to gather their own forces.

But how far would the debt of honor and treaty obligations take this shipment request?

On October 5, 1914, a break came. The British Board of Trade informed the Belgian minister that approval for the shipment had been given. But as historian George Nash explained, "At this point a misunderstanding occurred that was to shape the entire outcome of the relief mission and, indeed, the course of world history." The English made a "procedural suggestion" to the Belgian minister that the food be sent from the American Embassy in London to the US Legation in Brussels. But the Belgian minister, when conveying British approval, told Ambassador Page that this was a *condition*, not a suggestion, and asked if America would accept this responsibility.

Why was this of such major importance?

As Nash states, "It was an extraordinary, probably unprecedented, request in the history of warfare: that a neutral government, far from the scene of battle, oversee the provision of foodstuffs to the capital of a belligerent country under enemy occupation."

Page had no idea how to reply. He had been moved by the personal accounts from Gibson and Shaler of the pending food crisis, but faced with what he thought was the British demand for direct US patronage, he felt he could not officially act without instructions from Washington. The ambassador immediately cabled the State Department outlining the situation and asking that he be allowed to participate in such a necessary shipment to Brussels. He also added that if the State Department agreed to this, it should also seek additional guarantees from the German government in Berlin to reinforce the guarantee from Governor General von der Goltz in Brussels.

A long two days later, working faster than its usual snail's pace, the State Department contacted James W. Gerard, the US ambassador in Berlin, and asked that Gerard request German government approval of the plan and confirm von der Goltz's guarantees.

Meanwhile, Hoover—who was in the thick of things long before he ever officially took on Belgium relief—was in nearly constant discussions with Shaler and others. According to one historian, when he met for the first time with Page on Saturday, October 10, "the idea of the Commission for Relief in Belgium first took tangible form." Page later told others that this was the meeting at which Hoover asked if the ambassador would support him and his associates if they needed diplomatic assistance once they took up relief work for Belgium.

The ambassador "approved heartily of the plan and promised to render all possible assistance." He also told Hoover that representatives from other Belgian cities, such as Liège and Charleroi, had come to see him, asking for assistance to cut through British red tape and gain American support. Page told Hoover that from then on he would refer all Belgian delegations to him. Hoover would ultimately meet with representatives of multiple Belgian cities.

During the following days, Hoover had a lot to think about on a personal level. There was his immediate family of Lou and their two young sons. What about his mining interests all over the world? He knew that if he chose to tackle the job of feeding an entire nation ensnared within a war zone—something that had never been attempted before—he would have to turn his back on his businesses, and his family would take second position so he could focus solely on the humanitarian relief. Were such sacrifices worth an effort that had no guarantee of success?

Two days later, on October 12, Hoover met again with Page, and this time he had a more concrete relief plan that dealt with the entire country of Belgium, not just individual cities.

Arguably, that is the moment Hoover was all in, committed to taking on Belgium relief.

A later account dramatically told of how Hoover struggled over what he should do and what would happen to his mining interests if he took on the relief program. That account tells of him coming to his breakfast table one morning—ten days later on October 22—and telling his visiting friend and journalist Will Irwin that he would take on the project and "let the fortune go to hell."

That certainly makes for a dramatic story perfect for publication, and it probably did happen as reported, but Hoover's activities in the relief process days prior to making such a proclamation argue that he was already deeply committed to taking on the relief. In fact, his prewar contemplation of entering public service, coupled with his months of thorough and wholehearted tackling of American tourist aid, reflected a man primed for taking on Belgium relief.

When he sat down with Page on October 12 with a nationwide plan for Belgium relief, he was a man already dedicated to the cause. There was still no reply from the State Department to Page's October 6 cablegram, so what Hoover was suggesting was all predicated on the ultimate US acceptance of responsibility for the Shaler shipment. If that happened, other shipments would have to follow immediately if Belgium was to be saved. It was assumed these additional shipments would also fall under the protection and patronage of America and be allowed through the blockade by the British.

To organize these relief efforts, Hoover recommended to Page that a central non-governmental American committee be formed and authorized (with the patronage of the US government) to administer the entire program. That program would include everything from handling and spending all funds raised worldwide (which was already starting) to the purchasing, shipping, and distribution of all food in Belgium. Hoover also recommended that the new committee absorb the American committee then in Brussels and that Dannie Heineman be asked to take charge of the work of distributing food in Belgium as vice chairman of the new committee.

Page immediately approved the plan although his hands continued to be tied by the lack of news from the State Department.

Hoover didn't wait for State Department approval to act. He immediately began an international publicity campaign to bring to light the Belgian people's suffering and potential starvation. Hoover knew that the only way he could get governments to agree to any part of the Belgium food-relief plan was to gain worldwide public sympathy and support for the Belgians. Governments would find it difficult, if not impossible, to go against a relief program that was heartily supported by their citizens.

"The greatest hope," he wrote, "of maintaining the open door for the importation of foodstuffs into Belgium and the retention of native food, was to create the widest possible public opinion on the subject. We believed that if the rights of the civil population in the matter of food could be made a question of public interest second to the war itself, then the strongest bulwark in support of the Commission would have been created."

Hoover's understanding of this concept, and of the way the world's news media worked, would serve him and his cause extremely well from the very beginning.

Finally, on October 17, the German government in Berlin agreed not to impede or requisition any food imported by the neutral Americans into Belgium. That was followed two days later by the State Department's approval of the Shaler food shipment.

The ever-impatient Hoover knew that the key to the whole situation was the German guarantee, so on October 17—before the State Department's approval—he generated a major story that went out over the newswires. It announced "a comprehensive scheme for the organization of an American committee with the purpose of taking over the entire task of furnishing food and other supplies to the civil population of Belgium, so far as American relief measures are concerned, under the official supervision of the American Government." This committee would also "concentrate and systematize" all funds and food donated to Belgium relief. Page had "consulted" with Hoover, who "would be one of the leading members of the committee, which would also include leading Americans in Brussels." While the release did mention the committee was a "proposal," there was little doubt that creation of the entire committee was a fait accompli.

Hoover was going to save Belgium, and no one was going to stop him.

THE BIRTH OF THE CRB AND THE CN

Even with a determined Hoover steering the proposed relief, there was one more critical person needed before the Belgium relief program could be fully established—Émile Francqui.

As the concept of Belgium relief began taking shape in London, Dannie Heineman back in Brussels had come to the same conclusion as those in London: Brussels food relief had to become Belgium food relief, or the entire country would ultimately starve. It took him days to convince Francqui, the Comité Central, and the two neutral patrons, Whitlock and Villalobar.

On October 15, the committee met and decided to extend its operations to the country as a whole—even before the members had heard that Shaler's initial food shipment was approved. It was an audacious but critical move if Belgium was to be given any chance at all. The Comité Central immediately petitioned and received von der Goltz's approval to expand the program nationwide. The next step was to send a delegation of Francqui and Baron Léon Lambert, accompanied by Gibson, to London to secure British and American approval.

And thus, two major forces of nature—Herbert Hoover and Émile Francqui—were about to collide. In a surprising coincidence of life, they had met before at the turn of the century in China when they were on opposite sides of a major court battle. To say they disliked each other was a vast understatement. Now, in a fascinating twist of fate, their ability to work closely together would dictate the survival of a nation.

Reportedly, when Francqui was told before the London meeting that Hoover was the man leading the American relief for Belgium, he had shouted: "What! That man Hoover who was in China? He is a crude, vulgar sort of individual." While the recorder of that scene did not personally witness it, the words sound so Francqui-esque that it's more than likely they accurately reflected the Belgian's opinion, if not his exact words.

As for Hoover's personal reaction when he first saw Francqui again, he left behind no immediate personal recollection of how he really felt. Whitlock, who was not in London to witness their first meeting, wrote that "gossips" reported both men had stood silently for a long moment staring at each other; then, as if breaking a spell, they had shaken hands and gotten down to business. While they would each take strategic opportunities in the coming months and years to disadvantage the other—to the serious detriment of the relief—they never betrayed their public appearance of polite teamwork.

At this first gathering in London, these two highly pragmatic men realized they could not do the job without each other. Hoover had seen the entire operation as solely American because he had a neutral country's freedom and diplomatic influence to obtain the food and ship it into Belgium. But he also realized he lacked a practical way of distributing the food once it entered the country. Francqui, who believed the entire operation could be run by Belgians, knew he had the foundations of a nationwide distribution network, but he also knew the belligerents would not allow Belgians to have the necessary freedoms to buy and ship the food into Belgium.

On October 22—the day Hoover reportedly stated, "Let the fortune go to hell"—he and Francqui formally agreed to a cooperative relief program between the American Commission for Relief in Belgium (soon changed to the more-inclusive Commission for Relief in Belgium, CRB) and the Comité Central de Secours et d'Alimentation (soon to be transformed into the nationwide Comité National de Secours et d'Alimentation, commonly known as the Comité National, CN, when Francqui returned to Brussels).

Both Hoover and Francqui agreed that the relief would have two prongs: provide food at a slight profit for those who could pay and provide outright charity for those who couldn't. The profit from one should pay for the other. In essence, both wanted to reestablish commerce in a country where it had died. They wanted to restimulate the food chain so that it could become self-perpetuating while also providing funds for the charity portion of relief.

The organizational concepts behind the CRB and the CN sounded deceptively simple, more a matter of logistics than anything else: The CRB would buy and transport food to the neutral port of Rotterdam, where the supplies would be transferred onto canal barges and hauled to various central warehouses via Belgium's extensive canal network. Once at these distribution centers, the food would be transferred from CRB supervision to CN responsibility. The CN would prepare and distribute the food through its extensive communal network to more than seven million Belgians in a ration system that would sell the food to those who could pay and give free sustenance to those who could not.

The whole operation hinged on two critical agreements with the belligerents: British approval to allow such imports through its blockade and German guarantees not to take any imports for themselves.

In theory, the entire relief program as envisioned by Hoover and Francqui was straightforward and clear-cut.

In reality, nothing was further from the truth.

ENGLISH DEMAND CREATES THE CRB DELEGATES

Because the English did not trust the Germans to keep their hands off any imported food, they stipulated that an unspecified number of Americans be in Belgium to act as US minister Whitlock's "delegates" to guarantee the Germans honored their nonrequisition commitment and to supervise the food until it was turned over to the CN for distribution. From this one stipulation came CRB delegates, a uniquely fascinating group that would end up representing to most Belgians the true heart and soul of the American side of relief.

But where could Hoover find US volunteers ready to drop everything, work for free, go into the unknown prison of German-occupied Belgium, and do a job that had never been done before? With a transatlantic crossing taking a week or two, coupled with recruitment time, it might be months before Americans with the right experience could be found and brought over. Hoover needed people immediately.

Hoover found willing recruits through two channels.

The first was serendipity. By November, ten to fifteen men had floated into the CRB like driftwood onto a beach and become delegates, including Edward Curtis, who had helped Hoover in tourist aid before the CRB; Frederick W. Meert, who had attended universities in Belgium before the war; Robinson Smith, author of *The Life of Cervantes*, who appeared one day in Brussels and offered his help; James Dangerfield, who had worked two years in Ghent; John Fleming, who was a businessman working and living in Brussels; and E. E. (Edward Eyre) Hunt, a freelance war correspondent, who would soon join the group through contacts in Holland.

These first responders were businessmen and artists, journalists and book authors—bound together and driven by the common desire to aid a nation in trouble. Some had lived in Belgium for years, started families, and loved the country like a second home. Others had helped Hoover with his American tourist relief program in London before volunteering for the CRB. A few were simply in Europe, had heard of the proposed relief program, and volunteered to help.

While each one of them was critical at the time for helping the organization move forward, they represented a haphazard way of recruiting that was not practical or reliable for the huge relief program on the horizon.

That could also be said for the second pathway from which Hoover found early recruits, and it was nearly as unorthodox—Oxford University. The school term was almost over, and numerous American students (most in the Rhodes Scholar program) were about to start six weeks of winter break.

One student, twenty-five-year-old Perrin C. Galpin, saw articles about the CRB and its need for volunteers to go into Belgium. He wrote Hoover and was immediately enlisted by the CRB's executive team in London to recruit more students. Galpin had no difficulty finding willing participants, as their youthful spirit of adventure was aroused by the thought of walking into the unknown to help a starving people trapped in a brutal occupation. As the student organizer, Galpin even decided which students would go—in direct contradiction to later assertions that Hoover had approved every delegate.

By early December, twenty-five Oxford students had signed up. These idealistic, enthusiastic, rather naïve young men—one of them was only nineteen years old—would have to deal with battle-hardened German officers and conservative Belgian business executives as they tried to discern what they were supposed to do. Their entry into international humanitarian relief work would not be an easy one.

Before the first group of ten students left Britain, they met with Hoover. Their biggest challenge, Hoover believed, was to remain neutral no matter what they saw, heard, or felt. He cautioned them: "You must forget that the greatest war in history is being waged. You have no interest in it other than the feeding of the Belgian people, and you must school yourselves to a realization that you have to us and to your country a sacred obligation of absolute neutrality in every word and deed."

How those student volunteers would react to Belgium—and how Belgium would react to them—was a huge unknown. That was just one of many uncertainties that plagued Hoover, the CRB, Francqui, and the CN as 1914 came to an end. Every day brought new challenges that threatened to shut down the operation. How would the relief be funded? Would the military men from both sides who opposed the program allow it to survive? Who would provide ships? Where to find a steady stream of reliable CRB delegates? Could the delegates remain neutral in the face of the Germans' harsh rule? Would Hoover and Francqui truly put aside their animosity?

It was anyone's guess whether or not the relief—and the people of Belgium—would last through the winter, let alone the war.

2

First Challenges, First Steps

Within the first few months of operations, much was accomplished by the CRB and CN. The Germans agreed to three critical components of relief: allow CRB imports into Belgium, not requisition any of that food, and permit CRB delegates free movement throughout Belgium to supervise the program.

In turn, the Allied governments permitted food through their blockade against Germany, the British government granted an initial subsidy of £100,000, and the Belgian government advanced large sums to the CRB.

To run the ever-growing relief program, Hoover and his executive team established four main offices in four different countries. In London, the CRB's administrative headquarters was at 3 London Wall Buildings, next door to Hoover's mining office. In the port of Rotterdam, a transshipping office was created to direct the flow of food from oceangoing ships into canal barges bound for Belgium. In Brussels, the operational office for Belgium and later northern France took up multiple stories. And in New York City, the American office of the CRB was charged with handling US donations, shipping, public relations, and the coordination of efforts within the vast network of CRB local and state committees that had grown out of Hoover's America-wide plea for help.

Even with these positive movements, however, long-term security was far from assured. CRB delegate Robinson Smith wrote in an article about Hoover, "The supreme test of the man was in those first months of the Belgian Relief. Then he had no certain government support, his responsibility continued to the actual feeding of the people, and the whole thing was new."

The situation was compounded by worldwide perception of the war's duration. The Kaiser had told his troops at the start, "You will be home before the leaves have fallen from the trees." But even before the Western Front was finalized in December 1914, people began questioning the initial consensus that the war would be over in no time. Many had thought that any conflict between the European powers would bring such devastating results that the war would not be allowed to last. They were right on the first part but horribly wrong on the second.

The CRB's and the CN's relief efforts had a similar shift in perspective. During the first few months of operations, their work was seen more as a temporary humanitarian aid program than as a long-term solution to a need that would last through a prolonged war. But when worldwide opinion about the war's duration began to shift, people also began to understand that the humanitarian aid would not be a temporary operation.

That realization brought the need to resolve key issues so the relief program could move forward in the most effective ways possible. Those foundational issues included long-term government approval from both the Allies and the Germans, a permanent way of financing the entire operation, and securing ships for the transportation of food from around the world (all detailed in this chapter).

As the fledgling CRB executive team tackled those formidable tasks, Hoover knew that the only way he would be allowed by any government to stay in business would be if he had worldwide public opinion on his side. But first, civilians and governments had to understand what the CRB actually was.

THE CRB, THE US GOVERNMENT, AND NEUTRALITY

Officially, the CRB was established as an American-owned, nongovernmental, private-citizen-run company to provide food relief for Belgium. Unofficially, in the minds of most people and governments, the CRB quickly became an American quasi-governmental institution, and its leader, Herbert Hoover, was given a level of respect, prestige, and freedom usually reserved for only official diplomats.

In fact, after the first year of operations, Hoover had somehow created what others might have called a nation of relief that boasted its own flag, a fleet of ships, international agreements, and a civil administration. One British official termed the CRB a "piratical state organized for benevolence." And the head of that state was probably one of only a few individuals in the world who could travel freely across all warring lines from Berlin to London, Brussels to Paris.

According to Tracy B. Kittredge (a CRB delegate and later author of an unauthorized CRB history), "The chief significance of the Commission, and most of the difficulties, arose because of the fact that it was a diplomatic compromise, not only in the beginning but throughout the whole of its activities. As a tremendous business organization it had to carry on its work in a way satisfactory to Powers that were struggling with each other for life and death. It was only Mr. Hoover's ingenuity in persuading or bullying the various Powers into making the concessions demanded by the other groups that made possible the continuance of relief work."

Kittredge went on to explain, "In carrying on these negotiations, the Commission acted from the first as a semi-diplomatic body, sometimes dealing with the governments concerned through its diplomatic patrons, more often acting through personal interviews or correspondence of members of the Commission, and especially of Mr. Hoover, with the competent officials of the various governments."

This was all made possible, some might say, when President Wilson declared America neutral on August 4, 1914, which created a neutral juggernaut that was courted by both warring sides. None of the belligerents wanted to lose the sympathies and unofficial support of the most powerful neutral country in the world—and the CRB seemed to be an extension of America.

The belligerents were well aware that any action they took or policy they implemented that was perceived by the American public as against human decency and the rules of war (set forth by the Hague Conventions of 1899 and 1907) would have a negative impact on the US government's official position. Simply put, the German civilian government would do practically anything to keep America from joining the Allies, while the Allies' civilian governments would do practically anything to gain sympathetic support in hopes of eventual US entry into the war.

Meanwhile, the American government and its officials tried to walk the difficult tightrope of neutrality, always diligent in not indicating any bias toward one side or the other—an almost impossible task for even the best diplomats. (It became much harder to do so when the implementation of America's official policy of allowing both sides to purchase US goods heavily favored the Allies over the Germans.)

The CRB reaped the benefit from the neutral tightrope-walking. President Wilson wanted to avoid even the appearance of taking sides, but he could stand firmly behind what was considered a completely neutral humanitarian relief program. He praised the efforts of the CRB and Hoover, both in private meetings at the White House and in public statements.

On the front lines of the relief program, four US officials became staunch supporters of the humanitarian relief. These Americans acted more in their capacity as patrons of the relief program (there were three major neutral patrons of the CRB: America, the Netherlands, and Spain) than in their official capacity as US diplomats.

The first of the four was the ambassador to Great Britain, Walter H. Page, who quickly embraced Hoover's efforts and aided the CRB in securing numerous approvals and support from the British government. Page would remain a strong ally of Hoover's up until he became ill in the autumn of 1918 and had to resign his post.

Brand Whitlock, the US minister to the legation in Belgium (headquartered in Brussels), always believed firmly in the need for Belgium food relief and came to be an admirer of Hoover, although not always a fan of Hoover's bull-in-a-china-shop tactics. Hoover had little patience for Whitlock because he felt he was not strong enough to stand up to the Germans or to powerful Belgians such as Émile Francqui. Despite Hoover's desire to have him reassigned, Whitlock remained at his Belgian post throughout the war.

Hugh Gibson was more to Hoover's liking. Initially the secretary of the legation in Belgium, Gibson later joined Page's team in the embassy in Britain. From the beginning, Gibson embraced the work of the CRB as if he were a delegate. He spent much of his time in Belgium working to help the CRB gain better relations with the Germans and with Francqui and the CN. He knew all the players and was a wise counselor to Hoover throughout the war.

The fourth US official was James W. Gerard, the ambassador of the American Embassy in Germany. At critical times during the worst CRB crises, Gerard was able to save the day by going directly to the German civilian government and gaining the necessary support or agreement to keep the humanitarian relief going.

To those four American diplomats and to Hoover, neutrality had nothing to do with sitting back and avoiding conflict; it had everything to do with saving innocent lives. Kittredge wrote that the CRB "was an example of applied Americanism at its best, and in reality marked a new departure in international relations and gave a new significance to neutrality." Hoover, he wrote, had "a high conception of America's opportunity, as a neutral, to make neutrality more than a passive banality."

Hoover understood how important America's neutrality was and that if he could get both American and worldwide public opinion on his side, then civilian governments on both sides would have little choice but to accept the CRB's work. In the creation and sustaining of the CRB, Hoover seemed to use neutrality as his shield and public opinion as his sword. He became extremely adept at wielding both.

MASTER MANIPULATOR OF THE PRESS

From his career as a mining engineer and his more recent work with stranded Americans, Hoover had learned about the power of the press and how it could shape the mighty force of public opinion. He understood that if the CRB could tell the Belgium food story in a compelling way, it would garner major public support. Armed with such backing, he hoped he could force all the governments to support long-term relief for Belgium.

He immediately went to those in the press he knew and trusted. In the mining industry, his strongest ally and friend was Edgar Rickard, who lived in London with his wife and was the editor and publisher of *The Mining Magazine*. Journalists outside the industry whom Hoover liked included Ben S. Allen, a fellow Stanford graduate and reporter for the Associated Press; Melville Stone, general manager of the Associated Press (AP); and Will Irwin, another Stanford grad and personal friend who had become famous for his coverage of the 1906 San Francisco earthquake and numerous investigative pieces.

While it was true that Belgium had been in the news all over the world since the war began, that news consisted of its broken neutrality treaty; heroic stands by the small, determined army led by courageous King Albert; the occupation of Brussels; the fall of Antwerp; and the heartbreaking stories of refugees fleeing the German onslaught.

With the CRB, a new story arose, just as compelling as the others but with a surefire way for readers to become actively involved. Previous stories about Belgium had generated great sympathy and empathy, but there was little that the saddened, frustrated readers could do. This was something different: readers could give money, donate food, and even put pressure on their government to support CRB relief efforts. As historian Richard Norton Smith put it, "Starving Belgium was on its way to becoming an international cause célèbre."

To focus and amplify his press efforts, Hoover immediately established a public relations department at the CRB headquarters in London. Soon after, when a CRB office was started in New York City, it developed its own highly efficient and successful PR department. At every opportunity, Hoover and his team issued press releases; reported activities of the London, Rotterdam, NYC, and Brussels offices; and forwarded messages or information the CRB received from inside Belgium. He also gave speeches whenever and wherever possible, despite the fact he didn't seem to like public speaking.

"I employed myself," Hoover later recalled, "from the first of December until Feb. 17th [1915] in constant proselytizing with Englishmen of importance, and with the [British] Cabinet ministers on this issue. In the meantime, we have worked up a sentiment in the United States, Canada, Australia and other countries in favour of the feeding of the Belgian people to such an extent that it became a worldwide movement of interest, second only to the war itself. We carried on the most active campaign of publicity by every device we could invent in England as well as in those countries."

While Hoover wanted Belgium to be in the news as much as possible, he also wanted the information to come only from him or the CRB publicity offices. He knew that not all press was good press, and he wanted complete control over what reached the general public. Unable to impose such authority over the world's two major types of news providers—newspapers and magazines (radio was not yet in public use)—he demanded that absolute control over all the articles, press releases, and bulletins sent out by the CRB's PR offices.

Hoover's media efforts and the positive public opinion they brought would serve him well when he came face-to-face with British government reluctance to support the relief.

BRITISH OPPOSITION BEHIND CLOSED DOORS

Only a few months after the official founding of the CRB, Hoover could sense, according to historian Nash, that "the British posture toward his relief project was hardening." Opposition was gaining momentum as individuals like First Lord of the Admiralty Winston Churchill, Chancellor of the Exchequer David Lloyd George, and Secretary of State for War Lord Horatio Herbert Kitchener insisted that any relief to Belgium was assisting the enemy. Their contention was that the food simply replaced what the Germans were requisitioning; it relieved the Germans from feeding the civilians; and without the CRB the Germans would, no doubt, feed the Belgians.

Outside the public's earshot, another argument circulated among British military leaders. In a startling statement, Hoover later told Whitlock that "Kitchener had made the cynical and brutal statement that if the Belgians were to be let to starve it would then require more German troops to subdue the revolutions that would break out as a result of hunger, and thereby so much weaken the German forces." In other words, Belgian starvation would create such havoc behind the lines that the Germans would pull troops from the Western Front to maintain order.

Much of this was laid on the table at a hastily arranged meeting between Hoover and British prime minister Herbert Henry Asquith on December 4, 1914. Hoover later wrote that Asquith was not very sympathetic to the Belgian cause. The prime minister felt the Germans were obligated to take care of the Belgians, and food relief would relieve them of their obligations. He saw no way that the British government could sanction such assistance to the enemy.

By all accounts, Hoover stood up to Asquith. He even hinted—if not downright threatened, depending upon which source is consulted—that the British government could not afford to oppose the relief work because it might jeopardize favorable American public opinion. Hoover told Whitlock later that before the Asquith meeting he had sent to his journalist friend and CRB executive Will Irwin in New York a long letter exposing the Kitchener argument. Hoover had instructed Irwin to "hold this until I send a cablegram releasing it, then blow the gaff, and let the work of revictualing go up in a loud report that shall resound over the world to England's detriment."

Walking into the meeting, Hoover supposedly had in his pocket a copy of the Irwin letter, which represented the hammer of public opinion. He had been carefully forging that hammer since October. It was time to see if it had the power he thought it did.

Hoover wasted no time in preliminaries. Once Asquith finished stating that his government would not support Belgium relief, Hoover launched his counteroffensive: "You have America's sympathy only because America feels pity for the suffering Belgians." He showed the Irwin letter to the prime minister. "I will send a telegram at once, and tomorrow morning the last vestige of pity for England in America will disappear. Do you want me to do it?"

Asquith was stunned. Hoover said the prime minister told him he was not used to being addressed in such a way, adding, "You told me you were no diplomat, but I think you are an excellent one, only your methods are not diplomatic."

Three things about this story indicate the meeting probably didn't take place so dramatically: the prepared cablegram to Irwin has never been found; Hoover was, at times, prone to dramatic retelling for the PR effect; and Whitlock was a born storyteller with a flair for literary drama. No matter the details, however, the result was that Hoover got Asquith to be more supportive of Belgium relief and the CRB.

Throughout the four years of CRB operations, public opinion would time and again save the humanitarian relief program from near-fatal moves by various governments. That was the case only because Hoover and his team never let up on courting the press and using positive media spins to elicit worldwide public support.

Establishing permanent financing for the CRB was equally challenging.

SECURING LONG-TERM FINANCING

In early December 1914, Hoover faced two major issues regarding the financing of the ever-growing CRB:

1. Where to find steady financial support: donations from around the world were substantial, but they did not begin to cover the nearly £1.5 million per month that was needed to ship the goal of eighty thousand tons of food per month into Belgium; and
2. how to get the money that was made from selling the food *inside* Belgium to the CRB *outside* Belgium so more food could be bought: the Germans would not allow any physical transfer of currency or gold in or out of occupied Belgium.

The first food shipments into Belgium in late November 1914 had established an initial structure and process. The CRB-imported food was sold to the Belgians in a chain that included consumers, local communes, provincial committees, the CN, and the CRB within Belgium. Everyone in the chain paid whenever possible and at a price slightly above cost so that the profit could pay for those who needed charity.

Unfortunately, no matter the line of sale, the result created the same problem: money generated from the imported relief was stuck in Belgium. Somehow, the money had to get back out of Belgium and to the CRB so it could purchase more food.

The key to solving the exchange problem came from Aloys Van de Vyvere, minister of finance of the exiled Belgian government operating out of Le Havre, France. Hoover met with him in late November 1914, and Van de Vyvere told him that the Belgian government had certain financial obligations within Belgium that it could no longer pay. These included salaries to Belgian state employees, civil service pensions, old-age pensions, allowances to soldiers, and military pensions. Together, these obligations totaled 10.5 million francs per month.

Hoover's plan was a straightforward monetary exchange. Money generated in Belgium by the imported food could pay the Belgian government's salary and pension obligations while the equivalent of those payments *inside* Belgium could be advanced to the CRB *outside* Belgium by the exiled Belgian government. It was a financial exchange without the physical transfer of any currency or gold. Additional subsidies would be needed to fully fund the CRB's efforts, but the exchange would provide the critical vehicle needed to shift any large sums in and out of the country.

Such an exchange, however, did not solve another underlying problem: the exiled Belgian government did not have the large sums that the exchange—and the CRB—needed. Hoover believed the problem could be solved by Allied subsidies advanced to the Belgian government as loans. In essence, the Allies would fund the CRB through those loans.

By the end of 1914, the Germans had agreed to Hoover's monetary exchange concept.

The biggest hurdle, however, was getting the British to agree to the substantial government subsidies needed to fully fund the exchange plan and the CRB. The British were the key (as opposed to the French) because the British government was "the banker of the Allies." A major concern was that the Germans were still requisitioning supplies throughout Belgium. The British refused to support food relief that they thought would simply be replacing what the Germans were taking. Hoover was told he would get British support for his relief program only if the Germans would agree to stop taking Belgian supplies.

Hoover set to work. Finding no sympathetic ear or help from the new governor general in Belgium, Baron Moritz Ferdinand von Bissing (who had replaced Baron von der Goltz in early December), Hoover decided to go over von Bissing's head. It was a move he no doubt knew would incense the German and rattle Whitlock (both of whom were sticklers for following traditional protocols). Hoover turned to Ambassador Gerard and asked that he petition the German civil government for a nonrequisition guarantee in Belgium.

While that process was continuing, von Bissing threw a different wrench into the diplomatic works. Only seven days after von Bissing's appointment, he decreed that Belgians must pay as a "contribution of war" 480 million francs per year. (This was the equivalent of $96 million 1915 US dollars; the Belgian peacetime budget was only $120 million–$160 million.)

An agreement was ultimately reached, Kittredge explained, whereby the sum "was to be guaranteed by the Deputations Permanentes of the various provinces, and to be paid to the Germans in the form of notes issued by the Société Générale de Belgique [Émile Francqui's bank] on the security of the promises of repayment of the Deputations Permanentes."

Besides the burden this indemnity placed on the Belgians, Kittredge said, it had an additional negative consequence: "This war tax was a further serious embarrassment to Mr. Hoover in his negotiations to secure subsidies from the allied governments."

Hoover's take on von Bissing's war tax was typically pragmatic. Money was one thing; food was altogether another. He and Gerard had received a New Year's Eve present in the form of a German government guarantee that no more Belgian foodstuffs would be taken, effective January 1, 1915. To Hoover, the new monetary war levy was not on the same par as the just-received foodstuffs guarantee. "If the Germans take money out of Belgium," Hoover said, "it may indirectly cause great hardship, but it does not starve the Belgians, because the whole problem of feeding Belgium is that of actual material foodstuff required."

Unfortunately, the Allies did not see it Hoover's way. Despite the securing of a German nonrequisition guarantee, the British were "much incensed at the German levy and were not disposed, so long as the Germans continued to exact money from Belgium, to assist the Commission by subsidies."

Hoover had another fight on his hands.

SHOWDOWN WITH BRITAIN'S LLOYD GEORGE

On January 13, 1915, Hoover met with British foreign secretary Sir Edward Grey, who reportedly began by saying "half-humourously" that Hoover better not hope to get financial support from the British as long as the Germans were levying indemnities in Belgium.

The American shot back with a "terse statement of the case." He reminded Grey that he had been told earlier that the British could not support Belgium relief because the Germans were requisitioning Belgian food, so he had secured from Berlin a nonrequisition guarantee. With that success, Hoover said the CRB was "entitled to [financial] support from the British Government, and he was disappointed that further stipulations were now raised." He left the room not knowing if he could get the Germans to give up the war indemnities and if the British would come through with financial support and acceptance of his monetary exchange.

When he hadn't heard from Grey for nearly a week, Hoover wrote asking for news and stating bluntly, "I am rapidly drifting into the most intense financial difficulties, having large payments to make at the end of the week, while I am just simply busted."

Grey's reply was to set up a meeting for January 21, 1915, with David Lloyd George, the chancellor of the Exchequer. As Hoover later wrote, he thought the meeting was to discuss "the question of the exchange of money with Belgium." Hoover knew that Lloyd George was an opponent of the CRB, but he also felt that the work and the CRB agreements had advanced far enough that this meeting would be about pounding out details regarding his financial exchange plan, nothing more.

Figure 2.1. British chancellor of the exchequer David Lloyd George was totally opposed to the CRB when he met Hoover on January 21, 1915. It would be a critical showdown with millions of lives at stake.
Public domain.

He was in for a rude surprise. As historian Nash wrote, "A routine appointment now turned into a battle of survival." Sitting with Lloyd George was Attorney General Sir John Simon, Lord Alfred Emmott of the Committee on Trading with the Enemy, and Lord Eustace Percy of the Foreign Office.

Hoover, not knowing he had walked into an ambush, began by detailing the substantial costs associated with importing food and how he and his team had hit on an exchange plan. Hoover was ready for a lively discussion on the pros and cons of that plan.

Instead, Lloyd George—the man who controlled Britain's purse strings—told Hoover outright that he was totally opposed to any relief to Belgium because, "indirect as it was, it was certainly assisting the enemy, and that this assistance would take place in several ways." The imported food would simply be requisitioned by the Germans. The food would give the Belgians "more resources generally" to help them pay German war levies. And overall, because the war would be won by economic pressures, Lloyd George believed the first one to cave under such financial weight would lose the war.

Hoover noted that Lloyd George then "expressed the belief that the Germans would, in the last resort, provision the people of Belgium; that our action was akin to the provisioning of the civil population of a besieged city and thus prolonging the resistance of the garrison; that he was wholly opposed to our operations, benevolent and humane as they were; and that therefore he could not see his way to grant our request."

One of Britain's toughest politicians, known for his strong stands on issues, had just told Hoover he was going to shut down the three-month-old CRB.

It would be a defining moment for Herbert Hoover, the CRB, and the Belgian people. He took a breath and turned to his powerful opponent. He quietly but forcefully laid out his case for the Belgian people, answering Lloyd George point-for-point.

Regarding the requisitioning of food, Hoover told the group that the Germans had agreed to requisition no more native foodstuffs after January 1. He also insisted that, to date, the Germans had "impressed none of our actual food."

As for the point that the food indirectly helped the Belgians deal with the war levies, Hoover was adamant: "We were introducing no new money into Belgium, but were simply giving circulation to the money already existing, and that there was no danger of the Germans taking the money which we collected for foodstuffs because that money was in the possession of the American Minister."

Hoover then explained, as he had done with Prime Minister Asquith, that all his dealings with the Germans had shown they would never feed the Belgians. The Germans reasoned that they had no legal obligation because they had *conquered*, not *annexed*, the country. As Hoover put it, the Germans believed "there was no clause in the Hague Convention obligating the Germans [as conquerors] to provision the civil population of Belgium."

Furthermore, the Germans felt that because the Belgians imported most of their goods, it was the British who were starving them with their blockade. They believed that if the Allies would agree to open the port of Antwerp for international trade with neutral countries, the Belgians would be fine. Hoover pointed out that the Germans had not changed their position even after a small amount of rioting in Belgium and that the northern French behind German lines were, in some cases, already starving.

"I did not offer these arguments as my own," Hoover argued, "but to illustrate the fixity of mind by which the German people justify their action in refusing to feed the Belgians."

Lloyd George, according to Hoover, "denounced the whole of this as a monstrous [German] attitude."

To further strengthen his case, especially to the argument that relief would prolong the war, Hoover tried to stir a sense of British pride and greatness within those listening. He maintained that the British had undertaken the war "for the avowed purpose of protecting the existence of small nations, of vindicating the guaranteed neutrality by which small nations might exist." It would, therefore, be an "empty victory if one of the most democratic of the world's races should be extinguished in the process and ultimate victory should be marked by an empty husk."

Hoover wrapped up with a final declaration that "the English people were great enough to disregard the doubtful military value of advantage in favor of assurances that these people should survive." He added that British approval would "add to their laurels by showing magnanimity toward these people, a magnanimity which would outlast all the bitterness of this war."

When Hoover finished his impassioned remarks, a silence fell upon the room. Lloyd George paused before speaking, and to the always-impatient Hoover, the pause was no doubt nearly interminable.

In an instant, it was done: "I am convinced," Lloyd George stated. "You have my permission." Standing up, he said he had to leave but was sure the group would "settle the details of the machinery necessary to carry it out." He then turned to Hoover and said "the world would yet be indebted to the American people for the most magnanimous action which neutrality had yet given way to."

In that moment, as Kittredge wrote, "Hoover scored the most signal triumph of his diplomatic career, for, by his clear concise statement of the situation and his eloquent advocacy of the cause of the Belgians, he won over Lloyd George, who had previously been an opponent of the Belgium relief work, and enlisted him as a hearty supporter of the Commission's activities." This also meant the German war indemnities ceased to be an issue.

Additionally, because Lloyd George would go on to become prime minister in 1916, the long-term consequences of his conversion were huge. "From this time on the attitude of the British Government became much more sympathetic toward the Commission and it gave, not only its approval, but its money and its ships and its constant co-operation to the Commission."

SHIPS AND THE BLOCKADES

From the beginning, finding ships to haul food from around the world to Rotterdam was one of the CRB's greatest difficulties. It was wartime, shipping was at a premium, and the British had established a blockade of German ports and declared the North Sea a war zone. When the British did allow through the first two vessels (the *Coblenz* and the *Iris*), their red-tape delays had shown how difficult providing a reliable flow of food into Belgium would be once the CRB was fully operational.

Hoover, with the diplomatic help of Ambassador Page, suggested to the British government that one person be appointed as liaison between the CRB and various British departments to smooth the way through governmental bureaucracy, not only with shipping but also with all other CRB matters. Lord Eustace Percy was appointed to the new position by his boss, Foreign Secretary Sir Edward Grey. As Hoover said of Percy, "He knew all the paths through the red tape of government. He quickly developed a friendship for the Commission, and he never flagged in supporting us among his official colleagues."

Percy was able to help in the first shipping challenge that came from the British. The government initially permitted only shipping from neutral countries to be used, which severely limited the number of ships available for charter. Early in 1915, however, Hoover—with the help of Page in London and Gerard in Berlin—was able to obtain an agreement from the German government that any ship flying the newly created CRB flag and carrying relief for Belgium was immune from being stopped, seized, or attacked. With that German guarantee, and Percy's help, Hoover was able to secure from the British the right to charter English shipping.

The number of ships the CRB needed was relatively small but would grow as the CRB enlarged its organization. The target of bringing approximately eighty thousand tons of foodstuffs each month into Belgium required approximately twenty vessels, depending on each ship's tonnage capacity. But to guarantee the monthly amount on a consistent basis, about three months' worth of foodstuffs would need to be in transit at all times—a total of fifty to sixty ships under CRB charter at any one time. As the CRB grew and the war dragged on, the international shipping situation became more competitive and the CRB ended up buying some vessels to complement the charters. At one time, more than seventy-five vessels, either owned or chartered, were flying the CRB flag.

Procedures for each ship were complex. Every CRB ship had to apply for and receive numerous passes and permits. From America, each ship was given a certificate from the US Customs Service stating its cargo and destination. The German ambassador in Washington would then use that certificate to issue a permit that, in turn, would secure a safe-conduct pass from the German consul of the port of departure. The British consul at the port would also issue a certificate.

On board, each vessel was provided with the CRB's large flag, which proclaimed, "Commission Belgium Relief, Rotterdam." Each vessel also had two huge cloth signs, five feet high by one hundred feet long, that were attached to each side of the hull and declared that the ship was sailing under the CRB. Electric lighting signs were also used at night.

In early February 1915, another shipping challenge arose. Germany declared a war-zone blockade around the British Isles that included merchant shipping even from neutral countries. The German government said it was in response to the British blockade of German ports—the militarists on both sides wanted to cut off their opponents from worldwide supplies. The German blockade would be enforced by a deadly submarine fleet, which was instructed that unrestricted warfare existed, meaning commanders no longer warned merchant ships before striking.

Upon hearing the news, Hoover rushed to reconfirm with the Germans that CRB ships had immunity. In Berlin at the time for another CRB issue, Hoover met with German chancellor Theobald von Bethmann-Hollweg and asked for confirmation that the CRB flag would be honored by submarine commanders. "I told him," Hoover said, "the story of a man who had a bulldog which he assured his neighbor would not bite. But the neighbor replied: 'You know the dog would not bite, but does the dog know it?'" The chancellor agreed to remind the submarine commanders that CRB shipping was off-limits.

Not long after, on April 10, 1915, the properly labeled CRB ship *Harpalyce* was torpedoed and sunk by a U-boat. It had already off-loaded its food cargo in Rotterdam and was heading back to Norfolk, Virginia. Attacked without warning at 10:00 a.m. in the English Channel, it sank quickly. Fifteen of the forty-four crew members were lost.

Hoover was incensed, and official protests were lodged. An inquiry brought German denials, but nothing official came of the incident, although it meant that the CRB had to work harder to secure shipping because ship owners became justifiably concerned.

Less than a month later, a much larger international incident occurred with the sinking of the British passenger liner *Lusitania* on May 7, 1915. German submarine U-boat 20 sank the massive ship in less than twenty minutes, killing 1,193 people (including 128 Americans).

Worldwide condemnation was swift and universal. Many in America called for the United States to enter the war. President Wilson, who had stood firmly to keep America out of the war, remained steadfast in that principle.

Ultimately, the concern over America entering the war on the side of the Allies prompted the Kaiser and von Bethmann-Hollweg to issue an apology and to curb the policy of unrestricted submarine warfare. For the moment, at least, the German civilian government had maintained its control over the military, which had few, if any, reservations about unleashing its U-boat fleet against all shipping.

Other issues that arose in late 1914 and early 1915 included obtaining war-risk insurance coverage; securing special sea routes from both sides to safely traverse minefields and stay as clear of U-boats as possible; and dealing with the British insistence that all CRB vessels stop at British ports before reaching Rotterdam since the Germans stated they would not guarantee the safety of any CRB ships that *did* stop at English ports. (This was resolved by Gerard, who convinced the German government to back down.) These and other issues were tackled as they arose by Hoover, Lord Percy, Page, Gerard, and the CRB shipping director, John Beaver White.

Even after resolving the start-up challenges and establishing general permissions, approvals, and procedures, shipping would be a never-ending issue that faced numerous crises—none bigger than the German *promise* of immunity, which was never a *surety* of safe passage.

The final crisis within the shipping arena arose in early 1917 with Germany's decision to reinitiate unrestricted submarine warfare in an attempt to end the war quickly. The strategy resulted in a significant loss of ships, including those run by the CRB. In the CRB's five years of operation (November 1914 to August 1919), 114,000 tons of cargo were lost and fifty-two CRB ships were attacked, torpedoed, mined, or wrecked, with thirty-eight of those completely lost. Many of those losses took place during the 1917 submarine campaign, as indicated by the drastic drop in CRB tonnage delivered from the second year (1,300,322 tons) to the third year (724,175 tons) when the U-boats were unrestrained.

Allied shipping and neutral countries' shipping were impacted even more than the CRB's. Losses ran so high that they came dangerously close to forcing a shift in the Allied position not to negotiate a peace.

In America, President Wilson and much of the general public found the German submarine strategy abhorrent, and it, coupled with the publication of the Zimmermann Telegram (see chapter 17), led to America declaring war on April 6, 1917. America's entry into the war went a long way toward mitigating the Germans' devastating submarine warfare, as did the creation of the convoy system in which merchant ships traveled in groups under the protection of military vessels. (See chapter 18 for shipping details through the end of the war.)

3

Hoover and Other Relief Efforts

When the Germans invaded Belgium in August 1914 and stories of Belgian devastation and refugees filled newspapers and magazines, spontaneous relief groups sprang up all around the world—most notably in Britain and America. The Belgian ministers within those two countries naturally aided and stimulated as much charitable activity as possible, leading to a multitude of relief efforts.

According to historian Branden Little, approximately 120 American relief committees were operating in 1914, including organizations such as "Father De Ville's Milk Fund for Belgian Babies; the Children of Flanders Rescue Committee . . . King Albert's Civilian Hospital Fund . . . the Belgian Relief Fund; the Belgian Relief Committee; and the Commission for Relief in Belgium."

Such abundance had unintended consequences. "The dizzying array of appeals for help beginning in August 1914," Little wrote, "confused many Americans who in low rumble started to voice concerns about the legitimacy and capacity of committees to make efficient use of donations."

A CRB history agreed, noting, "All these efforts . . . had been scattered and uncentralised. The various activities often overlapped. There was no common object to which the various committees were devoted. There even existed invidious jealousy and competition between the various committees."

When the CRB was formed October 22, 1914, Hoover immediately set out to establish his own CRB branches around America—introducing a relatively new concept to humanitarian aid, that of state and local committees to stimulate sustained interest and donations.

But Hoover also wanted to bring all existing independent relief efforts under his umbrella. His firm belief was that such a vast undertaking of feeding an entire nation, which required multiple international agreements during the waging of a world war, needed one organization to lead it. He had already been forced to accept a partnership with Francqui and the Comité National. He wasn't about to accept any others, especially within his own country.

Naturally, not everyone agreed. Putting it gently, CRB delegate Kittredge wrote, "During the first few months embarrassing complications were occasionally encountered."

TWO MAJOR COMPETITORS

Most of the spontaneous, early American relief efforts were small and localized, but two in particular, both headquartered in New York City, were substantial and had grown bigger every day: the Belgian Relief Committee and the Rockefeller Foundation.

The Belgian Relief Committee was founded in the late summer by a "few modest Belgians and their sympathizers," according to one magazine article. Its president was Rev. J. F. Stillemans, a Catholic priest of Belgian birth who had recently moved from Oklahoma to New York City and become involved in the relief group. Other Belgian members included the Belgian minister to the United States, Emmanuel Havenith, and a well-to-do patron, Madame Vandervelde.

The chairman of the executive committee, and the real power behind the group, was Robert W. de Forest, who also was the vice president of the American Red Cross. During a vacation in Europe that was interrupted by the start of the war, he had seen the Belgian devastation. When he returned home, he started the group outside the confines of the Red Cross.

(At the time, the American Red Cross was not the behemoth humanitarian organization it is today. In 1914, its pledge was to provide medical assistance to combatants, which it did on a small scale from 1914 until America entered the war in April 1917. As the United States geared up for war, however, the American Red Cross used as a template the CRB's structure of state and local committees to explode into an organization with thirty-two million members. Even so, the amount and value of supplies delivered by the CRB far surpassed the American Red Cross's donations during the war.)

A prominent American member of the Belgian Relief Committee was Thomas Fortune Ryan, a tobacco, insurance, and transportation mogul who had turned philanthropist. He was also a sore spot for Hoover. Ryan's prominence, business acumen, and charitable work had made him a perfect candidate for top CRB executive in the proposed New York office. Hoover, who had not known Ryan previously, offered him the position. Ryan surprised and annoyed him by joining the rival group.

Altogether, the Belgian Relief Committee's influential members were a potent combination of representatives of religion, professional charity, business, and politics. And they were a fundraising force to be reckoned with, having amassed nearly $200,000 by the end of October. On October 23, a day after the official founding of the CRB (but probably before most Americans had heard that news), the Belgian

Relief Committee cabled $50,000 to Ambassador Page asking that he put it to good use for Belgium relief.

In addition to the Belgian Relief Committee, there was the Rockefeller Foundation. Established in 1913 by thirty-nine-year-old John D. Rockefeller Jr., the foundation's mission was to "promote the wellbeing of mankind throughout the world." The foundation's first grant of $100,000 was given to the American Red Cross to purchase property for its headquarters in Washington, D.C. When Rockefeller learned of the Belgian plight, he was ready to throw the financial resources of his new organization behind the relief effort. On Sunday, November 1, he issued a statement declaring his foundation would "give millions of dollars, if necessary, for the relief of non-combatants in countries involved in this war." It had already chartered the steamship *Massapequa* to take four thousand tons of supplies to Belgium.

With the previous Rockefeller Foundation grant to the American Red Cross, and de Forest's positions as Red Cross vice president and chairman of the Belgian Relief Committee, it was natural that the Belgian Relief Committee and the Rockefeller Foundation would join forces. It also appears that de Forest thought the CRB could be a European satellite, or distribution arm, of his Belgian Relief Committee.

A November 3 *New York Times* article, "Plan Co-Operation in Belgian Relief," said that Belgian Minister Havenith and de Forest had had a meeting "in regard to co-operation between the Belgian Relief Committee and the Rockefeller Foundation." De Forest said after the meeting that while the Rockefeller Foundation's statement on November 1 about spending millions on Belgian relief was "on its own initiative . . . there is complete co-operation between it and the New York Committee."

De Forest also said that "complete international co-operation" was taking place among his Belgian Relief Committee, the Belgian minister, and the "American Committee in London, in which our Ambassador in London, Mr. Page; our Minister in Belgian [*sic*], Brand Whitlock, and our Minister in The Hague, Dr. Henry van Dyke, are members, and of which Herbert Hoover is Chairman."

While de Forest did acknowledge Hoover and his group, it was only as a piece in de Forest's organization, not the other way around. He told the *Times* that "all American contributions for the immediate relief of Belgians in Belgium, whether received by the Belgian Minister or the New York Committee, or any other Belgian Relief Committee, so far as the Belgian Minister and the New York Committee can control the same, will be placed in the hands of a supply committee, consisting of Thomas F. Ryan and Robert W. de Forest. This supply committee will purchase supplies and forward them direct by the steamer load as soon as they have sufficient amounts from time to time to make up a cargo."

In de Forest's organizational chart, it seemed as if Hoover and the CRB would be relegated to mere middlemen in the chain of distribution between de Forest's group and Francqui's CN—not exactly what Hoover had in mind.

De Forest finished his statement to the *Times* with a call to rally American relief efforts around him and his organization: "There are undoubtedly many committees organized and organizing in different parts of the country for Belgian relief. It is earnestly requested that these committees forward the amounts collected by them as promptly as possible."

Less than a week later, de Forest and the Rockefeller Foundation were back in the *Times*. The Rockefeller Foundation announced it had "arranged to provide a steamship pier, to charter ships, and to convey free of charge from New York to Belgium such supplies as the public may wish to contribute." This plan was "in co-operation with the Belgian Relief Committee of New York, of which Mr. Robert W. de Forest is Chairman."

Hoover was not happy to hear the news for multiple reasons. For one, according to a CRB history, "in these arrangements the Commission had no part, and indeed was hardly even consulted, as the New York committee and the Rockefeller Foundation regarded it merely as a distributing agency, and proposed to organise themselves the collecting end in America." More important, though, free shipping was a huge PR move that would go a long way in establishing dominance in the minds of the public.

The article also reported that the Rockefeller Foundation was preparing to send a "War Relief Commission" of experts to Europe "to advise as to time, place and means whereby relief can be best provided for needy non-combatants in all the warring countries." Three experts would sail for Europe on November 11, 1914. The chairman of the group was Wickliffe Rose, director general of the Rockefeller Foundation's International Health Commission. He would be accompanied by Henry James Jr., manager of the Rockefeller Institute for Medical Research, and Ernest P. Bicknell, national director of the American Red Cross.

Accompanying the article was another appeal to the American public to give money or supplies, and it was signed by Rockefeller, de Forest, and members of the Belgian Relief Committee. Lastly, the article made only one small mention of the "American Committee": "The arrangements for distribution have been made by the American Committee in London, of which Ambassador Page is Chairman, and provide for distributing stations in Belgium under the immediate supervision of the American Consuls in the afflicted region." There was no mention of Hoover, who was chairman, and the article erroneously assigned that position to Page.

Even worse, a four-page article that was probably written in early November and later published in a prestigious monthly journal, *American Review of Reviews*, featured de Forest and the Belgian Relief Committee. Only one sentence mentioned "the committee in London of which Ambassador Page is at the head," while another mentioned Brand Whitlock. Nowhere was Hoover's name to be found.

All this media coverage had an impact. One CRB historian noted, "The impression prevailed in America at this time that the Commission was only a London committee under Page's direction to forward supplies to Belgium. Hence the New York and other committees went on making independent appeals and arranging independent shipments variously consigned to the American Ambassador to London, the Minister at The Hague, the Consul in Rotterdam, or to the Commission."

MANEUVERING TO TAKE CHARGE

None of this—from minor slights and major omissions to the fact that the two New York groups were gathering serious momentum—was lost on Hoover. In a telegram to New York at the time, Hoover's frustration is clear, to the point where he let slip a highly unusual use of the word "myself": "To the embarrassment of the Ambassadors, people in America insist on cabling them instead of myself in these matters. We must centralise efforts and get people to recognize the Commission as the only channel for relief in Belgium."

But how was Hoover to get de Forest and the Belgian Relief Committee into the back seat—not only in the minds of the public but in the minds of US government officials—when de Forest wanted to drive?

Hoover would need some time to marshal his forces to deal with this threat to his organizational chart. That was especially true considering there was a major war raging, communications technology was limited to overseas cables, and it took an average of ten days to two weeks for ships to cross more than three thousand miles of ocean.

In the meantime, he knew he had to cooperate as best he could—if nothing else, for good public relations. He no doubt reminded himself that nothing really mattered except getting food into Belgium. A way of publicly showing cooperation and helping the Belgians, while privately planning how to deal with de Forest, came at the end of October. During the CRB's first official week of operations, Hoover committed to match funds with de Forest to buy a shipload of food. The *New York Times* reported on October 31 that each group had put in $150,000, and Hoover's first week's report of CRB activity showed £35,000 (the equivalent sum) as a joint purchase with the de Forest committee.

To gain his own momentum, Hoover knew he needed a strong CRB presence in New York. He turned to one of his closest friends and associates, Lindon W. Bates, an internationally known civil engineer.

When Bates had first read that Hoover was organizing a relief effort, he had cabled his friend on October 19: "It's a fine idea; you were always a born consolidator, and would consolidate the solar system if there was a chance to make a needed fundamental change in this wicked world."

On October 28, Hoover cabled Bates to see if he would be interested in working with the CRB. Bates immediately replied that he would and that his wife would try to organize all the women's organizations in America to aid Belgium.

On October 30, Hoover decided strong action was needed. He cabled Bates, "We are asking [for] the formation of a committee of leading New York men who will recognise that the situation requires a strong and important body in New York to control the expenditure of the various relief funds already raised and see that they reach Belgium in the shape of food, instead of being given independent application. . . . Under the various international agreements it is utterly impossible for any relief or foodstuffs to reach Belgium except through this Commission."

There, in the last sentence, was a major key to Hoover taking complete command. The multiple and complex agreements and guarantees that the CRB and CN—working with diplomats Page, Whitlock, Gibson, and Villalobar—had secured from Germany, England, and Belgium were proof, at least in Hoover's mind, that the CRB was the only authorized agent to bring relief into Belgium.

Hoover began to work on multiple fronts to counteract de Forest and the Rockefeller Foundation. He knew that the Belgian minister in Washington was a member of the Belgian Relief Committee and had not responded well to the CRB's direct appeals for cooperation. So Hoover went to the minister's bosses, Belgian officials in London and Le Havre, France, and "arranged to have positive and definite instructions sent to the Belgian Minister in Washington that all committees organised under this patronage should work through the Commission." While the minister was not so quick to roll over, he ultimately did after additional pressure was applied.

Hoover also added to all media releases, "The Commission for Relief in Belgium is the official body recognized by the various governments for the transmission of food shipments into Belgium; it is the only channel through which food can be introduced into Belgium; and has by its association with a committee in Belgium the only efficient agency for the distribution of food within the country."

Hoover also turned to his ally Page, who always seemed ready to go in any direction Hoover suggested. According to one CRB delegate, Page once remarked, "Mr. Hoover never did me the unkindness to accept my advice." This time, Page probably didn't need much convincing of Hoover's consolidation plan, for he had received numerous cables from various relief organizations asking the same questions about how they could help Belgium. He probably wouldn't have minded if they all went to Hoover rather than himself.

At Hoover's prompting, Page sent a request to the US State Department for official recognition of the CRB. Hoover wanted President Wilson to tell the American public that his organization was the only official, authorized group to handle Belgium relief.

On November 7, an indirect but nonetheless critical answer came when Robert Lansing, the legal adviser to the US secretary of state, replied to a request for information from the governor of Iowa. Lansing's reply, which was published in the *New York Times*, included: "The Commission for Relief in Belgium is the only agency that has machinery for the distribution of food in Belgium. It has the benefit of complete diplomatic arrangements with all the belligerent governments. It works with the only committee in Belgium that has machinery for local distribution in every community. No cargo is safe unless it is properly shipped and consigned. All shipping directions are given by Herbert Hoover, chairman of the Commission in London."

While not official presidential recognition, Lansing's statement was an important acknowledgment of preeminence. Despite Hoover's and Page's appeals, though, President Wilson would not go further at the time. In fact, Wilson actually viewed US diplomats Page, Whitlock, and Gibson as acting more as private citizens than representatives of America when working for Belgium relief—a finer point that was never fully publicized nor brought to the complete attention of the belligerents. There is little doubt that Wilson morally supported the CRB's plan, but his full endorsement at this embryotic stage could have been seen as foolhardy. Some might have also contended that an added benefit to this lack of official recognition was a potential legal defense—albeit flimsy—of the US government if anything went horribly wrong: "What! You thought these people were acting officially on America's behalf? Why, they were only private citizens."

In an ironic twist, Hoover was almost undone by his desire for official recognition and quest for dominance. The back-and-forth in the press between Hoover and de Forest and the Rockefeller Foundation was perceived by some as creating confusion in the minds of the general public and the government. Additionally, since October, there had been discussion within the government about establishing an overarching committee for relief. On November 12, the *Washington Post* ran a front-page article that said President Wilson was going to form a "central committee" to oversee the Belgium relief.

If Hoover had been frustrated and angry with two NYC relief groups in the picture, he was probably apoplectic at the thought of US bureaucrats mucking up his show. He scrambled through multiple levels of emissaries to get the message to Wilson that such governmental intervention was not necessary and would, in fact, hurt the cause.

In a rare show of solidarity, most of those already in Belgium relief agreed with Hoover. "Nobody, it seemed, wanted a single national committee," according to historian George Nash. The common thought was that such a move by the American government might be considered a breach of America's neutral stand (similar to officially recognizing one relief group over the others). Hoover agreed with that, but he also drove home to anyone who would listen the notion that the Midwest and the West would not give to Belgium relief through an East Coast–based governmental committee. This somewhat parochial argument, hitting two beloved targets of westerners (East Coast elites and the federal government), was a bit weak, but enough people felt it held some truth that it helped do the trick. The idea of a national relief committee died a quick death.

During this period of media battles, Hoover decided it was not enough to have an NYC-based committee led by Bates. He felt it had become critical to open a New York City office. In the initial October press release announcing the CRB, there had been no mention of that. But it was a logical move and one that had probably been discussed since the beginning. The charitable donations of literally hundreds of CRB-inspired relief groups could be collected with greater ease from New York than London. And a side benefit was that an NYC office established an American base from which the CRB presence could become better known and, it was hoped, put into proper Hoover perspective de Forest's Belgian Relief Committee.

On November 13, with pressure building from the Belgian Relief Committee's media campaign, Hoover asked Bates if he would open a New York City office and serve as vice chairman of the CRB. Bates quickly agreed.

FRANCQUI PROVIDES THE KEY

Through all these machinations, the general public would have wondered, no doubt, what all the fuss was about. Why was Hoover so opposed to de Forest and the Rockefeller Foundation when they were raising money, gathering food, and shipping it to Rotterdam?

To Hoover, it all came down to control over shipping. He would be happy if the two other NYC groups simply collected money and supplies. The shipping, which would ultimately be massive, was a different matter. Hoover believed that the organization that controlled the shipping would be perceived by the public and government officials as the preeminent relief organization. And taking charge of shipping would complete Hoover's chain of control for getting relief into Belgium. There was also a very practical consideration for that—multiple relief committees competing to charter ships would simply drive up the cost of shipping.

For Hoover and the CRB, the biggest hurdle to the control of shipping had come when the Rockefeller Foundation and de Forest had announced they would provide free shipping from American shores to Rotterdam.

At first, there didn't seem to be much Hoover could do to counteract such a tremendous move. The generosity was overwhelming, and the tide of American support for de Forest and the Rockefeller Foundation surely swelled.

Hoover was near his wits' end as to how to counteract that move when salvation arrived from a highly unlikely source: Émile Francqui. Hoover received word of Francqui's securing of Belgian bank loans of £600,000 ($3 million) for the relief efforts (see chapter 8). Finally, Hoover had something concrete to work with.

In a huge strategic gamble, Hoover checkmated de Forest and Rockefeller by publicly announcing that Francqui's money was strictly for transportation costs and if the NYC groups continued with their plan, their actions would jeopardize the $3 million. Hoover maintained they needed to back away from shipping to guarantee that this money would go toward helping the Belgians.

The only problem with Hoover's statement was that there was no such stipulation on Francqui's money. In fact, on November 12, as historian Nash wrote, "Hoover informed Francqui that he and his colleagues had *decided* to apply the fund for this purpose and to announce that it had been given with this proviso, lest (he said) the loan discourage charitable giving."

To sweeten the pot, Hoover added that all shipping of gifts via rail within the United States would be covered for free—an offer not made by the two other groups. When Hoover made that announcement, he had nothing to back it up. The Belgian minister in America had already secured free rail services for Belgium relief, but he had so far refused to transfer that gift to the CRB. By the end of November, though, Hoover was able to honor his commitment because the minister finally relented under serious pressure from his government.

How did de Forest and the Rockefeller Foundation take the news? They begrudgingly backed away from providing shipping. With great understatement, a history of the CRB stated: "The New York Belgian Relief Committee and the Rockefeller Foundation were at first loath to abandon the scheme they had devised for collecting and shipping themselves the food to be contributed in America, but they were soon convinced of the wisdom of leaving all such matters to the expert services of the Commission, and of devoting their efforts to the collecting of funds."

By November 20, a meeting of Bates, de Forest, and the Rockefeller Foundation determined that de Forest's group would be the preeminent relief agency for New York and the surrounding area only. The Rockefeller Foundation would continue to provide funds but back away from shipping.

From this point on, "the Commission would, therefore, take over the entire control of all food from the time of shipment. This measure gave to the Commission immediately the necessary control of shipments and made it possible to effectively manage the collecting and shipping of the food supplies contributed throughout the United States."

In the coming months, there would be a few bumps that would need smoothing out, but basically, from late November forward, the Rockefeller Foundation and the Belgian Relief Committee played just fundraising and supply-gathering roles for Belgium relief.

Once again, Hoover had somehow miraculously cleared away obstacles that had threatened his exclusive control of Belgium relief. As Nash put it, "With the securing of the Rockefeller Foundation's seal of approval, the principal challenge—real or imagined—thus far to Hoover's preeminence in Belgian relief work disappeared. But what a wearying struggle it had been."

Tired or not, Hoover was forever the tough pragmatist. He outlined what happened and the CRB's success in correspondence to Bates: "I do not wonder at all that the de Forest line contingent are sore, as they thought they could treat us like school-children, and have found that here has grown up the one organization which is pointed to with satisfaction by all of the belligerent Powers, and with pride by all good-feeling Americans. They might have enjoyed considerable participation in it if they had played the game with us, but they themselves, by their own acts, put themselves out of court, and I am not at all sorry."

Hoover followed with a strong summary to Bates: "You can always bear in mind that the people who are going to control this Commission are the people who control the money and the people who control the international agreements, and that we have both of these things in our grip."

Arguably, it was Francqui (by securing the £600,000 loan) and Bates (by establishing the NYC office) who had saved Hoover from being just another also-ran in the Belgium relief race.

Within a year, however, both would turn on him, causing serious trouble for the CRB and himself.

4

Rotterdam: The Transshipping Hub

Choice was never an option when it came to determining where a CRB transshipping hub should be located. Facts dictated that the port of Rotterdam was the only suitable place: Belgium was cut off from the rest of the world; any food shipments would have to be delivered via Belgium's extensive canal system (Belgian trains were used primarily by the German military); and no port owned by either warring side would be acceptable to the other.

Figure 4.1. Each CRB ship was outfitted with large signs on both sides to alert German U-boats that it was not an enemy vessel.

Public domain; Hugh Gibson, *A Journal from Our Legation in Belgium* (New York: Doubleday, Page & Co., 1917).

The port of Rotterdam in the neutral country of the Netherlands was not only physically close to Belgium and directly linked to the Belgian canal system, it was also the fourth-busiest harbor in the world (the five busiest were New York, Hamburg, Antwerp, Rotterdam, and London). Located less than forty-five miles (seventy-two km) from the Belgian border, Rotterdam with its 420,000 residents was the country's second-largest city and sat on the northern edge of a massive river delta where three major European rivers emptied into the North Sea: the Scheldt River from Belgium; the Meuse, or Maas, River from France and Belgium; and the Rhine River flowing from Switzerland, Liechtenstein, Austria, France, and Germany.

As a major international port, Rotterdam had a sufficient number of stevedores, modern harbor facilities, and specialized equipment to handle the projected eighty thousand to one hundred thousand tons of CRB food that would be necessary every month for the Belgians to survive. A critical state-of-the-art piece of equipment available was the floating elevator, which could pull alongside an oceangoing ship and vacuum wheat (the principal CRB import) from the cargo hold and transfer it to the holds of small lighters, or barges, saving days of laborious transferring by hand.

THE CRB COMES TO ROTTERDAM

On Sunday, October 25, 1914, with the first two shipments of CRB food already loading on the Thames River in London, Hoover sent Millard Shaler and Captain John F. Lucey to Rotterdam to begin the arduous task of setting up the main CRB shipping office between the outside world and German-occupied Belgium. Shaler would stay in Rotterdam for a few days and then go back into Belgium, but Lucey would remain to spearhead the initial setup and operations.

Hoover couldn't have picked a better, more resourceful, and more hardworking man than Lucey. Born in County Kerry, Ireland, he and his family had moved to America when he was very young and settled in New York City. From a young age, Lucey was independent. After years of serving in the army and seeking his fortune in the Alaskan gold rush and the US oil fields, he started his own firm, Lucey Manufacturing Corporation, which became the second-largest oil-well supply company in the world in twelve short years.

In August 1914, when the Germans invaded Belgium, Lucey was just another American businessman in Europe trying to expand his business. He was still in London in October when Hoover asked him to join the CRB. He liked being addressed as Captain Lucey and shared an important trait with Hoover: impatience.

When Lucey and Shaler arrived in Rotterdam, they hit the ground running, setting up a temporary office in their living quarters. With the help of US minister to Holland Henry van Dyke, who was just returning from a two-day diplomatic trip into Belgium, and the US Legation secretary to Holland Marshall Langhorne, permission was secured from the Dutch government to import all the supplies needed for Belgium relief. The Dutch government also provided free use of the state telegraph lines to the CRB and even agreed to carry free of charge a definite amount of food per day from Rotterdam south to Liège once the system was set up. The two Americans conferred with the German Consulate in Rotterdam and found waiting there 150 safe-conduct passes for the first shipments, already signed and stamped by the German authorities in Brussels.

Lucey and Shaler also secured the services of the local office of the British Furness shipping company to temporarily handle receipt of the supplies and transportation into Belgium. Stevedores, cranes, and floating elevators would transfer the cargoes from the oceangoing vessels to either trains or canal barges that would carry the supplies throughout Belgium. The two men also started searching for clerical staff for what they envisioned would be the blizzard of paperwork necessary to ensure Hoover's demand for scrupulous accounting of all transactions and activities was met.

After Lucey and Shaler learned that transporting the food by train would be out of the question—rail service in Belgium for civilians had not been restarted and any running trains were used by the military—they began to map out the best routes of canal entry into Belgium. They didn't need to worry about finding barges for the work. Since the start of the war and the disruption of commerce, hundreds of Dutch lightermen and their craft were sitting idle. Added to that were hundreds of Belgian lighters that had been taken into Holland to evade seizure by the Germans.

But where to send what to whom once the food began arriving in Rotterdam?

Lucey knew he needed practical information about the situation in Belgium before he could answer that complex question. With Belgium cut off from the outside world, however, any news was nearly impossible to get. The Germans allowed only neutral diplomats and a handful of others in or out.

Lucey spent a great deal of time conferring with as many people as he could, but much of what he heard was conflicting. So much so, in fact, that he had "neither definite information regarding the internal relief organization nor specific recommendations as to where to direct the first shipments of food," according to a CRB history. That wasn't from lack of people asking, begging, and pleading. "Appeals, rumors, orders, suggestions came in showers from local [Belgian] committees, refugees, American consuls in Belgian cities, from the American Legation in Brussels and the Comité Central."

To help Lucey, Shaler left for home in Brussels via Ostend, Ghent, and Antwerp, accompanied by the Dutch consul at Ghent and Henry Albert Johnson, the US consul at Ostend. They would try to get word back to Lucey about the conditions in each area and to inform the Belgians that help was coming.

On the same day, Belgian Monsieur Van den Branden was allowed out of Belgium to be the Comité Central's (later renamed the Comité National) liaison with Lucey and the CRB. But Lucey quickly discovered that "he brought no definite instructions as to shipping . . . nor as to destinations to which the first shipments should be directed."

Into all this confusion steamed the little *Coblenz.*

THE FIRST SHIPMENT ARRIVES

The world press had reported that the first cargo of relief aboard the *Coblenz* had sailed from London on October 28, but no one was sure when it would arrive in Rotterdam. Finally, in the pre-dawn hour of 3 a.m., on Sunday, November 1, the small steamship pulled into Rotterdam harbor with its precious cargo earmarked for Belgium.

The Dutch government waived its rule against work on Sunday, as did the local labor union, so that the one thousand tons of supplies could be handled as quickly as possible. All through the day, the sacks of beans, rice, and flour were hauled by hand and by cranes out of the *Coblenz* and into barges that hugged each side of the ship.

Lucey, no doubt, was there directing, supervising, and urging on any who didn't have the proper sense of urgency. He knew that this food had been needed weeks ago. Throughout the day, onlookers watched from shore because they knew this was the first ship to arrive with Belgium relief supplies and wanted to see the historic event unfold.

Lucey was still desperate for information regarding what was happening in Belgium—everything from the organization of distribution and a determination of what areas needed what supplies the most to the condition of the country's canal network. That Sunday, November 1, he sent Edward D. Curtis from Rotterdam south to Brussels with a letter to Whitlock and an urgent request for reports on the organization of distribution within Belgium.

Figure 4.2. Rotterdam harbor: A US cargo ship in the process of off-loading wheat into a canal barge as other barges wait their turn.

Public domain; Herbert Hoover Presidential Library Archives, West Branch, Iowa.

Curtis's trip represented a momentous occasion that no one had time or interest in marking. It was the first trip into Belgium of the first CRB courier—a critically important job when there was no public telegraph, telephone, or postal service in or out of occupied Belgium. The Germans had agreed, however, to allow the CRB to send mail to and from Belgium but by special courier, similar to the permission they had given Whitlock and Gibson as neutral diplomats. The CRB courier would become an indispensable part of the relief organization's communications network and a rigorous, demanding job throughout. Traveling in and out of Belgium numerous times a week, the courier would constantly be in contact with German officers, sentries, Belgian officials, and citizens. This would have demanded at least competency, if not fluency, in both French and German, with a bonus for knowledge of Dutch and Flemish.

On that first Sunday in November, as Curtis, his chauffeur, and motorcar were stopped at numerous German checkpoints on his trip to Brussels, Dutch stevedores kept laboring to unload the *Coblenz*. By Monday morning, November 2, the ship was empty, and eight barges, or lighters, were ready to go. Towed by four tugs, they slowly made their way out of Rotterdam harbor bound for Brussels.

These small barges and tugs represented an incredible feat—food was heading into Belgium only eleven days after the official founding of the CRB.

The holds of each barge were sealed, and a large sign stated in English, "Consigned to the American Minister in Brussels for the Comité National de Secours d'Alimentation." On the door of each lighter captain's cabin was a copy of von der Goltz's guarantee and his request that German officials give the shipment safe conduct. The crews were all neutral Dutchmen who carried with them individual German passes allowing them to travel to Brussels and back.

This "Flotilla of Mercy," as one British newspaper christened it, was shadowed by a motorcar that contained three men. Marshall Langhorne represented Whitlock as the neutral diplomatic patron of the shipment; Jarvis E. Bell was a newly designated CRB delegate; Mr. Wyman was the European manager of the American Express Company and presumably along as an observer. They carried with them the German guarantee, signed by von der Goltz, and the Berlin government's agreement not to requisition the food.

The tug and barges made it successfully to Brussels traveling along Belgium's incredible network of canals.

AN EXTENSIVE WATERWAY SYSTEM

Belgium, like Holland, boasted a vast network of canals that covered practically the entire country. There were three main arteries from Holland into Belgium, with some continuing into France. Before the war, these canals had been freely used, but with the German occupation, they were under tight controls and some were highly restricted because they were in the Etape Zone, a subzone of the German Army Zone (see Reader Aids: Map of the Region), which was controlled by the military, not the German civil government in Brussels.

The first major canal was from the Dutch towns of Terneuzen and Sas van Gent to the Belgian city of Ghent (which was in the Etape). This was a large canal that could handle big barges carrying 1,200 tons. At Ghent, the cargos from the larger barges had to be reloaded into three-hundred- and four-hundred-ton lighters to go north to Ostend and Bruges or south to Courtrai (Kortrijk in Flemish), Tournai, Mons, or Charleroi, with branches leading to the French cities of Lille and Valenciennes.

The second major canal ran from the Dutch town of Roosendaal to Antwerp and from there to Brussels or Louvain. It was large enough to handle thousand-ton barges. This canal was doubly important because most of Belgium's chief flour mills were around Brussels or Louvain. Much of the imported CRB wheat ended up heading down this canal to the mills for processing before leaving again as flour. At Antwerp, smaller canals led to Mons and the surrounding area.

The third major canal came from Rotterdam and flowed to the Dutch town of Weert and on into the Belgian province of Limbourg (now spelled Limburg). It branched west to Turnhout and Antwerp, south into Holland again at Maastricht, and then back into Belgium to Liège and Namur. Depending upon the water levels, lighters could be sent from Namur along the Sambre River to Charleroi, or south on the Meuse River to Dinant, and ultimately to Charleville in France.

The extensive Belgian waterway network meant that all the major centers of the provinces (except Luxembourg) could be supplied from Rotterdam. Depending upon the final destination, however, a barge could take days if not a week to complete its journey. Before the war, tugs were used to haul barges through the larger canals, while horses were used to pull them through smaller ones. When the war started, however, most horses were requisitioned by the military of both sides. That meant, in some cases, that men were hired to haul the barges by hand through the smaller canals, and in a few cases, women were used as well.

Additionally, the war created major problems within the canals. CRB delegate E. E. Hunt wrote, "As for the canals, some of the dykes had been cut and were not yet repaired; bridges had been blown up for military reasons; barges had been sunk; and at important points the Belgians were not permitted to approach the canal embankments for fear they might attempt to damage the system to the detriment of the German armies."

No one knew for sure which canals were clear and which were blocked. Hunt noted, by middle to late December, "The Rotterdam office had been in operation for eight weeks, yet in that time it had secured practically no information regarding the condition of the Belgian waterways. In sheer desperation Captain Lucey had dispatched canal-boats of flour, rice, peas, and beans, without knowing whether the canals were navigable or blocked."

Hunt, who was in charge of the Antwerp CRB office, was determined to help Captain Lucey gain tight control of barge activity. He knew what was needed was a system to track lighters as they moved through Belgium. This was especially obvious to Hunt because there had been times when he and his Antwerp delegates had "spent days patrolling the canals in search of a lighter which had dropped from sight almost as if swallowed up by Father Scheldt [River] himself."

Hunt came up with a plan. If he could find a spot overlooking the Scheldt River where the lighters could be seen as they entered Belgium, that information, if approved by the Germans, could be telegraphed to Rotterdam and Brussels for tracking. The lighters would be easy to identify because they all had distinctive names, such as "Marie Germaine," "Louisa," "Ariel," "Deo Gloria," "Dorothea," "Madonna," and "Frederika." He sent one of his new delegates, William W. Flint, to find such a lookout along the shores of the Scheldt. Flint "set out on a river boat and disappeared for five days. Then he returned to Antwerp with a tale of great adventures, arrests, detentions, conferences, and agreements."

The delegate had also found Fort Lillo, an ideal place to spot incoming barges. Close to the Dutch border, Fort Lillo was situated high above the river on old earthworks. The only things there were "a few trees, a few small Flemish houses in orderly rows, [and] a single customs house overlooking the river." Hunt and Flint motored out to negotiate for the job they needed.

When they got there, "our limousine completely blocked the narrow lane before the customs house and drew all the civil and military population about us. Several Landsturm soldiers [older Germans used for non-combat duties] strolled up, puffing away at their pipes and staring. The Belgian population ranged itself silently about the car. The dead silence, the dropped jaws, the fixed eyes of such crowds were always disconcerting to us, but our Belgian chauffeur seemed as indifferent as a good actor before a crowded house."

Out of the customs house came two officials in their green uniforms and box caps. They "touched their foreheads, and bowed gravely." Hunt and Flint told them what they were after. Once the customs officers knew the two were with the CRB, the Belgians said they would be happy to provide all the names and shipping numbers of passing barges. But how to get the information back to the Antwerp office? The Belgians suggested asking the German officer in charge of the area, who had been helpful in the past.

"We lifted our hats, shook hands all round, and motored to a small bar-room—the office of the commandant." When Hunt saw the German, he was sure of success. "He was a lonely young under-officer who greeted us with obvious pleasure because we broke the monotony of his exile." Once Hunt explained the situation, the German replied: "Certainly, certainly . . . I am pleased to help. I will telephone every day what lighters pass Lillo. It is a pleasure to help."

From a coupling of such CRB delegate initiative with Belgian and German assistance, a comprehensive system of barge tracking was established throughout Belgium that would work successfully for the rest of the war.

EARLY SUCCESS CONTINUES

Approximately three weeks after first arriving in Rotterdam, Captain Lucey was able to secure CRB offices at 98 Haringvliet, a hundred-year-old mansion previously owned by a successful Dutch merchant. The offices were "commodious quarters" on "a tree bordered street beside a busy canal in the heart of the city." From the windows, Lucey and his staff could see the Meuse River and countless canal barges of the working harbor.

While the house maintained some of its previous accoutrements, it was no longer a quiet, stately mansion; it was the bustling business office of the rapidly growing shipping arm of the CRB. A large staff of Dutch, Belgian, and American clerks were scattered throughout the building, and Dutch and Flemish barge captains and dock laborers were always waiting in line for an audience with someone who could either put them to work or solve a problem they had encountered while employed by the commission. The halls and various offices were filled with a nearly constant cacophony of ringing phones, clattering typewriters, and buzzing conversations.

By the end of November 1914, the Rotterdam office had received and unloaded 26,431 tons of foodstuffs. It was a far cry from the goal of eighty thousand tons that was the minimum needed to sustain more than seven million Belgians a month.

However, after the start-up months, Rotterdam witnessed an average of four full oceangoing cargo ships arriving every week. And within the first full year of operations, the statistics had grown to be impressive. According to Kittredge's CRB history, from October 22, 1914, to October 31, 1915, a total 988,852 tons of foodstuffs had arrived in Rotterdam from 186 full cargoes, averaging 4,637 tons each, and 308 partial cargoes, averaging 209 tons each. The total expenditures of the CRB in the first year were a staggering £17,257,591 (nearly $2 billion 2020 dollars), which included the cost of cargoes on route to Rotterdam on October 31.

As for the food getting from Rotterdam into Belgium and northern France (which became part of the food relief in April 1915; see chapter 9), from the 988,852 tons of food delivered to Rotterdam in the first year, 906,875 tons had been transported into the occupied territories and delivered to the individual provinces in already-agreed-upon proportions and percentages.

The Rotterdam office's efficiency was matched by its lack of internal upheavals within the director's position. During the life the CRB, the Rotterdam office had only three directors while the Brussels office suffered through eight. The three Rotterdam directors were Captain John Lucey, October to December 1914; Carl A. Young, January 1915 to June 1916; and W. Lyman Brown, July 1916 to the end of the war.

For the remainder of the war, the Rotterdam office and its extensive procedures of processing, distributing, and tracking would successfully get food into Belgium and northern France in the fastest and most efficient ways possible.

5

Life in German-Occupied Belgium

The whole world had followed the German invasion of Belgium like no other conflict before. From the fields of battle, an unprecedented number of war correspondents had filed countless dispatches about Belgium, describing everything from civilian executions to entire towns being torched. While some of the Belgian atrocity stories had been exaggerated or even fabricated, many had been all too real.

Figure 5.1. A major thoroughfare in Brussels crowded with civilians waiting in line for the food relief provided by the CRB and CN.
Public domain; Herbert Hoover Presidential Library Archives, West Branch, Iowa.

But the reality of 1915 occupied Belgium and northern France was much more of a mystery, hidden behind what Herbert Hoover called the "ring of steel" that Germany created to cut off the conquered lands from the rest of the world. For the most part, the Germans succeeded—the world knew little of civilian conditions behind the lines.

For those who wanted to know, it was first helpful to understand Belgium's underlying makeup. Even though the country had been officially formed less than eighty-five years before (in 1830), the residents were distinctly different from those living in neighboring countries.

POLITICAL, LINGUISTIC, AND RELIGIOUS DIFFERENCES

Belgium's political situation before the war had always been highly charged, if not explosive. The three major parties were Catholic, Liberal, and Socialist, with numerous factions such as the Flemish Movement striving to find a place at the parliamentary table.

Much of Belgium's political landscape was shaped by the country's substantial language divide. The French-speaking Walloons, who lived predominately in the south, had more control over Belgium's affairs than the Flemish-speaking Flemings, who lived mostly in the north. As a result, French was the predominant language and was used throughout the country in politics, education, and commerce. Most educated Flemings were bilingual but in many cases resented speaking French. Many Walloons in southern Belgium had only limited understanding of Flemish (a Dutch derivative).

The war and occupation had brought a superficial end to the bickering between the two groups because, as CRB delegate Hunt stated, "The Flemings are as loyal as any other portion of the people to the ideal of a free and united Belgium." But taking a break from arguing the language issue did not mean the underlying issues and their attendant emotions had disappeared. They still simmered just below the surface that was shown to the Germans.

The Germans—and von Bissing in particular—wanted to exploit the language difference. The ultimate goal, according to the governor general in a memorandum not meant for public release, was not to have the Flemings gain an independent state but to make it easier for Germany to absorb the Flemish territory into the German Empire. "Among the German interests in Belgium," he wrote, "is also the Flemish movement, which has already made good progress. . . . We have among the Flemings many open and very many still undeclared friends, who are ready to join in the great circle of German world-interest."

Von Bissing stressed, however, that the German occupation must "repress boundless hopes on the part of the Flemings. Some of them dream of an independent State of Flanders, with a King to govern it, and of complete separation. It is true that we must protect the Flemish movement, but never must we lend a hand to make the

Flemings completely independent. The Flemings, with their antagonistic attitude to the Walloons, will as a Germanic tribe constitute a strengthening of Germanism."

With the invasion, however, the multilingual Belgians had surprised even themselves by coming together into a stubborn front opposed to the Germans. While the Flemings were appreciative that the Germans ran all their official *affiches* in three languages—German, French, and Flemish—that did not mean they would take the bait of division.

As Émile Cammaerts, a renowned Belgian playwright and poet of the time, explained, "Not being able to stir the people against the Allies or against their own Government, the German Press Bureau attempted to revive the language quarrel to provoke internal dissensions." His scorn was obvious when he went on to write, "Germany, who had never troubled much before about the Flemish movement and Flemish literature, suddenly discovered a great affection for her Flemish brothers who had so long been exposed to [what the Germans called] 'the insults of the Walloons.'"

Von Bissing and his civil occupation government strategically gave preferential treatment to Flemings and acknowledged them and their authority whenever possible. Throughout the war, von Bissing actively supported the policy known as *Flamenpolitik*, or separation of the Flemings from the Walloons. His efforts led to the autumn 1916 reopening of the University of Ghent as an all-Flemish institution, although so many Flemings were opposed to the school that it never had the support and significance that von Bissing hoped it would.

Religion also played a significant role in Belgian life. The majority of Belgians in 1914 were Catholic, and the religion was a driving force in the country, more so in the Walloon south than in the Flemish north. In fact, religion was such a strong influence in Belgium that it mitigated many of the differences that existed over language. And in the critical arena of politics—which seemed to dominate nearly every Belgian's body and soul before the war—the Catholic Party had been in power for nearly thirty years.

CRB delegate Earl Osborn explained, "It takes quite a while for an American to realize that in Belgium political beliefs are the standard by which men judge each other and on which they form their friendships and enmities; the first question that a man asks about another is whether he is a liberal or a Catholic."

Regardless of which religion was followed, the vast majority of Belgians would have agreed that within a year of German occupation, the one spiritual and moral voice that spoke for the entire nation was Cardinal Désiré Félicien François Joseph Mercier, who resided in Malines (Flemish Mechelen) in the Flemish province of Antwerp. Cardinal Mercier had been born in Braine-l'Alleud, twenty miles (thirty-two km) south of Brussels, and been educated in Louvain. In 1906, he had become archbishop of Malines and a year later was elevated to cardinal, making him both a bishop and a cardinal.

Standing well over six feet, Cardinal Mercier stood out in any crowd and had been an outspoken critic of German actions and policies throughout the invasion and from the moment the occupation began. He rose to international prominence in early 1915 after his defiant Christmas 1914 pastoral letter was smuggled out of Belgium and printed around the globe. He would continue throughout the war to be a constant, vocal thorn in the side of von Bissing, who restricted the cardinal only by placing him under house arrest for fear that his imprisonment or execution would lead to civil unrest. Numerous times in various ways, the cardinal was able to circumvent von Bissing's restrictions and stimulate deeply patriotic, hopeful feelings in all Belgians.

With the world little understanding conditions under German occupation, Belgian playwright Cammaerts expressed the difference between the invasion and the occupation in his book *Through the Iron Bars*. The world, he wrote, "had lived, for months, under the impression that 'things were not so bad' in the conquered [occupied Belgium]. After the outcry caused by the atrocities of August 1914, there came a natural reaction, a sort of anti-climax. Fines, requisitions, petty persecutions do not strike the imagination in the same way as the burnings of towns and the wholesale massacre of peaceful citizens. It had become necessary to follow things closely in order to understand that, instead of suffering less, the Belgian population was suffering more and more every day."

As the occupation took hold, a feeling of national desperation gradually enveloped Belgium. Initially, Cammaerts wrote, before the October 1914 fall of Antwerp, "the hope of prompt deliverance was still vivid in every heart." But after Antwerp's surrender, throughout the entire country, "the yoke of the conqueror weighed more heavily on the vanquished shoulders, and [it was] when the Belgian population, grim and resolute, began to struggle to preserve its honour and loyalty and to resist the ever increasing pressure of the enemy to bring it into complete submission and to use it as a tool against its own army and its own King."

By that time (the winter of 1914–1915), the Germans had divided the conquered territories into three major zones: the Occupation Zone and two Army Zones. The Occupation Zone included the majority of Belgium (a sliver of Belgium remained free) and was controlled by the German civil government headed by Governor General Baron von Bissing in Brussels. Two Army Zones, each named Etape, were controlled by a regional army commander. The French Etape contained six districts named after their major city or commune: Longwy, Charleville, Vervins, St. Quentin, Valenciennes, and Lille. The Belgian Etape had two districts: West Flanders and East Flanders. Within each Etape district was a thin strip of land directly behind the trenches that was called the Operations Zone. (See Reader Aids: Map of Region.)

Compounding the situation was Germany's new method of locking Belgium away from the rest of the world.

THE BELGIAN–DUTCH BORDER EVOLVES DANGEROUSLY

When the war started, the border between Belgium and Holland was overrun with refugees and retreating Belgian soldiers. Some estimates had the number as high as a million who fled north to the Netherlands or south to France. The Dutch and Belgians put aside their traditional dislike of one another as Holland opened its collective arms to the refugees, and the Belgians responded with grateful appreciation. Many Dutch homes spontaneously took in as many as they could while tent cities, some housing as many as twenty-five thousand people, sprang up nearly overnight.

In December 1914, after the German occupation of Belgium had had a few months to settle in, Governor General von Bissing issued a proclamation promising no retribution to those who wanted to return to their homes. More important, Belgian men of military age were promised they would not be taken prisoner or held accountable for their past military service.

The Germans' seemingly benevolent beckoning of Belgians to return home was viewed by many as a blatant attempt to curry favor with worldwide public opinion. To the refugees, it was a welcome call to go back home, and hundreds of thousands did so (approximately one hundred thousand stayed in Holland through the war).

Such a fluid border in those first months of the war would not be seen again until the end of hostilities. By late 1914, Belgium was effectively sealed off to all those who did not have an official pass issued by the German authorities.

This did not stop the continued clandestine attempts to get people and goods in and out of Belgium. People trying to get *out* of Belgium included Allied soldiers and downed airmen trapped in enemy territory, as well as young Belgian men eager to join the Belgian or Allied armies. People trying to get *into* Belgium without proper paperwork were either Allied spies or smugglers dealing in food or material outlawed by the Germans. Smugglers knew that the imprisoned Belgians wanted one other item nearly as much as food: information about the war and the free world. The Germans were determined to stop such information—in the form of newspapers and magazines—from entering occupied territory.

After the border had been tightened, von Bissing issued another proclamation that reflected how seriously the Germans took illegal border activity. He decreed that any who attempted to cross would "run the risk of being killed by the sentinels on the frontier." Those caught would be sent to Germany as prisoners of war. "This applies equally to members of the family of any Belgian capable of military service . . . who do not prevent the latter from entering Holland." Von Bissing's message was clear—the innocent would pay the price for the guilty party's actions.

Even with a tighter border, the Germans wanted even more control by the spring of 1915 because too many people and materials were still slipping through. But they faced two primary challenges: the checkpoints and the land itself.

The checkpoints along the 280-mile (450-km) border were at major and minor roads. The major checkpoints—which monitored foot traffic, vehicles, and trams—were manned by German officers and soldiers. Some of the small posts were initially maintained by Belgian customs officials who had guarded them before the war. By early 1915, however, it had become obvious that many of those Belgians were too easily bribed, so they were replaced by German landsturmers (older soldiers used for noncombat duties).

The other border challenge—the land—was not as easily addressed. Much of the border traversed the Campine, which was flat, desolate, and dotted with scrub pines and purple heather. The Campine's inhospitable, wind-swept countryside was difficult to monitor and harder to guard.

An idea to deal with such terrain came from a Prussian army officer, Captain Schutte, who worked with German Intelligence in Belgium. He suggested an electrified wire barrier be built along the entire border. The concept was tried in early 1915 along part of the Swiss border and had been "enthusiastically received by the army command," according to Belgian historian Jan Ingelbrecht.

So, in April 1915, work began on installing what the Germans called "Grenzhochspannung hindernis," or border high-voltage wire, along the Belgian–Dutch border. Many Belgians came to call it the "dead thread." The main electricity for the wire came from feeder lines that tapped into already-established power stations or large facilities nearby. But the border's extreme length dictated that a *schalthaus* (switching house)—run by gas generators and used as rest stations for the landsturmers—be built every two kilometers (1.2 miles) to keep the electricity at a sufficient level. That level was two-thousand volts—enough to kill.

To lower the cost of construction and to make it easier to monitor, the Germans did not follow the exact border and reconfigured it around the new electric wire. Certain bulges and parts of the country were cut off, and only about 196 miles

Figure 5.2. An unidentified victim of the German electric fence, which sealed off Belgium from Holland and the rest of the world. No date or location is known.

Public domain; Roger Van den Bleeken, Archives Heemkring Hoghescote vzw, Kapellen, Belgium.

(316 km) of the border were electrified. Additionally, a large swath of no-man's-land was established so that the entire border was defined by a line of traditional barbed wire, an open space, the electric wire, another open space, then another line of barbed wire. In populated areas, the width of the open spaces around the electric wire was relatively narrow. In the less densely populated frontier, the open spaces were wide enough to accommodate roving patrols of German cavalry. The electric wire itself stood on tall poles with barbed wire on each side. In a number of villages, the electric wire ran straight through the residential center. Altogether, it was an imposing and frightening barrier.

After months of work, when the electrification was complete, many civilians and even some soldiers were unsure of exactly how the electric wire worked. Electricity had only come to Belgium less than thirty years before, and many in rural areas had little, if any, experience with it. Was the wire truly live or just a ploy to scare people from trying to cross? If it was live, would the wire give only a small shock or would it kill? Did a person have to touch it to be shocked, or was the electricity able to jump out of the wire?

The one sure thing was that from then on only the serious-minded would take the risk of trying to cross the border.

GERMAN OCCUPATION HAS DIFFERING IMPACTS

For those trapped behind the electric fence, life became a complicated mix of physical and emotional hardships that were spread unevenly through the Belgian population. The Germans wanted and demanded total control of civilian life, and they achieved that for many. But class distinction and who could pay for what played a major role in how seriously occupation affected daily life.

Not surprisingly, the aristocracy and the wealthy merchant and middle classes were better off than most, but they generally tried to compensate by giving much of their time and resources to relief efforts (see chapter 8).

The less fortunate, on the bottom rungs of the socioeconomic ladder, suffered the most. Those who had a job that paid even a little felt they were lucky, but coal miners and others involved in heavy physical labor struggled to maintain their strength and stamina since food minimums were hard for the CRB and CN to maintain and black-market food became more and more expensive. Those who lived in cities and major towns had different hardships and challenges from those who lived in villages or on farms, but both groups experienced the full range of scenarios, from best-possible to worst-case.

No matter who you were or where you lived, the food restrictions had far-reaching consequences for the health of the population. The threat of epidemics was something that concerned local doctors, national health officials, the CN, and the CRB. Efforts at the beginning of the war were sporadic and uncoordinated, but later they became systematic and nationwide.

PROCLAMATION.

Inhabitants of both sexes are strictly forbidden to leave their houses so far as this is not absolutely necessary for making short rounds, in order to buy provisions or water their cattle. They are absolutely forbidden to leave their houses at night under any circumstances whatever.

Whoever attempts to leave the place, by night or day, upon any pretext whatever, will be shot.

Potatoes can only be dug with the Commandant's consent and under military supervision.

The German troops have orders to carry out these directions strictly, by sentinels and patrols, who are authorised to fire on anyone departing from these directions.

THE GENERAL COMMANDING.

Figure 5.3. A German *affiche* (French for "poster") displayed in occupied Belgium. It reflects how completely the Germans wanted to control civilian life.
Public domain; Joseph Green papers, Seeley G. Mudd Manuscript Library, Princeton University, New Jersey.

While the CRB was officially concerned only with the importation of food, the delegates could not ignore what was happening in all the communes, villages, and towns within their territory. E. E. Hunt, like many other delegates, quickly saw how the stress of war, the lack of a complete and healthy diet, and the ensuing cold in the winter of 1914–1915 was a recipe for the spread of diseases.

"Belgium needed far more than bread," Hunt said. "Thousands had neither clothes nor dwellings; millions were out of work; people of all classes were cold and idle and ill. The task of the Commission for Relief in Belgium could not long remain a simple doling out of rations, for food was almost useless without other things as well—clothing, fuel, dwelling houses, money, and good health."

By the beginning of 1915, two epidemics had already been reported in Antwerp Province: typhoid and black measles. Hunt stated that seventy-five cases of typhoid were known and others suspected in the town of Willebroeck (now spelled Willebroek), twelve miles (twenty km) south of Antwerp. As the province's CRB chief delegate, Hunt took it upon himself to deal with the situation.

Hunt knew of two American women working in the Rockefeller relief station in Rotterdam. They were Dr. Caroline Hedger and Miss Janet A. Hall, both of whom had served with the Chicago Health Department, had volunteered to work in Rotterdam, and had come over in 1914. "At my request these ladies came to the province of Antwerp as volunteer health officers."

No one had told Hunt to do so, and no one had asked him to deal with typhoid or any other health issues in Antwerp Province. He had simply seen the need and acted, gaining the approval of the Belgians and the travel permissions from the German authorities for both women.

The women arrived in Willebroeck with their own supply of typhoid vaccine. For two weeks, they lived above a tavern in a small suite of rooms where "mould was so thick on the walls that one could scrape it off with one's fingers," Hunt related. They started work immediately, helping local physicians and going into every house where typhoid had been reported or was suspected to be. They inoculated as many people as possible and ended up donating $3,000 worth of vaccine to the CRB, which used it to help eradicate typhoid in other areas.

Hunt's action and the women's efforts not only helped Belgium; they also helped the CRB realize that health issues were a major concern, especially as the war dragged on. Quickly the delegates—both those already on the job and those arriving—were inoculated with four separate injections for typhoid, and health reports became part of a delegate's duties.

A greater concern was also shown for other opportunistic diseases, such as tuberculosis, which had found footholds within Belgium and northern France as the long-term lack of plentiful food began to take its toll. (CRB delegates were not immune. Delegate Robert M. Dutton died in the United States on February 19, 1918, at forty-eight from tuberculosis that he probably contracted while in the CRB.)

On April 1, 1916, Francqui wrote to Hoover about the food situation and included a report from leading Belgian medical professionals and the chiefs of hospital services that showed a serious increase in mortality and in the occurrence of diseases brought on by malnutrition.

Hoover responded by sending to Belgium Dr. William Lucas, a children's specialist and professor of pediatrics at the University of California, Berkeley. After a three-month investigation that was aided by Belgian physicians, Dr. Lucas wrote an extensive report highlighting the growing spread of multiple diseases such as tuberculosis and rickets. He divided the population into three classifications: the well-to-do, the farmers, and the "industrial and shop-keeping class." He reported that it was the latter group, approximately five million people, that was suffering the most from malnutrition—particularly the children.

Dr. Lucas made numerous recommendations, most notably that children receive supplemental food from what was already being provided. The CRB and CN responded by establishing a network of canteens—mostly in schools—that provided a midday meal to infants, children, expectant mothers, and the elderly. Hoover also circulated the Lucas report widely and used it to reinvigorate Allied support for food imports. Other CRB and CN reports would follow as concern for the health of civilians would remain a top priority for both groups throughout the life of the relief.

Figure 5.4. Belgian children were impacted the most by the war and needed the relief program more than any others.
Public domain; Herbert Hoover Presidential Library Archives, West Branch, Iowa.

URBAN LIFE UNDER THE GERMANS

Because Belgium was the most industrialized country in Europe and had the highest population density, most of its citizens lived in cities and towns. They all were under the heavy hand of German occupation, with the country's two largest cities, Brussels and Antwerp, being representative of what most experienced.

In Brussels, occupation fell over the city like a black mourning shawl.

Before the war, the city had been the "proud Paris of the North," boasting an air of gaiety and refinement that was heightened by magnificent architecture. The charming old section of town had crooked little streets and the stunning *grand place* (main square), which Baedeker's tour book proclaimed was "one of the finest medieval squares in existence." The square was anchored by the city's inspiring fifteenth-century *hôtel de ville* (town hall). Fashionable cafés, luxurious restaurants, wine rooms, and simpler brasseries (taverns) offered a wide variety of food and drink. On the edges of the old part of town were beautiful, broad, tree-lined boulevards where ancient city walls used to stand. To the west, along a slight ridge, was the fashionable upper section of town, and to the south and southeast were the "new quarters."

By the winter of 1914–1915, occupied Brussels was a totally different city. The change had started the moment the German Army had marched in. All communications were cut off—telephones and telegraphs were shut down, postal service was suspended, and newspaper offices were closed and their presses seized. Transportation was stopped—automobiles were banned, most horses were requisitioned, streetcars were shut down, and all trains were suspended. Civilians were not allowed to leave their neighborhoods without a German pass and had to abide by numerous restrictions and curfews.

"We were thus pretty thoroughly cut off from the world," Legation Secretary Hugh Gibson said. "Most of the conveniences which we had come to take for granted in our modern life were stopped without warning, a hundred restrictions were put upon us and several millions of people had to adapt themselves over night to an entirely new and abnormal mode of life." And at night, shops, restaurants, and bars were emptied early by German curfews, while most streets were darkened in anticipation of raids by Allied biplanes.

Meanwhile, German troops were everywhere, patrolling the streets, eating and drinking in the cafés, marching and singing up and down the wide avenues and boulevards, and commandeering park bridle paths for cavalry officers and their well-groomed mounts. Many of the soldiers were simply tourists on furlough from the Western Front.

The Germans, famous for their precision and eye for detail, even went so far as to change the time in Brussels and throughout occupied Belgium. Before the war, Belgium had been on Greenwich Mean Time, while Germany had set its clocks one hour earlier. When the Germans took over, they insisted that the country convert to German time and that all town clocks be set to the new time.

Immediately, towns all over Belgium reported faulty tower clocks that couldn't be repaired. Most Belgians began referring to all appointments in Belgian time, as opposed to German, or "hour of the clock," time.

Occupation also brought a startling new image to Brussels. Legation Minister Brand Whitlock said, "We began to note a new phenomenon, new at least to Brussels—women begging in the streets. Hunger, another of war's companions, had come to town."

Thousands of other Belgians, Whitlock continued, "besieged the [German] Pass Bureau for permits to travel. The soup kitchens and bread lines were thronged. There was no work to do. The rust of idleness was on everything. An occasional aeroplane from the Allies dropped little celluloid tubes containing encouraging news, but the Germans, waging a successful war, insolently published all the news, even the official reports of the Allies."

As fall wore down into the winter, the Belgians began to feel a more permanent and oppressive sense of occupation. Joining the ever-present German soldiers were German bureaucrats and civil service personnel, who came to the city to run the German civil government of occupation. They filled the streets, crowded onto trams (which had resumed service), and took many of the seats in the city's cafés. They were unwanted and unwelcomed people who most residents hoped were only short-term visitors, not new residents.

Adding to the feeling that the city was being taken over was another new sight, German *affiches*. These posters were plastered daily around Brussels and all over occupied Belgium. Belgians were used to the occasional local government placards,

Figure 5.5. Belgians from all walks of life wait patiently outside a Brussels soup kitchen.
Public domain; E. E. Hunt, *War Bread* (New York: Henry Holt & Co., 1916).

which gave residents neighborhood information, but these German posters were new. They carried war news or rules and regulations of the occupation and in many inferior ways took the place newspapers held before the war.

The first *affiche* was posted on the first afternoon the German Army marched into Brussels (August 20, 1914) and was indicative of what was to come. It was signed by the commanding general of the army, General Friedrich Bertram Sixt von Armin, and began innocently enough with a call for residents to stay calm and go about their business. That changed quickly, however, when it declared, "Resistance and disobedience will be punished with extreme severity. The owners of houses where ammunition and explosives are found may expect to be shot and have their houses burned. Whoever offers armed resistance will be shot. Whoever opposes the German troops, whoever attacks them, whoever is found with arms will be shot."

On September 2, 1914, an *affiche* appeared that was the first proclamation of the new German governor general in Belgium, Field Marshal Baron Wilhelm Leopold Colmar von der Goltz. The placard stated that a new civil administration would be installed, and both it and the already-present military government in Belgium would be headquartered in Brussels.

"My task will be to preserve quiet and public order in Belgium," von der Goltz stated frankly in the *affiche*. "Every act of the population against the German military forces, every attempt to interfere with their communications with Germany, to trouble or cut railway, telegraph or telephone communications, will be punished severely. Any resistance or revolt against the German administration will be suppressed without pity." If such sabotage did occur, von der Goltz warned, the innocent would be punished along with the guilty.

He finished the *affiche* with what he probably thought was a reasonable, compassionate note: "I do not ask any one to forgo his patriotic sentiments, but I do expect from all of you a sensible submission and absolute obedience to the orders of the German Government."

The impact of this proclamation on residents of Brussels was significant. Since the start of the war, most Belgians had felt that the Germans were only passing through. But here was a proclamation announcing the formation of a civilian government. Such a thing screamed the dirty word "annexation."

Outwardly, Brussels—and Belgium—complied with von der Goltz's proclamation, but inwardly the story was quite different. The very nature of a people who had been continually invaded but never conquered in spirit was to fight back in creative ways that would not bring the wrath of retaliation. In short order, citizens everywhere began tactics of subterfuge, passive-aggressive compliance, and occasional outright defiance. On the streetcars, the Belgians did the only thing they could do in protest: they "proudly turned their backs, or refused to sit beside the hated [German] uniforms." It was the same in the cafés, where many residents preferred to leave "rather than sip beer or coffee beside the enemy."

Clandestine activities included brave civilians around the country producing leaflets, flyers, or broadsides that criticized the Germans or relayed outside news of the war. The one that rose to international prominence was the Brussels-based *La Libre Belgique* (*The Free Belgium*), which was produced every week and never failed to somehow reach an enraged Governor General von Bissing, who placed a 10,000-franc reward on the capture of those responsible. The scrappy little paper would inspire a nation but lead to the imprisonment of many and the execution of a few, including twenty-three-old Gabrielle Petit (later to become a national hero). Throughout the war, the paper never missed a weekly issue.

Residents of Brussels also struck back by using their own flag. Because von der Goltz had specifically stated no one needed to "forgo his patriotic sentiments," Belgians began displaying their country's flag wherever and whenever possible. From balconies, on doors, outside windows, hanging from carts, and as lapel pins, hat pins, and parcel wrappings—Belgian flags were practically everywhere the Germans looked.

On September 18, only three weeks after von der Goltz's statement, a new *affiche* appeared ordering the Belgians to take down their flags. Signed by Baron Arthur von Lüttwitz, the military governor of Brussels (different from the occupation governor general von der Goltz), it stated that the order had been made to protect residents because the display of Belgian flags was "regarded as a provocation by the German troops living in or passing through Brussels."

In the spirit of passive resistance, the Belgians obediently took down their flags, then promptly began using the Belgian flag's colors (black, yellow, and red) as hair ribbons, parcel string, and other adornments.

The war of wills had just begun.

Brussels's occupation—and transformation—grew worse when in December 1914, Baron von Bissing replaced von der Goltz as the new governor general. Under the baron's harsh rule, the occupation took on deeper and darker tones. As one history explained, "Since von Bissing's arrival . . . Brussels had become to all intents a vast concentration camp under a harsh and tyrannical rule."

Figure 5.6. Gabrielle Petit, a twenty-three-year-old Belgian woman who had worked in the underground ferrying men to the border and distributing copies of the underground newspaper *La Libre Belgique*, was executed by the Germans on Saturday morning, April 1, 1916. She died relatively unknown, but after the war, she became a national hero. Public domain.

This meant that to enter or leave the city required a pass, which was difficult and costly to obtain from the Germans. All citizens had to carry an identity card bearing a photograph, and Belgian men eighteen to forty had to register and regularly report to the German Kommandantur (commandant's headquarters). Day and night the streets were patrolled by armed soldiers as well as by the Belgian city police force. Reportedly, the Germans also employed three special brigades of secret police that used agents provocateurs and Belgian informers to gather incriminating information against unsuspecting civilians.

In Belgium's second-largest city and largest port, Antwerp, the scenes of occupation took on slightly different hues, although the palette was the same. According to Hunt, "The hum and the throb of industry were gone; the quays were empty; factories were shut; acres of rusting wagons and rotting ships lined the northern basins; the warehouses were sealed and guarded by German soldiers; labor was dispersed; and the very air was idle and noisome." To him, Antwerp had become "a dead city."

Before the war, Antwerp had been one of the largest commercial ports in the world. Even though it had a metropolitan population of only four hundred thousand, its port was the third-busiest in the world and served "as an outlet for the commerce of Germany as well as of Belgium." In the northern section of the city were six huge man-made *bassins* (basins) that handled the loading and unloading of everything from seagoing ships and canal barges to pleasure boats. The *bassins* were linked not only with one another but to the River Scheldt to the east and a large canal to the west. Once the war began, the activity within the basins instantly died. When the CRB began shipping food in canal barges from Rotterdam, it used only the Bassin Guillaume for operations.

In early 1916, new CRB delegate Prentiss Gray walked along the waterfront and was "struck with the absolute desolation and desertion. Twenty-five thousand dock workers are idle in this city alone, and since Antwerp fell, none of the magnificent dock equipment has turned a wheel. Not a steamer or a barge discharges any of the wharves except the Bassin Guillaume, where our relief barges are unloaded. The entire water front is deserted." In contrast, because of the CRB, Bassin Guillaume "presented a scene of feverish activity," according to Gray.

A few days later, Gray saw a more personal side to the occupation and the effect it was having on Antwerp's residents. He was invited to dinner at the home of Monsieur Blaess, who worked in the ship-owning department of the CRB. Gray arrived at eight that night. The husband had not arrived home by the time the group sat down to eat at nine. "Madame Blaess and her three daughters, although exceedingly nervous, repressed their feelings in an effort to make us feel at home. As the evening progressed their growing fear that M. Blaess had been thrown into jail was perfectly evident. When he finally came in at ten-thirty, their joy simply carried them off their feet."

Later that night, Gray wrote in his journal: "What a terrible thing this dread must be! Imagine living in the constant fear that, when anyone dear to you is out of sight for more than a few hours, the news may eventually come that he had been transported to Germany for some minor offense, or is lying incommunicado in prison!"

Outside Belgian cities, life could be much worse. As the new chief delegate to Antwerp Province, Gray wanted to see how the Belgian poor lived outside the city. He found more than he expected when he visited the town of Boom, less than nine miles (fifteen km) south of Antwerp. Worthy of only a phrase in a tour book—"a town with 16,800 inhabitants and numerous brick-kilns"—Boom was described by Gray as "a dirty little town supported before the war by its brick yards. The brick company absolutely controlled the town by owning all of the land and most of the houses of the workingmen." The brick company's doctor had reported to Gray that all residents were in "exceedingly good health and doing very well under our system of feeding." Gray wanted to see for himself.

During the next four hours, the American went door-to-door and visited twenty families in their homes. Even with his limited French skills and nonexistent knowledge of Flemish, he was able to ascertain the situation.

"All but three," Gray wrote, "had been without meat, except for the bacon supplied by the Commission, since the beginning of the war. None had any stock of food in the house, and all were living from week to week on what they drew from the communal warehouse. This is not difficult to understand as the brick company pays only from fourteen to sixteen francs per week for an adult's labor, and from seven to eight francs for that of a child. Employees work from twelve to sixteen hours a day."

Those facts were nothing compared to what he saw, which overwhelmed him. "I have never seen people in a sadder state of health, nor living in more squalor and filthiness. Even in peace time, I understand Boom has been considered a poor town. Nevertheless, unless something is done to relieve this situation we shall have a death rate here that is perfectly appalling."

NORMALCY SLIPS AWAY

Within a few months of occupation, the Germans allowed certain parts of daily life to resume. Outwardly, throughout the country, there was an appearance of near normalcy to much of daily living, especially in the first year or so of occupation. The trams and trains ran again, the censored mail was delivered, people with jobs still went to work, and those who could afford to pay still sat in cafés talking and drinking watered-down imitation coffee or reading with disgust one of the German-sanctioned newspapers. Those on farms lived generally quieter lives as they eked out survival by coaxing as much edible produce as possible from the land and butchering their livestock as a last resort.

But as the war dragged on, the appearance of normalcy wore thin or disappeared altogether. Despite the tremendous efforts of the CRB and CN, four long years of occupation led to food getting scarcer, clothes and shoes literally disintegrating from wear, longer lines at the daily soup kitchens, and more and more shops, restaurants, bars, and cafés closing because they had nothing to sell. The ranks of the destitute increased in direct proportion to the decrease of those who could pay for food and clothes.

By May 1917, when the last Americans had to leave Belgium because of America's April entry into the war, Germany's unrestricted submarine warfare had taken a tremendous toll on shipping. This meant the average daily caloric intake per capita for the Belgians was a meager 1,522, which was less than half the prewar normal. And for many, according to Hoover, that average fell far short because "those who did heavy work had to have a minimum of 2,500 calories a day or there would have been no economic life; thus the rations for others fell far below 1,500 calories." Additionally, the calorie average was "totally inadequate in fats and proteins."

It would be another year before the precarious food situation would improve, due in large part to a 1918 bountiful American harvest and the development of the convoy system of shipping that minimized the effect of Germany's submarine warfare.

With food supplies stabilizing in Belgium and northern France by mid-1918, civilians in the occupied territories struggled on, although a sense—and appearance—of normalcy would not be truly reestablished until well after the war concluded.

6

The CRB Delegates

Arriving in Rotterdam on Saturday evening, December 5, 1914, the first ten Oxford students who had agreed to become CRB delegates were a bit stunned by how quickly events had transpired. A few days before they had been university students, most of them Rhodes Scholars. Suddenly, they were in neutral Holland preparing to go into German-occupied Belgium to do a job that was anything but clear.

"What we were to do, no one exactly knew," said Emil Hollmann. "We had visions of sitting on the top of box cars or sleeping on the decks of small canal barges in their long journeys from Rotterdam into Belgium. . . . We expected to see German savages prowling around ready at the slightest provocation to scalp women and children and perhaps provoke a quarrel with us for the same purpose!"

They had more questions than answers. Neither Hoover nor anyone else was able to say what the work would entail. The CRB was—by the necessity of attempting such massive relief for the first time—making it up as it went along. And because conditions within sealed-off Belgium were sketchy at best, few outside the country knew what to expect inside the country.

The ten newly minted delegates were Carlton G. Bowden (University of the South); Emil Hollmann (Stanford University); David T. Nelson (University of North Dakota); Tracy B. Kittredge (University of California, the only non–Rhodes Scholar); Walter C. Lowdermilk (University of Arizona); Scott H. Paradise (Yale University); Richard H. Simpson (Indiana University); George F. Spaulding (University of Arizona); William W. Stratton (University of Utah); and Laurence C. "Duke" Wellington (Williams College).

All of them—and the next wave of fifteen who would follow a week later—had been chosen by a fellow Oxford student, Perrin Galpin, who went to Belgium in the second wave. Hoover had telegraphed Galpin back on November 30, 1914, "We propose to leave the selection of the ten men entirely in your hands as we have confidence in your ability, and, furthermore after our conversation on Friday you are aware of the conditions which we impose."

Practically speaking, Hoover simply didn't have the time to choose delegates as he dealt with much larger issues and challenges. He knew these young, inexperienced students weren't the ideal candidates for such a job, but he had no choice. The time and distance from America made it impossible to wait for the perfect CRB delegates. For that matter, what constituted a "perfect" delegate was still unknown.

Each of the students carried only a small valise, something they were unaccustomed to as Oxford students. In England, they were expected to be properly attired at all times for numerous and varied events. German-occupied Belgium was a bit different. George Spaulding wrote, "We had been warned before leaving Oxford that we might have to ride canal boats to guard food shipments and to be prepared for hardships. So we had not taken our best clothes, not to mention dinner jackets which were de rigueur in those days whenever asked out for dinner." His suitcase contained only his toiletries, "a couple of ties, handkerchiefs and socks," some shirts, "extra underwear and a sweater . . . extra trousers and my College blazer—a scanty wardrobe, indeed."

Regardless of such clothing limitations, these early CRB delegates were rarely, if ever, seen in public without the proper day attire of a businessman: jacket or suit, stiff collar, and tie. They would maintain that standard even in Belgium, with the added benefit of a long, thick overcoat to combat the weather, which was always uncertain at any time of the year.

Even though Hoover was not a clothes-conscious man, the Chief, as the delegates came to call him, would never abide his men being out of form. That went double for most of the other CRB executives, and especially for the Belgian men of industry who were members of the provincial committees and the CN. Most of them were a product of the times and felt that a person dressed inappropriately could not be taken seriously.

FIRST ENTRY INTO BELGIUM

Properly attired, the ten delegates reported to Captain Lucey at the Rotterdam office on Sunday morning, December 6, for assignments. The shipping director gave them a quick overview of what little he knew of conditions in Belgium. He made a few specific assignments, but most of the new recruits were sent to Brussels to attend orientation meetings before receiving their assignments from the Brussels office.

One of those who did receive an assignment from Lucey was David T. Nelson. Recently turned twenty-three, he had been born and raised in North Dakota by parents who had emigrated from Norway. He was about five foot ten inches tall with a face that at rest was as unreadable as the prairies he had grown up around. But his smile was open and straightforward, and he was known to be trustworthy, hardworking, and ruggedly self-reliant.

Nelson's journey into Belgium would not be the easiest and reflected just how confusing the situation still was. He was assigned to be a delegate in Liège, a large city in southeast Belgium. He first traveled by train to the Dutch town of Maastricht with Hollmann, who had been tasked with establishing a CRB transshipping office in that town for supplies destined for southeastern Belgium. When they arrived in Maastricht, Nelson was supposed to smooth the way for a train of supplies that was coming from Rotterdam and meant for Liège. He quickly discovered that the train would not be allowed through the Dutch border because of a decision by some stationmasters south of Maastricht.

Quickly learning that one of the most important characteristics for a CRB delegate was improvisation, Nelson decided to talk directly with those stationmasters. He found a ride the next day in a motorcar from Maastricht south seven miles (eleven km) to the small Dutch town of Eijsden (not to be confused with the Belgian town of Eisden, which was north of Maastricht), where the train's permits were being held up. Once there, "after scouring the town I got to the burgomaster's [mayor's] chateau and managed to secure a man who could speak English as well as Dutch, French, and German. You need all to deal with a Dutch official. A Dutchman is without question the slowest person on earth."

Once Nelson and his volunteer had convinced the stationmasters to allow the train through and secured clearances, permits, and scheduling for the oncoming train, another problem arose. The motorcar that had given him a ride had left, and he had no way to get to his next stop, the Belgian village of Visé, which was across the border and about five miles (eight km) south of Eijsden. There were no motorcars to be had, and the Dutch stationmaster in Eijsden would not allow him to ride on the train that would come through later.

The only thing to do was walk. But he had his valise with him, and it was too heavy to carry such a distance. With little confidence he'd ever see it again, he left the suitcase at the station to be forwarded whenever possible. "I shall entertain no hope till I actually lay my hands on it again."

So, on that cold afternoon, December 9, as the sun was settling low in the sky, Nelson—sans suitcase and carrying only the clothes on his back, his wallet, identity papers, and permits to enter Belgium—began his lonely walk into German-held territory.

Having no idea what to expect, he was happily surprised to find the border crossing and travel to Visé, and then on to Liège, much easier than expected. Later, he would be reunited with his suitcase.

THE INITIAL WORK

As delegates began to enter Belgium, they were assigned to various regions throughout Belgium's provinces. Some of them had to make their own arrangements for office space, hire staff, and even secure their own housing. Most, though, were aided by private individuals and members of the provincial and local committees, who found them all they needed, sometimes for free. Belgians were eager to provide facilities and services to the CRB, not only out of kindness but also because they thought association with the neutral Americans might give added protection from the Germans (usually true).

Most of the CRB's offices out in the provinces ended up being manned by one to two delegates, with larger offices having four or five, and the Brussels office containing the most. Collectively, when the CRB was fully operational, the average number of delegates at any one time in Belgium and northern France ranged from forty to fifty-five.

For each of the delegates scattered throughout the provinces, the job was a bit different, and each faced the specific challenges as best as he could—especially in the early days.

In December 1914, Tracey Kittredge and Richard Simpson received their assignment from Captain Lucey. They traveled by car to Hasselt, the capital of the Flemish province of Limburg, which was in the northeast corner of Belgium.

When Kittredge and Simpson arrived, they checked into a hotel and began working. Kittredge had been designated as the chief delegate, but that didn't carry much weight, status, or privileges. They both did whatever was needed to move relief efforts forward, including contacting local and provincial officials, setting up an office, and filing reports with Brussels.

Kittredge wrote that all the CRB delegates had "come into Belgium keyed up with heroic resolve to devote their whole energy and ability to the work. . . . In those first days they seldom stopped to enquire what their specific duties were. The food was to be distributed to every household in Belgium, and an infinite amount of detailed organization had to be accomplished before this end could be attained. The delegates almost to a man threw themselves into the breach and did what was to be done without enquiring what their authority was, or whether they were expected to attack the problems to which they devoted themselves."

Kittredge went on to describe some of what they did. "Ships to be helped through damaged canals; sunken bridges and barges to be lifted out; lightermen to be cajoled or intimidated into obeying orders; warehouses and depots to be installed, filled/and protected; communication within the provinces and with Brussels to be established; mills to be controlled; bakers to be constrained into living up to their contracts; systems of distribution, administrative forms, ration cards to be devised and put into effect; local committees to be organized and induced to distribute food according to instructions; complaints to be investigated and difficulties with the Germans to be smoothed out."

With great understatement, he concluded, "The task was a formidable one."

Kittredge and Simpson were at a distinct disadvantage when it came to understanding their region, the food needed, and the details of how the distribution worked, but they did have two aces in the hole: they were neutral, and they could move about relatively unrestricted.

Neutrality afforded them the ability to work with both the Belgians and the Germans.

The freedom of movement was also special because at this early stage in the German occupation, very few Belgians were allowed to leave their own towns or villages. By December, some areas and cities were seeing tram and train services restarted, but Belgian communication was still nearly nonexistent, and personal movement was highly restricted.

Because Kittredge and Simpson, along with every other CRB man, were able to obtain German passes to travel, they became vital lifelines of communications between Belgian relief officials in the larger cities and their counterparts in villages and towns within the surrounding countryside. The Americans could help collect and disseminate information about food stores, canal viability, and soup kitchens, particularly statistics regarding those able to pay for their daily rations and those on complete charity. By providing such invaluable services, these December delegates were able to help prove the CRB's worth in the eyes of many Belgians beyond the food that the Americans could provide.

Delegate transportation was by motorcar whenever available. They were generally the only civilians allowed to use automobiles in Belgium. US-based Willys-Overland Motors had donated a fleet of machines for CRB use, but the cars had not yet arrived in early December. This did not stop the delegates, who always found a ride, either with a motorcar and driver donated by a prominent local person or with a sympathetic

Figure 6.1. The CRB delegates and their Belgian drivers were some of the only civilians allowed to use motorcars in Belgium. When the delegates first arrived in 1914, they flew small US flags on their cars. Later, as this photo taken after 1914 shows, CRB banners were created and flown in their place because of German demands.

Public domain; Herbert Hoover Presidential Library Archives, West Branch, Iowa.

German officer. Ultimately, all Belgian and US motorcars used by the CRB were provided with Belgian drivers. This not only gave much-needed employment to Belgians, but it also displayed to the public and the Germans the proper appearance of respect and professionalism that the CRB hoped to achieve in Belgium.

When in use by the CRB, most of the vehicles were initially decked out with American flags on the front fenders and a placard labeled CRB on the engine cowling. A motorcar so decorated never failed to draw crowds of Belgians and even cheers as it traveled throughout the cities and countryside. After the Germans became irked by such demonstrations, the American flags were removed from the vehicles and CRB pennants took their place.

GETTING THINGS DONE

On December 11, 1914, E. E. Hunt arrived in Antwerp as the new CRB chief delegate for Antwerp Province, which contained roughly one million civilians. There were no blueprints or manuals, no experts to instruct him on what needed to be done or how to work with the members of the Antwerp provincial committee or the CN. He was on his own to figure it out as he went along.

The basics were obvious. Food shipments that were starting to appear in Belgium via canal barges from Holland had to be processed, paid for, and distributed in a fair and equitable way, regardless of anyone's status, position, politics, or religion. And the Germans were not supposed to touch any of it, even though they ruled occupied Belgium ruthlessly.

Additionally, in these early days, details big and small were still being worked out within the CRB. As more delegates had joined—volunteering their time and energy to the work—it became obvious to Hoover and the other executives that they deserved compensation for at least any expenses they incurred while in Belgium. It was finally established that each man would receive 20 francs a day, or 600 francs a month, to cover his expenses. But the policy was never officially announced throughout the network, and a few delegates heard only rumors about it.

Hunt had to face this situation when one of the delegates assigned to him, William Stratton, officially wrote on February 3, 1915, urging Hunt to "use your influence at Brussels [office] toward ascertaining who, if anyone, knows anything about the 20 francs per day that is supposed to be paid to Americans in Belgium for defraying personal expenses. I have been broke since God knows when; the landlady has threatened to throw me out and has already interdicted me from the use of the bathroom and laundry until my bill is paid. I do not know how or where the Relief Commission could do any more useful work than in my case." In the bottom left corner of Stratton's letter, fellow delegate Richard Simpson had added, "Endorsed: Absolument d'accord. Same here. R.H.S."

Hunt quickly remedied the situation, Stratton paid his bills, and the delegates' housing situation would be later rectified in a luxurious way as Antwerp merchant

Edouard Bunge donated the use of his townhouse as a residence for CRB delegates (as many other wealthy Belgians did).

Besides dealing with such internal issues, Hunt's first order of business was to determine how he and the CRB fit into the Belgian way of doing things. Working with diverse groups of men in the numerous Belgian committees and communes, he quickly realized he was standing in a hurricane's eye, surrounded by the swirling winds of Belgium's social, religious, and political attitudes. He knew he would have to understand and acknowledge the powers of each to effectively fashion a coordinated relief effort.

Because Belgium was a relatively new country, Hunt learned that "the commune, not the nation, was the Belgian fatherland." And at odds, he wrote, were "Republicanism against Monarchy, Clericalism against Anti-Clericalism, Flemings against French-speaking Walloons, Socialism against Capitalism. Business, society, every department of life, was divided and subdivided into self-contained cliques. The bitterness of the struggle and the disunion were almost unbelievable."

The Germans had inadvertently changed all that with the invasion and converted the country's fierce factions into "tenacious patriotism," but Hunt acknowledged that it wasn't enough to wipe out the divisions. "Even in the midst of war men could not be expected to lay aside fundamental principles." The Belgians "still feared and distrusted their fellow Belgians. War exaggerated certain of their suspicions, instead of allaying them."

The CRB was supposed to be above all that. It was, in theory, working for all Belgians, no matter what their religion, political affiliation, or social standing. That concept was tested when in late December 1914, the members of the city district of Turnhout told Hunt privately they did not want to be on the CN's Antwerp provincial committee; they wanted to deal with Brussels directly or just with Hunt when it came to providing relief supplies to their district. They had not yet received any food from Antwerp and did not trust that a provincial committee could represent them and their needs to the headquarters in Brussels.

As Hunt wrote, the town of Turnhout was "rustic, old-fashioned, and Clerical" and did not trust the "merchants of Antwerp." In fact, the Turnhout delegation was not even clear on what the CRB was supposed to do. "It looked on us as an association of benevolent grain-dealers," Hunt wrote, "selling flour to a body of Antwerp business men, who, in turn, would resell it to the Turnhout delegation, of course at a profit to themselves!"

The issue came to a head at a provincial committee meeting. "There was an exciting moment when all the Turnhout delegates were on their feet at once, speaking Flemish instead of French, as they usually did when much excited, protesting . . . and adding that they were appealing to Brussels for complete separation from Antwerp."

The representatives of Turnhout petitioned the CN and the CRB in Brussels to permit a division of the province. Hunt was adamant that his province not be divided. He wrote multiple reports about the issue and why it was not a good idea to allow the secession of Turnhout.

With major communication difficulties still existing throughout Belgium, Hunt's reports did not reach Brussels in time to affect the decision. The CRB Brussels office said Turnhout was allowed to break away from the Antwerp provincial committee.

Hunt refused to accept the verdict. He pleaded his case with greater intensity, and the Brussels office reversed its decision. He then assigned Simpson to deal exclusively with Turnhout as a way of alleviating the city's fears of not being properly represented.

Hunt did not stop there. He knew there was truth in what the Turnhout representatives had been saying. The city of Antwerp had too much control over what was happening in the entire province of Antwerp. Hunt decided to take a bold next step—it was time to take on the powerhouse of Antwerp.

The city had been running relief efforts since the beginning of the war. City officials had always seen the work as a municipal matter. These officials, however, were "party men. They belonged to the Liberal or Socialist party. No Catholics were among them." They saw no reason "why they should surrender their favored position at the center of supplies when food began to come from America instead of the municipal warehouses."

Hunt stated diplomatically, "As an American delegate I was pledged to a different point of view." To correct the situation, he realized that "the Antwerp Provincial Relief Committee must be divorced from the Antwerp Town Hall and the group of party men who had so ably ministered to the wants lying close at hand."

The separation began, as Hunt noted, rather comically. His youngest assistant, nineteen-year-old Bennett H. (Harvie) Branscomb from Alabama, was designated as delegate to the city. One of his first jobs had been to reprimand the local committee for the reports it had been handing in. Hunt recounted that Branscomb had stood before some of the most prominent men of one of the greatest Flemish cities, held up one of their reports, and spoken in a quiet, southern drawl: "We cannot and we will not send another such report as this to Brussels. Reports must have our signature as American delegates. We will not give our signatures to tardy and un-businesslike reports."

The men were taken aback. The controller of Antwerp told a friend, "I have been accustomed to handle millions of francs every day, and now these young Americans come and ask me what became of such-and-such bag of flour last week!"

If they were surprised by Branscomb's remarks, they were shocked by what Hunt announced. He told the assembly that he had transferred the entire relief work for the city of Antwerp from the town hall to offices in Edouard Bunge's Bank of the Union of Antwerp and had designated a new delegate, Thomas O. Connett, to serve as the representative for the city. Hunt added that Connett had been instructed to create a census of all bread and flour consumers in the district. While the transfer was completed in four days, "such precipitate action appalled some of our supporters in the Committee."

After some time, however, their reaction became muted and then turned to praise once they saw what Connett was able to do. As Hunt noted, the "quiet, unobtrusive young Cambridge student, about twenty-two years old," with the help of numerous bank clerks, "had card-indexed the city of Antwerp and reorganized the system of control over food distributions with a saving of about one-fifth of the supplies."

Despite their youth, the American delegates were getting things done. Hunt noted, "None of us was out of his twenties. We were beardless boys in the assemblies of our elders, but young or old, we were equal participators in a thrilling undertaking and we intended to do our part."

DELEGATE RESPONSIBILITIES EVOLVE

Because of the initial war crisis, the Americans had been welcomed by the Belgians into the humanitarian relief process, especially when it came to establishing the international agreements and the purchasing of food outside of Belgium. "At first there was little difficulty," Kittredge wrote. "The country had been so near the threat of famine, the work of the organisation was so difficult and so engrossing, that the Comité National and the Commission alike threw themselves wholeheartedly in the work of organisation."

But as Hoover's publicity machine began to generate worldwide press about what the CRB was doing in Belgium, and as the American delegates became highly visible symbols of relief, motoring around Belgium bringing barge loads of foodstuffs into every province, the Belgian people took notice.

So did Francqui and his associates. They were stung by their countrymen's feeling that the entire relief work was being done by the Americans when, in fact, it was Francqui, the CN, and the provincial committees that had admirably set up the complex systems for food preparation, rationing, and distribution.

And then there was the issue of the role the delegates played in Belgium. "The Comité National did not intend that the Commission or its representatives should have any executive voice in the control of the distribution of food or of relief in Belgium." Kittredge put it, "The activities of certain of the American delegates began to rather annoy and irritate certain of the members of the Comité National and of the provincial committees. . . . [They] found no very keen pleasure in having their ideas overruled and the conduct of their organisation controlled by striplings from across the seas who, though capable and amiable enough, yet had as a rule but little practical or business experience."

This was not to say there was objection to the Americans in Belgium. Everyone—even Francqui—welcomed them because they lent diplomatic weight and protection to relations with the Germans. They just didn't want the "striplings" making any decisions or taking executive actions within Belgium.

Naturally, then, the delegates' duties in the provinces became a point of contention between the CRB and the CN—and even among the delegates themselves. Despite a December 1914 memorandum from Hoover that outlined many of the duties and responsibilities, the reality was that the individual "power, influence and duties of the provincial delegates differed according to the efficiency of the provincial committees, the difficulties of the local situation and the personality of the delegate," according to Kittredge.

Within the ranks of the CRB, this boiled down to two opposing points of view. "On the one hand was the group led in the beginning by [E. E.] Hunt and Robinson Smith," Kittredge explained, "that believed that the work of relief should be essentially an American affair; that the responsibility for the direction of relief operations rested on the American members of the Commission; that its methods should be those of American business efficiency; and that consequently the head delegate in each province was to be regarded as the manager of relief operations in his province."

On the other side of the discussion "were the majority of . . . delegates and all of the successive directors of the Commission in Brussels. They agreed the work of the Commission was indispensable to the success of the relief operations, and that the American delegates should exercise such supervision and control as to make sure that the food supplies and benevolent funds were efficiently handled, that they were fairly distributed and that they went solely to the Belgian civil population. But, according to this second point of view, the actual work of distribution was essentially a Belgian domestic problem; the work could be best done by Belgians who, because of their acquaintance with local conditions, habits and ideas, were in a position to conduct the work in a manner agreeable to the Belgians themselves."

Most critical of all, Hoover and the majority felt that "it was not the duty nor the function of the Americans to reform the Belgians or revolutionise their business methods and their social habits." Therefore, "the delegate should use his power with extreme discretion, should act as a diplomatic intermediary between the Germans and the Belgians and between the various conflicting groups of Belgian committees."

It was easy to know which side Francqui and the CN took—the latter. The few delegates like Hunt and Smith who supported the former were causing quite a concern for Francqui and his group, despite Francqui's occasional public compliments about these Americans.

While Hoover and most of the delegates understood they were not there to change Belgian ways, this awareness did not mean they agreed that they served no useful function within Belgium. They knew their presence was necessary for the relief to function at all because of the responsibilities imposed upon the CRB by the Allied governments. Hoover had personally agreed to, and the CRB had officially accepted, the job through the Allied guarantees of buying, shipping, and supervising the distribution of food and clothes down to the commune level, with no German requisitioning of foodstuffs. Hoover and his sometimes-strident delegates would accept nothing less.

This point was not lost among the everyday operations of the delegates out in a war-ravaged countryside dealing with Belgian businessmen of varying social, religious, and political affiliations. Kittredge honestly assessed, "In the end, as in the beginning, no definite decision was ever reached as to the exact function of the delegate. . . . His position continued to depend largely upon his personality and upon that of the heads of the province to which he was assigned."

The disagreements between the CRB and the CN, which Kittredge termed "rather painful misunderstandings," sprang from a CN viewpoint that would basically never change: Francqui and some of the other members of the CN felt the entire relief work was a domestic issue that they were quite capable of handling themselves, and thus there was no need for CRB delegates to be wandering around their country supervising relief operations.

In this regard, the Belgians and Germans agreed. The Germans felt relief efforts could be handled by the CN under German supervision, and they "regarded the Americans of the Commission as rather troublesome intruders, who were not to be allowed to have an active voice in the distribution of food and who were to be induced to be content with seeing that the food did not go to the Germans."

By the summer of 1915, resentment toward the CRB would bubble up into a full-blown crisis that was led by Francqui but supported by Baron von Bissing. (See chapter 11.)

HARASSMENT BY GERMAN SENTRIES

One of the ongoing problems CRB delegates faced as they traveled around Belgium was German sentries who continually stopped, searched, and generally harassed them. The Americans carried with them multiple documents, including a US passport, a letter in German stating the carrier was a member of the CRB, and always a *Passierschein* (a German safe conduct pass) for that particular trip. The passes usually stated that the Americans were not to be detained, searched, or questioned without cause.

Unfortunately, many times the passes were not honored or even looked at. Instead, the sentries ordered the Americans out of their automobiles, interrogated them extensively, and physically searched them. In some cases, the Germans even took apart the CRB cars looking for contraband. Any complaints about treatment or questions about the guards' authority to take such actions could mean rough handling or jail. Once in jail, the only way out was to somehow get a message to someone in the CRB or the American diplomatic corps.

The Americans were, however, not totally blameless when it came to sentry post incidents. Hugh Gibson wrote about two new Rhodes Scholar delegates and a stenographer who were entering Belgium for the first time. They had been pulled out of their car at the frontier and searched. The three had been warned back in Holland that it was illegal to transport letters in or out of Belgium, but the men were still found carrying numerous letters. They were immediately tossed in the local jail. There, they made their situation even worse. The stenographer had written a letter to his girlfriend back home, which he decided to tear up. "Of course that meant that he was caught red-handed 'destroying documents' and the whole crowd was in bad," according to Gibson.

Figure 6.2. Two German landsturmers—older Germans used for noncombat duties such as sentry duty.

Public domain; Roger Van den Bleeken, Archives Heemkring Houghescote vzw, Kapellen, Belgium.

The CRB car was confiscated, and the men were brought to Brussels under guard. Before Gibson and Hoover (who was then in Brussels) went to the political bureau to get them out, Gibson wrote: "It is astounding how grown men can be such fools. We shall probably succeed in getting them off but it is almost more than they deserve."

Hoover was continually faced with such youthful indiscretions as he tried to get the inexperienced delegates to understand they must remain absolutely neutral in both thought and deed if the relief was to continue.

The sentry situation did not improve until a somewhat comical event occurred. Governor General von Bissing refused to believe the stories of sentry harassment because he had specifically ordered that no CRB personnel should be stopped and searched. After the harassment issue was once again brought up to the governor general, an idea was suggested. Why not have one of von Bissing's staff officers travel in civilian clothes with a delegate and see how the sentries treated them?

A young staff officer quickly volunteered, and off they motored. At one sentry post, all those in the car were ordered to get out and wait in the guardhouse to be searched. The sentries would not review any documents being offered. After the disguised German refused to exit the vehicle, he was yanked out by his legs. In the guardhouse, when the German finally announced who he was, the guards didn't believe him and promptly beat and kicked him with fists, boots, and rifle butts. The badly injured man was then taken to Antwerp and thrown in jail with his papers still unopened. His ordeal ended only after someone finally read his documents.

When von Bissing heard, he was furious and a court-martial was quickly convened for those responsible. Meanwhile, according to Hugh Gibson, "everybody in Brussels was chortling over the fact that one of the Boches [derogatory name for Germans] had got a taste for it."

From that event, a few changes were made, and the situation did improve for delegates. They began carrying a CRB "passport" as well as their own US passport. Additionally, any CRB courier would be required to hang around his neck a large pouch (nearly eighteen inches by eighteen inches) with clear plastic on the front so that sentries could easily see and read all relevant documents for that particular trip.

FINDING GOOD RECRUITS

Hoover believed that the key element to successfully maintaining neutrality and continuing relief within Belgium was the CRB delegate. Without honorable, trustworthy American delegates to uphold the many guarantees made with the Allies and the Germans, the relief would be quickly shut down. So high-quality delegates were important, but the finding and maintaining of good delegates remained a constant struggle throughout the life of the relief.

In the founding few months of the CRB, when Hoover was desperate to find neutral Americans who would drop everything, work for free, go into unknown German-occupied Belgium, and do a job that no one could adequately describe, his personnel standards had been relatively low. "We are badly in need of Americans to take charge of our work in various Relief Stations in Belgium," Hoover had written to Oxford student Galpin. "We want people with some experience roughing it, who speak French, have tact, and can get on with the Germans." That was it—all the skills necessary for a position that had not yet been clearly defined.

The American Legation staff and CRB executives in Brussels quickly discovered that some of the first student delegates were not up to the task. At least six of the first twenty-five Oxford students to enter Belgium were never officially listed by the CRB as having served as delegates. The assumption is that they either did not complete their agreed-upon service or they did so to such an unsatisfactory degree that the CRB did not want to include them in official records.

Throughout 1915, personnel problems persisted as the New York CRB office sent over numerous recruits. Most were good, hard workers who fit into the relief program, but a few did not. CRB director in Brussels William Poland explained to new recruit John "Pink" Simpson, "You know, this is a delicate situation here. Some people come and don't get along very well and have to be sent home."

Simpson—who became a well-respected delegate—had a simple description of what was needed: "The requirements were common sense, reasonable intelligence, and ability to get along with people."

Even so, some washed out. For those, there were numerous ways that their departure would be arranged. Hoover and CRB executives walked a fine line with the unacceptable delegates, primarily because all the men were volunteers who were giving their time and, in some cases, their own money to do the work. Some were simply invited to leave and given a ticket back to America. Others, who were not appropriate for behind-the-lines work but might be useful elsewhere, were transferred, usually to the London office, where they could be better supervised and have less potential to do any damage to the relief program.

Such delegate problems were relatively rare in the small organization that saw only about 185 Americans who served as delegates in Belgium or northern France from 1914 until May 1917, when the last Americans had to leave because of America's April entry into the war. (With multiple membership lists having numerous errors and omissions, an accurate account is difficult.) Ten unacceptable delegates have been identified (by this author), leading to a realistic estimate of between 5 and 10 percent who washed out during the life of the CRB.

Delegate problems continued through the life of the CRB. In one cable from Hoover to the New York office in November 1916, he declared, "We don't need more boys." In the same message, Hoover asked that previous delegate Robert Arrowsmith, fifty-six years old, be convinced to return to Belgium. His request showed what kind of men Hoover was hoping to recruit. "We are greatly in need of Arrowsmith's services for very important work [stop] Previous experience and maturity are so vital to us for certain positions that we beg of you to secure him if he can possibly come [stop] Should have two or three more men of maturity."

Hoover acknowledged to Gibson the difficulty of finding good men. "I am full of apologies for failure to deliver new men, but to find men speaking French, of good character and position, who are willing to volunteer in an old story like this, is getting perfectly appalling. There is no longer the romance attached to it that there was in the early days, and I am simply having to beg men to go."

For an organization that was justifiably proud of bringing sound business practices to food relief, the CRB never seemed to completely systematize the recruiting part of the operation. In many ways, it would always remain a who-you-know men's club built on delegate recommendations and periodically prodded into swift action by the simple need for bodies in Belgium.

WOMEN IN THE CRB AND THE RELIEF EFFORTS

The CRB was definitely a product of its time, as evidenced by the lack of women within the ranks of delegates. The only woman officially recognized as a delegate was Charlotte Hoffman Kellogg, the wife of CRB director Vernon Kellogg.

Born in Grand Island, Nebraska, Charlotte graduated from the University of California and became the head of the English department at a private school. In 1908, she married Vernon Kellogg, a professor at Stanford University. When the CRB

Figure 6.3. Forty-year-old Charlotte Kellogg was the only official female delegate in the CRB. Her job behind the lines was to document the lives of Belgian women during the occupation, which she did in numerous books.

Public domain; passport photo; Hoover Institution Archives, Stanford University, Stanford, California.

began establishing state and local committees, Charlotte helped Lou Henry Hoover start the California and San Francisco groups and organized fundraising events. In early 1916, Charlotte, her husband, and daughter Jean traveled to German-occupied Belgium to join the CRB. Her husband ultimately became director of the CRB Brussels office. Charlotte was asked by Hoover to document the experiences and hardships of Belgian women during the occupation.

As Hoover noted in the foreword to her later book *Women of Belgium*, "She has done more than record in simple terms passing impressions of the varied facts of the great work of these women, for she spent months in loving sympathy with them."

Charlotte took the time to learn about the Belgian lace industry (see chapter 8), and she became well-acquainted with Cardinal Mercier. As a result, she later wrote two more books about her time in Belgium: *Bobbins of Belgium: A Book of Belgian Lace, Lace-workers, Lace-schools and Lace-villages* and *Mercier, The Fighting Cardinal of Belgium*. She would earn the admiration and respect of most CRB delegates, one of whom later wrote, "Everyone is crazy about her; she is a delightfully charming woman of tireless energy."

Charlotte Kellogg was not the only American woman heavily involved in the CRB and food relief. Two notables included the wife of Brand Whitlock, Ella Whitlock (known to some as Nell), who was extremely active, especially in the Belgian lace industry; and Lou Henry Hoover, who did a great deal to start and sustain the relief efforts of the CRB state committees by reaching out to prominent women all across America asking for their support. Her husband supported her in all her efforts, especially when it came to organizing the American side of relief.

Another woman who played a significant role in the early development of the American side of food relief was Josephine Bates, wife of Lindon Bates, director of the NYC office. Josephine helped develop what was named the "Woman's Section" of the CRB. Headquartered at 1 Madison Avenue in New York City, the Woman's Section became an integral part of the state and local committees, helping to stimulate and coordinate donations of food, clothes, and money.

The CRB letterhead stationery for the Woman's Section illustrated how extensive and important women's support was in America—more than half the page was taken up with listings of groups and their chairwomen actively involved. Organizations included: the National Council of Women; the International Woman's Suffrage Alliance; the Needlework Guild of America; National Congress of Mothers & Parent-Teachers Association; Daughters of the American Revolution, National Association Opposed to Women Suffrage; and the women's section of the National Conference of Catholic Charities. The letterhead also listed the CRB's chairperson for each of the Woman's Section's state committees but identified them as "State Chairmen," even though all of them were women.

In November 1914, Josephine received a cable from Belgium's Queen Elisabeth. "It gives me great pleasure to accept the invitation which has been transmitted to me to become patroness of the Woman's Section of the Commission for Relief in

Belgium. I wish to extend to the women of America the deep gratitude of the women of Belgium for the work which they are doing for my people."

Tens of thousands of women—both in America and in Belgium—were on the front lines of food relief, from the initial petition for donations to the collection of supplies, to the packing and shipping of what was received, to the final preparation and the distribution to those in need.

LIFETIMES OF PUBLIC SERVICE

The CRB application process would never become completely organized or foolproof. Those flaws, however, did allow into the relief program young, idealistic men who learned the personal and societal value of public service. Many of those CRB delegates went on to lifetimes of public service in government agencies, political appointments, elected office, and nonprofit and charitable institutions. Two notables were William Hallam Tuck and Maurice Pate.

Tuck joined the CRB in September 1915. After witnessing the German deportations of Belgians, he left in December 1916 because he felt he could no longer remain neutral. He joined the British Army and later the US Army. After the war, he spent much of his life involved in food relief and the welfare of humanity (working side by side with Hoover), most prominently as the director general of the International Refugee Organization, charged with aiding the massive refugee problem caused by World War II.

Twenty-one-year-old Pate devoted nearly his entire life to improving the lives of children around the world (and also working with Hoover after World War II), culminating in becoming founding executive director of the United Nations International Children's Emergency Fund (UNICEF; later changed to the permanent United Nations Children's Fund, but the acronym stuck). He served in that position until his death in 1965. Pate was nominated for a Nobel Peace Prize in 1960 for his work with UNICEF but turned down the nomination because he felt the organization deserved it, not him. Nine months after he died, his beloved UNICEF won the Nobel Peace Prize in 1965. Once, at a UNICEF dinner, Hoover described Pate as "the most effective human angel I know."

7

The Mechanics of Relief

How foodstuffs found their way to the civilians behind the lines in Belgium and northern France was a complex orchestration of sometimes elaborate processes and procedures handled by multiples of people. And much of it was created on the go, developed and established only as the need became apparent. (See chapter 9 for the food situation in northern France.)

On the simplest level, the CRB bought and shipped foodstuffs from all over the world (most notably from America and Argentina) to Rotterdam and then via canal barges to Belgian mills and warehouses where it was officially turned over to the CN and its forty thousand workers, who prepared and distributed the food through a ration-card system.

The importation goal for the CRB and CN was initially established by Francqui in October 1914 at approximately 80,000 tons of food per month—far less than the 250,000 tons per month that Belgium had imported before the war. And 80,000 tons only equated to a meager ten ounces of food per person per day. The aim was for the 80,000 tons to be divided among approximately 3,000 tons of rice and dried peas, 15,000 tons of maize, and 60,000 tons of grains, primarily wheat.

Wheat was the most important import because it was the primary component of bread, and bread was a critical staple of the average Belgian's diet. The processing of the wheat shipments, and how the wheat was distributed and converted into bread, set the standard for how all other imported products would be handled and controlled.

TRANSPORTING WHEAT INTO BELGIUM

Using as an example an average-sized vessel carrying approximately nine thousand tons of wheat, such a ship could be unloaded at Rotterdam in thirty-six hours of nearly nonstop work. When the vessel first arrived in port, it was greeted by giant floating elevators and a multitude of lighters, or barges, ready for loading. Floating elevators would come alongside the supply vessel and pump the wheat that was in bulk out of the ship's forward hold and into the lighters. In the ship's stern, or back, the lighters would pull alongside and stevedores would come aboard, climb down into the aft hold, and shovel the wheat into sacks. The sacks would then be manhandled over the side and placed in the lighter's hold.

Once full, each lighter's cargo size would be recorded and then the hold would be secured with a Dutch and a CRB seal. Even the barge's depth in the water would be recorded as a way of spotting any unauthorized removal of wheat. A shipment number would be painted onto a large square of cotton and placed prominently on the barge. All the barge's details would then be transferred to the CRB Rotterdam office, which was within eyesight of the harbor, and a battery of clerks would dutifully record the information and begin tracking the precious wheat.

The destination of each barge was carefully planned from a complicated process that had started inside Belgium. Weeks before, local communes would have determined how much bread per week they needed to feed all the people who were enrolled in their local ration system.

Because each loaf of bread had been standardized as to size and weight, it was already known how much wheat was needed to make each loaf, so a quick calculation could determine the amount of wheat needed.

This was not as easy as it sounds. In German-occupied Belgium, needs changed rapidly. Robinson Smith, chief delegate in Mons for Hainaut Province, noted, "Two weeks ago there were stores of native wheat in certain parts of the province of Hainaut; enough to last fifteen days; the Commission therefore did not send into those parts. But those fifteen days are past and at once those parts have to be placed on the same footing as the rest of the province." And earlier he had warned, "Three months ago only the millers feared the exhaustion of supplies; everyone had his bread, why worry. Ten days ago the provincial committee here at Mons said they were being saddled with too much rice: it was too much of a charge for the province, the population were not used to its consumption. Last night there was not a sack left in the warehouse."

When the commune's wheat needs were estimated as best as possible, this information was then sent to the provincial committee, which processed all communal orders and transferred those to the CN in Brussels, which conveyed all provincial orders and its own recommendations to the CRB offices in Brussels, Rotterdam, and London. While the London CRB office would make any adjustments to its wheat buying to match the newly received needs, the Rotterdam office—knowing what wheat was currently available and projected to arrive in the next month—would match the kind of wheat (bulk or sacked) on hand with what was needed where.

But the uncertainty of specific needs at specific times led to the development of a warehouse system within Belgium to complement direct shipping to communes. Approximately forty CRB warehouses were established throughout the country so supplies could be brought in prior to knowing exactly where the need was greatest.

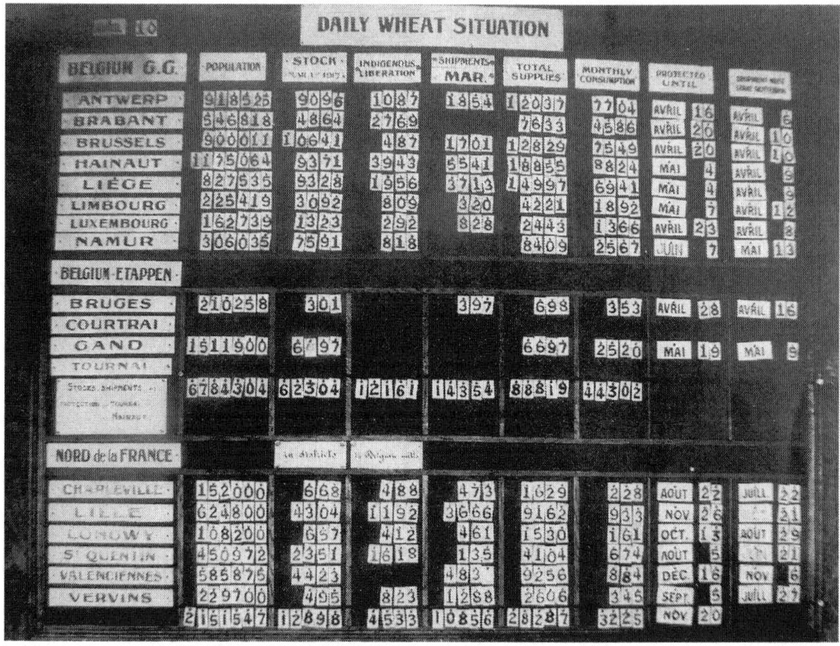

Figure 7.1. The massive size of relief operations, and Hoover's insistence on detailed record keeping, led to the creation of tote boards such as the "Daily Wheat Situation." Public domain; Herbert Hoover Presidential Library Archives, West Branch, Iowa.

Once the Rotterdam office knew where the wheat barges should go, it would secure from the local German diplomatic offices all the necessary authorizations for the barges to be sent into Belgium.

Loaded down with paperwork and wheat, the barges would then be pulled by tugs toward Belgium. When they reached the border, or frontier, each barge would be checked to confirm the seals were still in place and the barge's depth remained the same. CRB personnel positioned at the frontier would telegraph the Rotterdam office when the barges had passed Dutch and German checkpoints and were in Belgium. At all subsequent control stations along the way, more telegrams would be sent so the Rotterdam office had continual updates on where each barge was before reaching its final destination.

When a barge reached its destination, a CRB delegate would normally be there to record the breaking of the seals, the checking of the shipment size, and the unloading—all of which was carefully recorded and transmitted back to the Brussels and Rotterdam offices.

Usually at this point, the CRB would officially hand over responsibility for the shipment to the CN, which was officially in charge of distribution.

But because the CRB had agreed to Allied demands of true accountability throughout the entire process, Hoover insisted that CRB delegates continue to observe and supervise throughout the process to catch any oversights and/or abuses. (Such CRB meddling in what the CN considered to be its own affairs was a constant bone of contention between the CRB and the CN, and it would cause innumerable conflicts, both large and small, throughout the history of the relief. See chapter 11 for details.)

Once the wheat barge had reached its destination, any shipment discrepancies discovered during unloading were quickly investigated by the CRB delegate on hand.

Opportunities for theft during shipping were minimized by the rules and procedures, but the potential still existed. CRB delegate Joe Green—who was head of the critically important CRB Inspection and Control Department—related, "Thefts by the unloading gangs were of common occurrence. I made it a rule that each gang was to be collectively responsible for any thefts occurring while it was at work, and on one occasion when four workmen with a cart were carrying off sacks of maize, I discharged the entire gang and stuck by my refusal to reemploy the men under any consideration. That action had considerable effect upon the honesty of other gangs with which we contracted."

Another point of possible problems was with the lightermen and their families, who lived aboard the barges. "Lightermen were also notorious thieves," Green continued. "When the barge had been entirely unloaded, it was the duty of the chief [Belgian] surveillant to search it from top to bottom to see whether any sacks had been hidden away for the use of the lighterman and his family. From time to time the American representative was supposed to accompany him in these searches, in order to see that they were properly carried out. No part of the barge, even the sleeping cabin of the family, was sacred. On one occasion I discovered and confiscated a large sack of grain hidden under the bed of the lighterman's daughter."

The result of such a find could be devastating to the lighterman and his family. Any such theft resulted in the barge being placed on the CRB blacklist, and if a similar incident happened again, the lighterman would no longer get any CRB contracts for carrying relief supplies. In war-ravaged Belgium, where industry and commerce were basically dead, the cutting off of any steady work could spell financial disaster.

Once the wheat barges reached a mill and turned over their cargoes to a miller to be ground into flour, the controls became even tighter. The miller had to account for everything, from the initial cleaning of the wheat, to the grinding that created bran (used for cattle), to the refuse. He even had to account for whatever flour he might find when he cleaned his mill.

Because of the extraordinary wartime situation and the agreements that had been made with the Allied governments, any wheat that entered the mill had to be CRB wheat. If there was indigenous wheat available, it would first have to be sold to the CRB before being delivered to the mill, where the same rigid rules used for imported wheat would apply.

Since the beginning of the occupation, most of the country's smaller mills had been shut down and only larger ones were kept open to grind the CRB wheat. Most Belgian provinces had six to ten large mills in operation, with the exception of Luxembourg Province, which received its flour from Brussels mills. Each mill had a provincial committee bookkeeper to manage the large amount of paperwork involved in ensuring compliance with all regulations.

These mills and what they produced were so important to the relief effort that they were prominently marked with CRB placards to protect them from German soldiers who might want to buy or requisition flour. Additionally, German soldiers guarded each one at night. Even the wagons that delivered the flour from the mill to the bakers were protected by CRB placards. The CRB warehouses were similarly protected. The placards themselves were so valuable that they were numbered and recorded, and if one went missing, it was immediately reported to Brussels.

The flour was as tightly controlled when it reached individual bakers, and that control even included machinery to shake the empty sacks of flour to get the last bit from each. Bakers had to present their finished loaves to a central warehouse, where each loaf was weighed. And laboratories were used to determine moisture content and types of wheat used in the loaves.

All of that was necessary, according to CRB delegate Robinson Smith, because a baker, if left to his own devices, would "sift out the fine white flour left to make his loaf; and his loaf was almost never due weight. He did in many cases mix potato flour with the gray flour left to make his loaf; and his loaf was almost never due weight." Such abuses, according to Smith, had been going on "from time immemorial," so to prevent those activities the standardized loaves and warehouse checks were put into place. For the most part, those safeguards worked and curbed much of the baker abuse.

How much flour a baker received was dependent upon his customers. Within each commune, each family received a ticket good for 330 grams of bread per head per day from a baker the family had chosen. A hundred kilos of flour, when mixed with water, would produce 135 kilos of bread. The baker would, therefore, receive only enough flour to produce enough bread for the tickets allotted to him by his customers.

As the CRB controls were put into place, all sides settled into their respective roles in the relief system, although many players continued their attempts to scam the system.

DISTRIBUTING THE FOOD

The already complex relief system was compounded by the fact that conditions for individual Belgians were changing all the time. One day a person was able to pay for food; another day he or she was laid off from a job and could no longer pay. This meant the relief system had to be flexible enough to handle rapid changes. Fortunately for the Belgians, their commune form of government already contained much of that dexterity, and it ultimately evolved with the help of the input from provincial committees, the CN, and the CRB to accommodate the needs of more than seven million Belgians.

CRB delegate Robinson Smith helped the world understand how the system worked when he wrote a series of articles outlining the major components of the

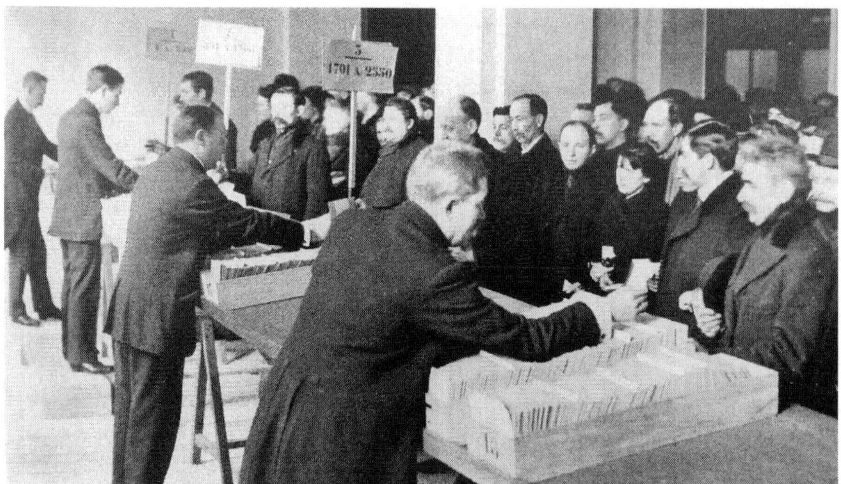

Figure 7.2. Each Belgian recipient of food relief had to have a ticket that was issued by the local commune or provincial committee.

Public domain; William C. Edgar, *The Millers' Belgian Relief Movement, Final Report, 1914–1915* (Minneapolis: Miller Publishing Co., 1916).

relief work. His articles were full of operational details, but they were also PR appeals for Americans to keep giving money to the cause. He humanized the explanation of how the soup kitchens worked by telling the story of an unnamed man living in Brussels who had a wife and three children.

The man suddenly found himself out of a job after his factory ran out of raw materials and shut down. With little savings, he applied for relief for himself and his family at his commune's local soup kitchen. The same day he applied, his application was investigated to verify what he had said. Because this was done locally in his commune where many people knew one another, his need was quickly confirmed, and he was issued a blue ticket with a large numeral "5" plainly stamped on it to indicate five recipients. The ticket was good for thirty days.

Once the man had the ticket in hand, he showed up every day at 11:00 a.m. at the local soup kitchen (also named canteen) with a large pitcher or other container. He was given five half-liters of meat-and-vegetable soup and five small loaves of bread, which he carried to his nearby home.

Each portion of the soup he received cost two cents to make, while the bread cost six cents per loaf. Initially, the man was proud and found a way to pay five cents a day, but after some time he could no longer pay and the color of his ticket changed to indicate full charity.

His commune paid half the cost of the meal, with the other half coming from provincial and CN subsidies and money collected from those who could pay. In addition to the daily soup and bread, the man received a ticket for a weekly supply of potatoes and coal. The communal personnel who did the actual work—from investigating cases to punching tickets to ladling out the soup and handing out the bread—were all volunteers.

To the Americans, the entire CN-operated system was a marvel of efficiency and, as Smith reported, showed its value by how nonexistent lines were, regardless of how many were served. "There is no eternal standing in line," Smith related. "Twelve hundred are dealt with in an hour at any table of any one station; there is no crowding or cursing or need of police."

Many of the other communes and provinces around the country had slightly different systems, but that was allowed as a way of acknowledging the fact that all provinces, communes, and Belgians were not the same.

The hypothetical man's local soup kitchen was part of a much larger citywide system. By early 1915, more than 400,000 meals a day were being served to residents from more than 130 canteens throughout Brussels. That meant approximately 200,000 people—a little less than a third of the city's population—were receiving a ration of bread, soup, and coffee every day. Brussels was divided into twenty-one districts, and each had a local committee that organized its own distribution. Bread and soup were delivered directly to those committees before ten o'clock every morning. These facilities were supplied by fourteen huge municipal kitchens that were run by many of the city's out-of-work chefs.

As reported by one British newspaper, "At the Central Kitchen 36 cooks and 50 assistants start at 2:30 every morning to make the soup. The cooks are divided into

Figure 7.3. Fourteen huge municipal kitchens in Brussels prepared the daily ration of soup.

Public domain; William C. Edgar, *The Millers' Belgian Relief Movement, Final Report, 1914–1915* (Minneapolis: Miller Publishing Co., 1916).

Figure 7.4. The soup was transported from the municipal kitchens to one of 130 canteens (also known as soup kitchens) via carts pulled by dogs, oxen, or humans.
Public domain; Herbert Hoover Presidential Library Archives, West Branch, Iowa.

two squads and are supervised by a special committee, which includes Senator Catteau, and the President of the Hotel and Restaurant Society of Brussels." The soup itself contained potatoes, meat, rice, onion, and leeks. Once the soup was ready, it would be transferred to manageable containers that were then carried by dog carts or horse carts to nearby canteens.

When Hoover visited Brussels for the first time in December 1914, he was mightily impressed and moved by seeing the Belgian system in person. On the morning he was taken around Brussels, it was cold and there was a "dismal rain." Whitlock, Francqui, Gibson, and a few others took Hoover on a journey that followed the food through to distribution.

The group first visited one of the municipal kitchens, which was in a large hangar of an express company that no longer existed. It was a bustle of activity as cooks prepared the food and attended to gigantic cauldrons where the soup was cooking.

The next stop for the group was a soup kitchen, or canteen. The one they visited was located in an old concert hall on the Rue Blaes, in the Quartier des Marolles. When the motorcars pulled up out front, Hoover and the group saw hundreds of people standing in line. As Whitlock related the scene, "They stood with the divine patience of the poor, there in the cold rain, shivering in shawls and old coats and wooden shoes, with bowls or pitchers and each with his number and his card, issued by his commune."

Hoover seemed touched by the quietly spoken "merci" as each person received a bowl of soup, loaf of bread, and a little coffee and chicory.

Whitlock wrote that each thank-you "somehow stabbed one to the heart, and brought an ache to the throat, and almost an annoying moisture to the eyes. One felt very humble in those human presences. . . . I knew what was going on in Mr. Hoover's heart when he turned away and fixed his gaze on something far down the street."

What struck an even stronger emotional chord were the canteens where the children and babies were fed. Before the war, children and babies of the poor had been fed at a few canteens operated by Les Petites Abeilles, or Little Bees. When Francqui and the CN were developing their soup kitchen organization in September 1914, they decided to simply subsidize and expand the Little Bees operation. By the time Hoover showed up in Brussels, there were thirty-two such canteens feeding children and babies every day. The Little Bees was a group that would operate numerous canteens around the country.

Hoover left Brussels with a new, even stronger resolve, if that was possible. He had seen the human side of the suffering. His first visit to Belgium and Brussels would stay with him forever. "German soldiers stood at every crossroads and every street corner. The depressed, unsmiling faces of the Belgians matched the mood of the dreary winter landscape. There were no children at play. The empty streets, the gaunt destroyed houses, the ruins of the fine old church of St. Pierre and the Library at Louvain, intensified the sense of suspended animation in the life of the people."

Whitlock wrote that when Hoover came to say good-bye: "He was very much moved by the sight of suffering he saw today, and very cordial and very fine. A remarkable man indeed."

THE CRB DIFFERENCE

In Robinson Smith's articles about the mechanics of relief, he gave readers an understanding of the overall picture of relief and how it was different from other forms of aid in times of suffering. He began by saying that the establishment of the CRB gave the delegates a true understanding of what relief really meant. "Relief means the putting into operations of such an extensive and well-ordered distribution of supplies that everyone will automatically and inevitably be taken care of." Smith clarified by saying this kind of relief "does not mean a house-to-house visiting. . . . What Belgium needed was forty huge warehouses into which the Commission food could pour by train and barge from Rotterdam. This the Commission prepared for, this the Commission achieved."

Smith explained that the CRB's massive efforts were different "radically from other large ventures in relief." He recalled the "spontaneous, magnificent" responses to American disasters still in the minds of many US readers: the 1889 Johnstown flood that killed more than 2,200 people, the 1900 Galveston hurricane where 6,000 died, and the San Francisco earthquake of 1906 that took the lives of more than

3,000. "These charities, called so quickly into being," Smith wrote, "were for the moment. They were of no avail unless their relief was brought to bear at once, as it was." As for the Red Cross, it was pledged to aid combatants on all sides during a war. Its military relief operations were different in goals, scope, and duration than civilian humanitarian aid.

The CRB was an organization specifically targeted to feed an entire nation caught in the middle of the largest war the world had ever seen—something that had never been attempted before or even thought to be achievable. As Smith explained, with the CRB, "the need was pressing, the only hope of coping with it was on deliberate, permanent lines. The Commission acted from the first as if it had come to stay."

And Hoover fashioned it in a completely different way from how other relief efforts had been established. He organized it like a big business, which had opened it up to criticism that Smith acknowledged and described. "Many people still think of it as a huge American concern, eager to sell its goods. Every delegate has that anxious down-town look for a new customer, precisely as if he were to get a certain percentage or rake-off from a sale."

"But that is where the difference comes in," Smith declared. "Though organized like a big business, where every account is scrupulously examined, every expenditure tallied, there is absolutely no diversion of funds [away from relief]. . . . Though the Commission acts like a commercial house in reducing its expenses to the very lowest and in bringing its efficiency to the very highest, it is in its motives and spirit wholly an experiment in ideality, and that is what lends to the work such an absorbing, not to say exciting, interest."

Moving quickly into hyperbole, Smith went on to say, "Almost every dream of the idealist comes true. People, for once in the world's history, are governed by purely unselfish motives."

To explain further, Smith wrote, "The Commission has a fairly free hand: what it says is law; and that law is never the slightest in favour of one class or party or province. It considers solely the general good. And every time it acts that way, the Commission succeeds. It is bound to win out. Given a fair field, justice and reasonableness are sure to win."

To prove his point, he told a couple of stories of when the CRB tried to make a "distinction" or distribute food in an unequal way and had failed. "It tried to give a little more food to the man that worked than the man out of work. But the man that worked, worked only three days a week, and the days he was home and still got more, the other man made trouble for him. We tried at the beginning to give more food to children over twelve than to those under, until one day a woman came and said that her daughter Marie Louise was big enough to be fourteen. After that every day-old baby in Belgium received as much as an adult. Its mother was weak and deserved it."

The CRB and CN worked hard to live up to that sense of fairness and equity for all recipients throughout its four years of life.

8

The Belgian Side of Food Relief

When Émile Francqui and Baron Lambert returned from their October 1914 trip to London, they hit the ground running. They had gone to Britain as representatives of a city-centric relief organization intent on securing food exclusively for Brussels. They returned as international partners in a never-before-attempted humanitarian aid program to save an entire nation from starvation. They knew that to receive, prepare, and distribute tons of food to more than seven million Belgians every day, they would need to quickly create a massive organization that was efficient and effective. To better reflect that national goal, the original Comité Central de Secours et d'Alimentation (CC) was renamed the Comité National de Secours et d'Alimentation (CN).

CN OPERATIONS COME TOGETHER QUICKLY

Francqui and his executive team immediately set up ten provincial committees, one to correspond roughly to each of the country's nine provinces and an additional one for Brussels. These provincial committees would become the middlemen between the CN on the top floor and the local communes' committees on the ground. Each provincial committee member, as one CRB history explained, "should be impartially chosen, and the committee should include representatives of each political party, and from each arrondissement [administrative district] so that the needs of all sections and districts would be known to the committees."

The CN would assign its own delegates to sit on each provincial committee, and each committee would assign one delegate to sit on the CN board. The provincial committees would "enjoy entire independence of action except for the general measures prescribed by the Committee National," but they needed to stay in constant communication with the CN and were required to have a bank account at the Société Générale (Francqui's bank) to ensure timely payments for food.

With dedication and determination, the Belgians were able to overcome the hardships of German occupation—restricted communications, limited movements, and myriad regulations—and make all the provincial committees operational by the end of November 1914.

The CN itself was divided into two departments, a commercial one (d'Alimentation, or provisioning) that dealt with all the issues regarding food for those who could pay and a charitable one (de Secours, or charity) for issues involving those who could not pay. Under the de Secours department were five divisions created to work on providing money, food, clothing and shoes, work, and housing. Beneath all of these, a large number of charitable committees grew up for the aid and protection of a number of groups, including refugees; military families; doctors and pharmacists; artists, children, and orphans of war; the homeless; and lace makers.

By strong force of will, Francqui established the CN organization in record time. He was a man who would have accepted nothing less.

At fifty-one, Francqui was a major force in the financial world and was director of the Société Générale de Belgique, arguably the most important banking institution in Belgium. He had been a driven, ambitious man all his life and had literally come up through the ranks to achieve his fame, fortune, and power.

An orphan at a young age (just like Hoover), he was sent to military school at fifteen. When he was an officer of twenty-one, he was appointed by King Leopold II to be in a group to organize and run the Congo Free State. After that, the king sent him to China to negotiate the awarding of a contract to Belgium for a large railway concession. While Francqui was there, his "main rival in these negotiations was Herbert Hoover." The bad blood between them would cause friction throughout the relief work, although publicly they always showed a united front.

Unlike Hoover—who wanted full control from behind the scenes—Francqui was a man who wanted full control from center stage. He was known for running businesses and meetings as a dictator who brooked no questioning of his commands. His physical appearance—big, burly, with mustache and cleft chin—was as imposing as his business methods. One man called him "the iron man of Belgium."

E. E. Hunt described him as "a big-businessman in the prime of life, self-made, brusque, bourgeois, sometimes intolerably rude, but always efficient. . . . He has no small ambitions, no cheap ideas of glory, and no sentimentality or cant."

While Francqui managed to get the CN functioning in a matter of weeks, this did not necessarily mean the Belgian communes at the bottom of the organizational ladder fully embraced the concept of the CN or of Francqui and what some people perceived as his grab for power. Most communes knew they didn't have the power the CN was mustering, and they couldn't even begin to achieve what the CN wanted to do, but that didn't mean they had to like it. Those not solidly behind Francqui sat back and bided their time, hoping he and his group would somehow slip up without jeopardizing the feeding of the country. (That never happened, as Francqui ruled the CN through the entire war.)

One of the first steps the CN had to make was determining how much food was needed to sustain more than seven million Belgians every day—most notably wheat for making bread that was a critical component of many Belgians' diets. It was understood that whatever figure was arrived at, it would ultimately be subservient to what could actually be provided.

In the beginning months, the CN received guidance from numerous doctors, scientists, and nutritionists, and initially it determined that a minimum of 250 grams (slightly more than half a pound) per person per day of bread was needed. Considered "extraordinarily low" by many experts, that amount was, by February 1915, increased to 330 grams (less than three-quarters of a pound).

As for the overall food importation goal, Francqui told Hoover on October 26, 1914, that starting December 1, the minimum foodstuffs required would be 60,000 tons of grains, 15,000 tons of maize, and 3,000 tons of rice and dried peas, or a total of nearly 80,000 tons a month—a significant amount but less than a third of what Belgium had normally imported. The 80,000 tons only equated to a meager 283 grams (ten ounces) of food per person per day. Even that amount, however, was difficult to obtain during the first three months of relief operations and would be a challenge to maintain throughout the war.

Another part of Francqui's CN organizational plan, which was required by both Hoover and the British, detailed how the CRB and its delegates fit in: "The Commission was to have offices in each of the provinces under the charge of delegates of American nationality, who should be assigned to work with the provincial committees. These delegates should act in cooperation with the delegates of the Comité National: they should reside in the chief place of the province, and should visit even the smallest hamlet to ensure the efficient working of the organization."

Francqui had to agree to such a statement to get British approval for relief, but just as Hoover had wanted a purely American relief program, Francqui had wanted a purely Belgian-run program within Belgium. He admitted publicly that the CRB was able to provide the critical services of organizing world charity, gaining diplomatic agreements from the belligerents, and buying and shipping food into Rotterdam, but he and a number of his associates were privately convinced that Belgians—and only Belgians—should do the work from the moment the food touched Belgian soil.

But being a military man who thought strategically, Francqui knew the tenuous position he and his country were in during this embryonic stage of relief, so he worked and waited. The issue would not go away, however, and "this attitude of the

Belgians in the Comité National who felt that the work, as a purely Belgian institution, should be carried on altogether by Belgians, was to lead to many complications and much difficulty later on," according to Kittredge. (See chapter 11.)

In early November 1914, however, with the CN organization mapped out and the Americans forced upon him, Francqui turned to the problem of securing financial backing that would keep the program going. The economic system of relief established earlier in Brussels with the Comité Central would be expanded to all of Belgium—ration cards would be used to provide a uniform daily ration delivered through soup kitchens (also known as canteens) to those who could pay and to those who needed complete charity. Everyone (except for the destitute) along the chain, from millers to bakers to consumers, would pay a price slightly over cost. Additionally, the CN and the local communes would subsidize a portion of the total costs. All of that meant the charitable portion of the work would be covered.

But this system needed major funding to prime the pump. After considerable efforts, Francqui was able to get Brussels bankers to put up a loan of £600,000 to add to the £100,000 from the British government and the £100,000 from the Belgian Relief Fund in France. But what he really needed was money to cover the necessary working capital for the CRB. As Hoover worked for the same goal in London, Francqui used his connections to put pressure on the exiled Belgian government in Le Havre, France, to provide those funds. In early November, the Belgian government agreed to advance £1 million to the CRB as "working capital and as a transportation fund."

Francqui's efforts inside Belgium and Hoover's efforts outside Belgium led to the complex financial transaction system and agreements that would fully fund the relief program throughout the war (see chapter 2).

By the end of the first year of operations, Francqui had whipped the CN and the provincial committees into the shape *he* wanted. Just like Hoover, he had either cleared the field of competitors or brought them under control and established himself as the driving force behind the CN.

Each week a Comité National meeting was held in Brussels at the Société Générale de Belgique bank, which Francqui controlled as its director. In attendance were forty Belgian men, mostly older, prominent businessmen, high government officers, or political leaders. At least a few Americans would also be there to observe. Francqui dominated every meeting, reading a long list of items, including weekly information from the CRB; notifications of new rules imposed by the relief's patrons because of German orders; information about shipments that had arrived in Rotterdam or that were en route to the provinces; a financial report; an agricultural report; and any instructions to the provincial committees. Everyone in the room knew that the real work had already been done by Francqui and a small executive group behind closed doors. It was generally considered for the best because he was one of the few Belgians who could control such a diverse group and get them to work together.

It would be that way through the life of the relief.

THE GERMAN POSITION ON RELIEF

Inside Belgium, no matter what Francqui and the CN planned or did, none of it would work if the German military and civilian authorities in Belgium did not agree. It was true that the first governor general, von der Goltz, had given guarantees, but many of the specifics of a large-scale relief program had not been ironed out.

Negotiations with the Germans fell mainly to the program's neutral patrons—Whitlock, Gibson, and Villalobar—and two of the CRB executives in Brussels, Heineman and his associate William Hulse. Numerous meetings and informal discussions led to a letter, sent on November 10, 1914, to the Germans by Whitlock and Villalobar that reviewed the program and detailed the points the Germans had to agree to before the humanitarian work would be firmly established.

The following day, Whitlock received a CN memorandum outlining what Francqui felt the Germans had to approve before the CN could do its job. The first part asked that the Germans stop all requisitions of native cereals until a countrywide inventory had been completed. The second section was about freedoms, including unrestricted movement for all material imported by the CRB, freedom of communications between the CN's various committees, and unlimited CRB use of telegraph services, especially to Rotterdam. Whitlock and Villalobar forwarded the CN's memorandum to Governor General von der Goltz with a letter that included "an appeal for favorable action."

A week later, the German reply came from Dr. Wilhelm von Sandt, the German civil administrator in Belgium. The Germans agreed not to requisition any more native food at least until December 10, when a nationwide inventory was to be complete. Von der Goltz agreed to all the requests, in hopes it would keep the civilian population peaceful.

Von der Goltz had gone so far as to write Whitlock a week before to acknowledge that the first consignment of food would only temporarily relieve the situation and that "in the interest of all concerned, an effort must be made to effect some permanent arrangement whereby foodstuffs purchased abroad may be brought for an indefinite period into Belgium upon the distinct understanding that they shall be devoted exclusively to the use of the civil population." He said he was speaking on behalf of the imperial government, which would agree to a permanent arrangement if the British did so.

Such German willingness to work with and accept the CRB and the CN seemed too good to be true. Everyone involved jumped at the opportunity and began developing better relations and guarantees. Time, however, would reveal that the devil was in the details and that the new governor general, von Bissing, would not be as cooperative as his predecessor.

A test of the Germans' official stand toward the relief work came quickly in the form of a newspaper article that nearly shut down the program. It also revealed that the news media, which Hoover relied on so heavily to create public opinion to support his efforts, was a double-edged sword.

On November 22, 1914, the *New York Times* ran a story that shocked many. The article was written by Cyril Brown, a staff correspondent in Europe, and it quoted "His Excellency von Frankenburg und Ludwigsdorf, personal adjutant to the military governor in Antwerp," who said that the Belgians were not "on the brink of starvation as a result of the German occupation. . . . The very contrary was the case." He agreed that Belgium was not a self-sustaining country, but imports had been secured, and the Germans had developed an idea to have an "inter-communistic commission" handle the imports to the localities that needed food. The commission the German referred to was the CN.

Making sure not to leave out Hoover and the Americans, von Frankenburg then stated rather starkly, "If America had not been so tender-hearted as to send foodstuffs, and if the food supply had not run out, we should certainly have considered it our duty to bring food from Germany, for we are for the time being the government here and it is our duty to see that the people do not starve."

Hoover was furious. In a telegram to Whitlock a day after the article appeared, he declared, "If it is true that the Germans intend to feed Belgium, America will withdraw instantly."

Whitlock immediately questioned the German authorities in Brussels. The same day Hoover telegraphed him, Whitlock replied: "It seems that a Captain von Frankenburg, a staff-officer, not authorized to speak, made statements to some person, claiming to be a newspaper man, relating to conditions in Germany, in which he said that there was no danger of starvation in Germany, and that Germany wanted no assistance in feeding its population. His remarks were therefore evidently entirely misunderstood. The German Government renews its official declaration that conditions in Belgium are as they have been represented, and views with great gratification the generous efforts of the American people to relieve the starving population here."

With that, the incident passed and the food relief continued.

CLOTHES, AN IMPORTANT PART OF RELIEF

With tremendous efficiency, Francqui, the CN, and the other Belgian committees brought standardized food preparation and fair distribution to all civilians. While food was always their focus, they did not neglect another vital component of relief—clothes. Time was the basic determinant of necessity—within months, it became obvious to most Belgians that clothes and shoes were wearing thin and retail shops across the country had run out or were about to.

Long before the CRB became actively involved in clothes, the Belgians tackled the issue. Nearly every village, town, and city had already created places called *comptoirs* (literally "counters"), where those who had registered could come in, get material and instructions on what garments to make, work on them at home, then bring back the finished pieces and be paid a small amount for the work. Added to the *comptoirs* were *ouvroirs* (work, or sewing, rooms). The finished clothes would go to people who could

Figure 8.1. During the war, Belgian schools taught young women how to sew so they could earn money in the country's network of *comptoirs* and *ouvroirs* (work or sewing rooms).

Public domain; Hoover Institution Archives, Stanford University, Stanford, California.

pay and to the destitute, whose numbers were growing every day and would reach approximately three million in Belgium (and one million in northern France) by 1916.

The system of *comptoirs* and *ouvroirs* was brilliant in its simplicity—provide labor to the unemployed by creating garments that were needed by those who could pay and those who were destitute. But there was a critical ingredient missing, native raw material. With Belgium cut off from the rest of the world, existing stocks were nearly exhausted by the autumn of 1915. While most of the initial clothing efforts had been locally begun, each of the communes realized that it would take a national effort to secure new stocks from outside Belgium. Over time, all the local efforts ultimately fell under the control of the CN.

To handle the growing need, the CN formed a clothing department, the Division du Vêtements, within its Secours section. Besides handling the importation and distribution of any clothes and clothing material brought in by the CRB, the Division du Vêtements administratively and financially supported and standardized the countrywide manufacture and distribution of clothes.

By late 1915, however, with available local stocks rapidly diminishing, the CN asked the CRB to begin importing raw materials for clothes.

The CRB had run a clothing donation campaign in the winter of 1914–1915 that had brought in a tremendous amount of clothes, but there was no effort to import a steady flow of clothing and raw materials into Belgium. Any clothing donations were passed through into Belgium with little thought as to what was needed or usable. The CRB didn't even have an official clothing department.

When the CRB received the CN's request, it quickly discovered that the Allies were opposed to the large-scale commercial importing of any textile raw materials because of their own needs. So the CRB then "turned to imports of second-hand clothing, and later we added large amounts of manufactured materials," according to Hoover. The CRB placed large orders in the United Kingdom and the United States, which were "forwarded as fast as import permits were granted, and as war conditions in the trade and in transportation would allow."

Goods from those orders began to arrive in Belgium in February 1916. A month before, the CRB had launched a major appeal to Americans for new clothes and raw materials. New clothes were preferable to used ones because of the multiple difficulties used clothes posed regarding cleanliness and transfer of pests such as lice and bedbugs. Before reaching Belgium, all the material—donated and ordered—had to be sorted, searched, and reviewed to ensure each item was appropriate, was useful, and contained no contraband.

The CRB not only handled clothing donations; it also ended up buying much-needed material to make clothes. Hoover explained, "Useful as these gifts of newly made and second-hand clothing were, they did not meet our problem. We were driven to importing cloth and material, needles, thread, buttons, shoes, and leather fittings. We started by buying 'mill-ends,' 'out-of-style goods,' and 'market gluts.' Soon we were obligated to give huge orders to manufacturers."

All these activities in and out of Belgium did not go unnoticed by the British. They quickly added cloth and clothes items to their demands and guarantees that were necessary for the humanitarian aid to continue. A problem quickly arose.

In April 1916, when the British found out the Germans were requisitioning some clothes and wool from the Belgians, they shut down all imports of cloth and clothing by the CRB. It took two months of negotiations for Hoover to get the clothing imports restarted on a limited basis. The agreement letter from British Foreign Secretary Grey to Ambassador Page stated that the clothing imports would be allowed as long as they were "distributed under the strict system of control guaranteed by the Commission."

This meant that the CRB needed more direct supervision of the CN's clothing operations. That was something Francqui and the CN were unwilling to grant—they had set up a perfectly fine system and felt no need to have the Americans looking over their shoulders.

In mid-1916, delegate Milton M. Brown was appointed to be the head of the CRB's new clothing department and tasked with collecting clothing information from the CN to assure the British that material was not being taken by the Germans. He would work with his Belgian counterpart, Madame F. M. Philippson-Wiener, whose husband was a member of the board of directors of the CN. Her boss was Emmanuel Janssen, one of three vice presidents of the CN, an ally of Francqui's, and, according to Whitlock, "anti-American."

Because of the CN's reluctance to share information about its massive clothing operations, Brown's job would become a contentious issue throughout the war.

Nevertheless, Brown was impressed with the CN's clothing operations, especially what he saw in Brussels.

BELGIAN EFFICIENCY AT ITS BEST

The CN's Brussels clothing operation had four major components to processing:

- The receiving center for all raw materials and imports, housed in an entertainment venue, Cirque Royal, which also served as the headquarters of the purchasing department of the Division du Vêtements.
- The central clothing warehouse in the Pôle Nord (North Pole), where clothes and materials were sorted and finished items were stored until distribution. The facility was also the headquarters of Madame Philippson-Wiener and her many departmental assistants.
- The cutting shops, where bolts of cloth were cut into pieces for garment making.
- The *comptoirs*. Twenty such *comptoirs* were scattered throughout Brussels and employed fifteen thousand workers. All finished clothes were then sent to Pôle Nord for cataloguing and storage.

The operations within Pôle Nord best illustrated the CN's tremendous organization and level of detail. The huge hall had been taken over by the Division du Vêtements and was "alive and humming with busy men and women," according to Brown. "An ice-skating rink in antebellum days, the seats have been taken out of the galleries which surround the rink, and the latter built over to provide space for sorting and inspecting of clothing—an area of perhaps some twenty thousand square feet. Where the tiers of seats in the balcony rise to the eaves of the roof innumerable long rows of shelving have been installed which hold their burdens of clothing neatly piled in classified order, of blankets, suits, underwear, hat, caps, waists, dresses, lingerie, and a hundred odd different kinds of garments."

A book of garment tables had been created with the statistical specifications for each of the 125 different kinds of items manufactured by the division. Brown explained, "For each man's shirt, size 36, for example, in bolt cloth of 90 cm. width, so many centimetres of cloth are necessary, also so many large buttons, so many small buttons, and any other accessories that may be needed." For maximizing every inch of cloth, standard patterns had been created and were used by the cutting shops.

The statistics told an incredible tale. The Brussels operation in its first month (September 1914) had distributed only 1,617 items, of which 1,065 were mattresses and blankets. By 1916, Brussels was distributing on average more than four hundred thousand garments a month. At one time, according to one delegate, there could be more than three million "pieces, yards and pairs" waiting to be dealt with. During the peak time of autumn, in preparation for winter, the facility could have hundreds of thousands of finished garments waiting for distribution.

Figure 8.2. The huge central supply station in Brussels for clothes. Delegate Milton M. Brown, who was appointed to head the CRB's clothing department, described the station as "humming with busy men and women."

Public domain; Vernon Kellogg, *Fighting Starvation in Belgium* (Mew York: Doubleday, Page and Co., 1918).

The level of detail was so amazing that Hoover later wrote, "So efficient were [the Belgian women in the *ouvroirs*] that one could stop a small boy on the street and note the indelible number on the inside of the collar of his blouse. With no questions asked of him, but from the records these women made, one could know his name, his address, the members of his family, their monetary resources, the date the material had arrived at the work room, and the name of the woman who had made the blouse."

BELGIAN LACE MAKING IS REVITALIZED

Clothes weren't the only items that fell under the responsibility of the CN's and CRB's clothing departments. Lace and lace making became critical. When the relief program first began enrolling people to receive assistance, more than forty-three thousand lace workers had applied for help.

For generations before the war, Belgium had been famous for both its fine needle lace and its fine bobbin lace. Various regions of the country were known for specific styles of handmade lace that had been developed in their locales over the centuries. Approximately fifty thousand women (and some men) made their living, or helped support their families, by the delicate, traditional art form.

A few years prior to the war, Belgium's Bavarian-born Queen Elisabeth had taken the industry under her protective patronage after learning of the industry's widespread and systematic exploitation of its workers and the growing threat of machine-made lace. The queen established a committee of prominent women, Amies de la Dentelle (Friends of the Lace), who led the movement for better working conditions, improved education, and higher standards.

After the war broke out, lace makers were instantly cut off from their raw material (thread) and from markets outside of Belgium. Members of the queen's committee continued to work but with the new effort of keeping the industry alive. Other lace committees sprang up around the country to help the workers. Efforts were ultimately centralized in a Brussels Lace Committee. Its honorary president was Ella Whitlock, wife of Brand Whitlock; patrons included Lou Henry Hoover, wife of Herbert Hoover, and four Belgian women: Comtesse Elizabeth d'Oultremont, lady-in-waiting to Queen Elisabeth; American-born Vicomtesse de Beughem, married to a Belgian aristocrat; Madame Josse Allard, wife of a Belgian banker; and Madame Kefer-Mali, related to the Belgian consul general of New York.

In early 1915, the Lace Committee requested that the CRB import linen thread and needles for the industry and then buy the pieces of lace produced for export out of Belgium. The CRB would sell the lace and gain back its money, and the lace workers would be paid for their services. The simple, direct plan, which involved a nonmilitary item, was something most could accept. Hoover was able to get the Allied governments to agree to import thread from England and Ireland and needles for lace making, as long as all such lace would be exported for sale in neutral or Allied countries. The Germans permitted the importation of thread into Belgium on the condition that all the moneys realized from the sale of the lace be turned back into the relief work. There were strict controls of the thread. For every kilo of lace thread imported, the CRB had to export an equivalent quantity of lace.

According to Brown, the entire operation developed into a substantial enterprise. "Our exports for the Lace Committee amount to something between three hundred thousand and half a million francs worth of lace per month, which lace is sold in Holland, England, France, the United States or elsewhere." Any lace not sold was warehoused in Rotterdam.

As for the workers, no person was allowed to work more than thirty hours a week or collect more than three francs a week. This way, more workers were given something to do and a little money. Each lace worker had to pay for any thread received to guarantee it would not be sold to someone else, and all thread was weighed so that worker was responsible for bringing back an equal weight in lace.

Designs in lace had always been important, but they took on new meaning during the German occupation. The Germans had outlawed any patriotic themes, so lace with images such as Allied flags or war slogans was carefully hidden from certain eyes. Or a subtler approach was used, such as utilizing the symbolic animals of certain countries—the lion for Belgium, the unicorn for the United Kingdom, the cock for France, and the eagle for America.

In a rare sign of détente between the CRB and the CN, disagreements over the Lace Committee and its operations were seldom recorded. It might be a coincidence that lace was one of the few areas of relief that was supervised mostly by women.

PRIVATE CITIZEN EFFORTS

While the CN was the official agency for food preparation and distribution in Belgium, many individuals in the privileged, wealthy classes—such as Baron Evence Coppée, Raoul Warocqué, and Baron Léon Lambert—found numerous other pathways to contribute. They sat on special committees, donated office space, loaned out business personnel for specific relief jobs, created make-work tasks for the unemployed, gave cash or material goods, and even volunteered at local soup kitchens. Many also loaned their cars and chauffeurs to the CRB and opened their homes to the CRB delegates as either residences or as places to catch a moment of much-needed relaxation.

A good example of individual Belgian philanthropy was shown by Antwerp merchant Edouard Bunge and three (of his five) grown daughters, Erica, Eva, and Hilda. Edouard's wife, Sophie, had died years before, and he had never remarried. Before the war, the family and accompanying servants had moved effortlessly between living in a large townhouse in Antwerp and in the Chateau Oude Gracht on the Hoogboom estate next to the village of Hoogboom and the town of Cappellen (now spelled Kapellen), a thirty-minute tram ride northeast of the city.

Figure 8.3. The CRB delegates found rest and relaxation with the Bunge family at the Chateau Oude Gracht. From left to right, CRB delegate E. E. Hunt and the Bunges: Eva, Edouard (father), Hilda, and Erica. Father Edouard and daughter Erica developed a dairy farm on their estate to feed the children of Antwerp.
Public domain; author's archives.

During the invasion and bombardment of Antwerp, the Bunges had remained in the city. The daughters had stayed because they worked in a makeshift hospital and would not leave their patients. They also continued to volunteer at soup kitchens and children's canteens. Edouard had stayed in hopes of helping his beloved city. He became one of only a dozen private citizens who aided in surrendering the city to the Germans.

After the city's surrender, the Bunge family lived in Chateau Oude Gracht, and the three daughters continued volunteering every day at local soup kitchens and children's canteens. Edouard's humanitarian relief activities included being the vice president of Antwerp's provincial committee, sitting on the board of the CN, and providing make-work jobs on his estate. He also helped the CRB by donating office space in his bank building for E. E. Hunt and his staff and providing his large townhouse as a residence for CRB delegates.

By early 1915, however, Erica wanted to do more than just volunteer. She and her father were aware that the hardest hit by lack of nutrition were newborns, who desperately needed fresh milk for proper development. They decided to start a dairy farm on their estate.

Since the Germans had restarted the local tramlines in and around Belgian cities, the Bunges knew there was reliable transportation from Cappellen to Antwerp, where members of the city's relief committee could distribute the milk. But would the Germans allow the Bunges to import dairy cows from Holland, bring in fodder for the herd, and create the facilities necessary to ramp up their estate's very limited current dairy production?

On Wednesday, March 3, 1915, a meeting of the Antwerp Economic Food Committee, comprised of influential Antwerp men, came together to address the issue of the milk supply for the city and most notably for the children. There were still dairy cows in the area, but their numbers had dwindled and production of milk was way down. It was proposed that Edouard Bunge would provide one hundred dairy cows and daily shipments of milk to Antwerp if the group would provide the fodder necessary for maintaining such a herd. The group quickly agreed.

A Dutch cattle trader was contacted to arrange the purchase and export license. The Dutch government needed proof, however, that the Germans would not requisition the cows or the milk. The German military governor for Antwerp, General von Hune, agreed to the project and provided a letter in April stating no dairy cows or milk would be taken by the Germans. Dairy cows were purchased at 1,300 francs per animal (equivalent to a little less than a year's wage for one farmworker), and the cows were delivered to the Hoogboom estate, only five miles (eight km) south of the Dutch border. Edouard Bunge and his business partner, Georges Born, paid for everything.

Erica Bunge stepped in to run the operation, and the Bunge estate supervisor Hendrik Verheyen became the dairy farm administrator. Others who worked on the project included Dr. Bonroy, the director of the Industry School of Antwerp, who volunteered as scientific and technical adviser; a man named Van Wallendael, who took on the purchasing of feed and monitoring of the stables; and Hélène Born, a close friend of Erica's and daughter of Georges Born, who volunteered to assist.

Erica was more qualified for the position than many young Belgian women. At an early age, she had shown an interest in business and had quickly become a business confidante to her father. Years before the war, she had graduated from an agricultural college in England—a rarity for women in the early 1900s. When the Bunges had moved into Chateau Oude Gracht, Erica began to participate in the management of the estate's two farms.

When it came to the dairy farm, the first order of business was that facilities had to be built. They included:

- a large, modern stable for one hundred head of cattle;
- a smaller structure that contained a stable for fifteen head of cattle, a storage room for all vehicles and equipment, a stable for four horses, and two saddleries; and
- a building that housed Erica and Verheyen's office, a laboratory, a room for cleaning the milk cans, a hall for filling the milk cans, the cooling equipment for the milk, and a locker room for the dairy farm's staff.

Three existing structures were incorporated into the new buildings to form the foundation of the dairy farm. When the new structures were completed, Edouard Bunge and Georges Born had paid more than 260,000 francs for construction.

On Tuesday, May 11, 1915, the dairy cows crossed the border in a long line of wagons that arrived safely at the estate. With the Bunges' existing small herd, the total livestock of the dairy farm came to one hundred and thirty dairy cows, one bull, three pull oxen, four horses, and thirty to forty heifers and female calves.

Erica and Verheyen managed a full complement of workers, including twelve milkers, two managers who controlled the cleaning and filling of the milk canisters and the maintenance of the cooling equipment, four transporters, two night guards, and one laundress. Their wages ranged from three francs up to more than four francs a day.

Within a few months, the dairy was producing 2,530 liters (668 gallons) a day. Every day the milk was collected and sealed in clean canisters, and four men then loaded the canisters onto horse- or oxen-drawn wagons that pulled them to the nearby tramline stop. The milk was then secured in a locked baggage car for its trip into Antwerp.

After the war, Edouard and Erica Bunge and Georges and Hélène Born received a commendation from the Belgian government for providing one million liters (26,417 gallons) of free milk during the occupation.

The Bunge family was just one of many Belgian families who contributed unselfishly to aid others throughout the war.

Figure 8.4. By the summer of 1915, the Bunge dairy farm was up and running and sending milk every day to the children of Antwerp. Two dairy workers carry one of the milk canisters. Note the *sabots* (wooden shoes).

Public domain; Raymond Roelands, *Geschiedenis van Kasteeldomein "Oude Gracht" in Hoogboom* (Kapellen, Belgium: Culturele Heemkring Hobonia v.z.w., 2016).

9

Food Relief in Northern France

On January 2, 1915, Hoover received a telegram in London from Ambassador Gerard. It told him about the need for food among the French citizens trapped behind German lines in the narrow strip of northern France between the trenches and Belgium's southern border. More than two million people lived in that area, and word had reached Gerard that they were about to starve. The mayor of Roubaix had said 250,000 residents would be starving within a few days if nothing was done. The ambassador also told Hoover that he had telegraphed the State Department requesting an arrangement be made with the German and British governments to allow the importation of one thousand sacks of flour a day for three cities (Roubaix, Tourcoing, and Lille) within the French territory.

The State Department's reply, which Gerard copied to Hoover, said that the British had no objections to the importation of food into northern France. So, the cable continued, "The question how far it is desirable that the Commission should extend its activities to districts in France, now in German occupation, seemed to be one primarily for submission to the French Government."

HOOVER TACKLES A NEW REGION

For the previous few months, Hoover and the CRB had heard stories about the food situation in northern France. In fact, in November and December 1914, the CRB and CN had agreed to feed those living in and around the two northern French towns of Maubeuge and Givet-Fumay because they had been placed under von Bissing's civil government control. (After making the exception to feed Maubeuge, Francqui had opposed feeding Givet-Fumay because he felt it should be the responsibility of the French government to do so, but the entire CN voted to provide relief.)

For administrative purposes, Maubeuge was attached to Hainaut Province, while Givet-Fumay was attached to Namur Province. (In December 1916, the region of Maubeuge was taken out of von Bissing's general government control and became part of the Army Zone, where it was merged into the St. Quentin District.) Beyond these two French areas, however, Hoover and the CRB could do no more because of the lack of resources and governmental approvals.

Hoover replied to Gerard, "We have had this called to our attention repeatedly." He wrote that the CRB was prepared to take on the work of finding and delivering the food needed, as long as the Germans agreed. With that said, however, Hoover also felt that the French had to support their own people and would have to "make a substantial subscription to our funds for Belgian work." He also informed the ambassador that "we are already sending some food into one section of France, but other sections we have been unable to undertake, as we have no resources with which to do so."

By mid-February 1915, Hoover grew concerned because repeated efforts to convince the French to make a financial commitment had fallen on deaf ears. The government's position was that Germany was responsible for the care and sustenance of those it had conquered and should be held accountable to do so.

Hoover decided to take direct action, as he had done before with the British. On February 17, he wrote to Raymond Poincaré, president of France. In a long letter, he outlined the brutal living conditions in the German Operations and Etape subzones, told of the limited efforts the CRB had made, and made a personal appeal to gain the support of the French government. His first sentence conveyed the urgency he felt, as did the unusual method of delivery for his missive by a fifty-year-old prominent American politician well-known in France: "I deem it my duty to lay before you the position of the French civil population north of the German lines, and I am asking Mr. Gifford Pinchot, one of our members, to deliver this letter to Your Excellency in person."

Hoover wrote how French representatives from the region had begged the CRB for food, and how CRB delegates who visited the region had found great need. He also explained that in mid-January he had extended the food relief into one area of France because "our investigation indicated that unless foodstuffs were introduced into this section the actual deaths from starvation, which had set in, would quickly decimate the population before outside arrangements could be made."

This meant, Hoover pointed out, that the limited amount of CRB food imported for the Belgians had to be reduced even further to provide for the French. This had not stopped the Belgians from agreeing to "divide their last morsel with this population until something could be done." But the generous gesture could not be continued for long, he stated, and he drove the point home with stark truths: "It is no use dividing the food between the Belgians and the French in order that all may die. We have no right to take money provided to feed the Belgians and give it to the French." He went further and declared that he had already directed that no more food would be sent into France after March 1, which was less than two weeks from the date of the letter.

Appealing to the president's humanity, he wrote, "If Your Excellency could see the mobs of French women and children which surround every German camp from daylight to dark to gather the refuse from the German soldiers, Your Excellency would then believe that these French people will pay the last penalty unless someone comes to their rescue."

He finished with a sentence full of repressed emotion: "In conclusion, before taking the heavy responsibility of saying to these people 'you shall not have bread,' I make this last appeal to the French people themselves in the name of their own country-women and children."

A few days later, Hoover sent a follow-up telegram to Pinchot at the American embassy in Paris outlining a bold course of action if the French would not agree to support the relief. It was a hardball move that he had used successfully against the British government—agree to support the relief, or worldwide public opinion will be called down upon the French government.

Two days later, on February 27, Pinchot wrote a memorandum to Hoover of a conversation he had had with Alexandre Ribot, the French minister of finance. In it, he stated that he had not given Hoover's letter to President Poincaré and that his interview with Ribot lasted not more than five minutes. But what an extraordinary five minutes.

In that time, the finance minister stated clearly that the French government would not give formal approval to any financing of aid to its people through the Belgian budget (as Hoover had proposed). However, unattributed money would be provided to the Belgian government and the Belgian government "would be asked no inconvenient questions," such as the origin of the funds.

The reason the French would not give money in their own name was "because to do so would be to put into the hands of the Germans the argument that since the French Government was permitted to feed its citizens therefore the German Government should be permitted to feed the people of Germany." The Allies had already been restricting many goods from going or coming from Germany, and on March 1, 1915, the British and French would announce a blockade that would effectively stop all goods from entering or leaving Germany. It was a retaliatory blockade for the February 4, 1915, German "War Zone" declaration, which declared that the North Sea was a war zone and ships within it, whether or not they be neutral, could be sunk without warning.

Ribot told Pinchot that the four hundred thousand French civilians already receiving aid from the CRB should go on being fed and that the CRB should expand the relief and simply ask the Belgian government for the necessary funds as needed, but "not," the minister stipulated, "to keep the French in the invaded provinces in luxury, but to give them what is necessary to prevent them dying of starvation."

Hoover—probably frustrated and angry that Pinchot had not delivered his letter—had to be relieved. Armed with this rather unorthodox assurance that financing would be ultimately available, Hoover began to stockpile flour for the French without reducing the Belgian ration. He also decided that when he began negotiating with the Germans, he would tell them that the additional food was being provided by "charitable institutions which we represent." It was a "fiction," as Kittredge noted, that was necessary because the French government refused to acknowledge its financial commitment.

With the financial situation resolved, Hoover moved on to negotiate an agreement with the Germans. He and his team were concerned about having to deal with the German Etape in northern France. The commanders in each of the six Army Zone districts had complete authority, and they severely limited the movements and actions of those involved in relief. Communications were so highly restricted that civilians were effectively cut off from anyone outside their neighborhood. There was no postal service and no communication allowed between communes, and even commune meetings were rarely permitted.

This imposing militarized zone did not seem to bode well for Hoover and his executive team, who had to secure nonrequisition guarantees from the German General Staff in Charleville, France, before regular shipments could begin. They only had to think about the difficulties they had faced with Governor General von Bissing in occupied Belgium to believe that the German high command would be even more formidable.

What they found surprised them. The German military was much more open to working with the CRB than von Bissing seemed to be. Major von Kessler, a CRB liaison in Charleville, was helpful and responsive. Kittredge noted, "Major von Kessler always maintained a sympathetic and friendly attitude toward the Commission, and in general the Commission did not have to encounter in its work in France the continual suspicion that was directed against it by many of the higher authorities in Belgium. In France its work went on for the most part very smoothly and without the dozens of petty annoyances and aggravating incidents that continually arose in the territory of [von Bissing's] General Government."

This didn't mean there weren't difficulties and crises that would occur, but the initial setup of nonrequisition guarantees came about relatively smoothly. On April 13, 1915, an agreement was signed by Major von Kessler, representing the supreme command of the German Army, and Oscar T. Crosby, then CRB director in Brussels representing the CRB.

The need in northern France had been so great, however, that the first shipment had gone out in early February. It was a trainload of flour from Namur to Charleville and the commune of Sedan. The food was personally escorted by two young CRB delegates. In dramatic and unnecessary collegiate fashion, twenty-two-year-old Rhodes Scholar John L. Glenn rode "perched on the engine to make sure the food reached its destination" while twenty-three-year-old friend and fellow Rhodes Scholar Carlton Bowden raced along in his Overland car to help pave the way. The flour was presented to the mayors of both towns with the insistence that cash be paid for the temporary one-off delivery.

A few more sporadic shipments were made before the official agreement for provisioning was signed and regular shipments were started.

What was at stake wasn't as large as the relief efforts in Belgium, but it was still substantial. Those newly covered by the humanitarian aid were:

	Communes	*Population*
Lille	107	622,696
Valenciennes	339	591,155
St. Quentin	511	450,424
Vervins	431	222,646
Charleville	339	150,476
Longwy	406	112,218
Total	2,133	2,149,615

After study and analysis, a minimum ration per person per day was determined to be:

Flour (bread)—190 grams	Salt—10 grams
Rice—20 grams	Sugar—10 grams
Legumes—20 grams	Lard—30 grams
Coffee—20 grams	Bacon—30 grams

Even with the early shipments, all the items needed were still not being fully delivered by summer and early fall of 1915. Because most of the food had to be bought and shipped from North and South America and those orders were in addition to the orders already placed for Belgium relief, it took two to three months after purchasing for delivery to be anticipated in northern France.

Similar to how relief was organized in Belgium, the actual distribution of food to the more than two million northern French would be handled by locals. Those workers would be part of a newly formed organization, the Comité d'Alimentation du Nord de la France, commonly referred to as the Comité Français (CF).

The CF resembled the CN in Belgium, but a major difference was that the actions of the CF were severely restricted by the military government. Because of those limitations, a central committee of the CF was headquartered in Brussels, but it was more an accounting group than an executive committee. Overall coordinating control was maintained by the Brussels CRB office. Within the Army Zone, the CF had committees at the district, regional, and communal levels that coordinated the distribution. Because the members of these committees were restricted even more than the CRB delegates, much of the communications between the groups was aided by the American delegate, who traveled extensively throughout his district.

Another major difference between relief in northern France and in Belgium was that in northern France there were no neutral diplomats such as Whitlock and Villalobar acting as the patrons of relief, and no German officials such as Baron von der Lancken (von Bissing's political director) representing the German civil government.

For all intents and purposes, the CRB was on its own. The delegates and the CRB executives had to deal directly with the military authorities within each of the six districts and with the overall German military headquarters in Charleville.

CRB DELEGATES ENTER THE PICTURE

As for the concept of CRB delegates working in the French Etape, there was much for the German high command to consider. Some of the places where relief personnel had to work were within eyesight of the trenches, where they could observe men training, see battle preparations, and watch general troop movements. Such unique frontline positioning was not lost on the German commanders, who subsequently demanded that strict military procedures and regulations be followed and that American personnel be subject to close observation, management, and even searches at any time.

This led to the condition that each CRB delegate working in the six French districts be accompanied by a German officer. Officially designated as a *Begleitsoffizier* (escorting or accompanying officer), they were chosen by the German General Staff primarily for their command of English and French. Their job was to protect the delegates from petty annoyances (usually from the local German forces), observe and report all interactions with the local French, and aid in any negotiations that were necessary with the local German authorities.

In early April 1915, the first CRB delegates to northern France met their German accompanying officers at German General Headquarters in Charleville. Not knowing how the job would play out, the CRB executives had sent as many men experienced in Belgium relief as they could spare—eight out of the initial ten had at least a few months' experience with the CRB. Carlton Bowden, Frank Gailor, David T. Nelson, Hardwood Stacy, and Richard Simpson had started with the CRB in December 1914. Frederick Dorsey Stephens had joined the CRB in January 1915, as had Lewis Richards, who had lived in Brussels for years before the war. H. G. Chasseaud had started with the CRB in February 1915, and W. H. Chadbourn had begun in March 1915. The only man assigned to northern France who was completely new to relief, having started in April 1915, was Robert Dutton, but at forty-five years old, he was nearly twice the age of the others, a graduate of the Naval Academy, and a seasoned war veteran. The northern France posting was his first CRB assignment.

A group photo taken in Charleville during the April meeting of German officers and CRB delegates shows the Germans in their uniforms of jodhpurs, polished Hussar boots, and peaked caps with polished bills, while most of the Americans are in three-piece suits and shiny leather shoes. (Chadbourn and Chasseaud are not present.) The mood seems casual, almost lighthearted, as a few hold cigarettes or cigars and some offer up slight smiles. Only the faces of Dutton and a few of the German officers reflect a more thoughtful, serious attitude. Not surprisingly, the only Belgian in the photo, Firmin Van Brée, representing the CN, stands stiffly and without expression as German officers pose so close as to be touching.

Figure 9.1. When the first CRB delegates assigned to northern France met their accompanying German officers, there was a lighthearted spirit that was illustrated in a comic photo taken then. Lieutenant Rumelin struck a dominating pose over Americans Stacy, Stephens, Nelson, Dutton, Richards (crouching), Simpson, Gailor, Van Brée (a Belgian), and Bowden. The lightheartedness would not last long.
Public domain; Herbert Hoover Presidential Library Archives, West Branch, Iowa.

Another photo was taken that day. It was a comically staged one, and the handwritten caption reads, "A mock atrocity photo at Charleville, German General Staff Headquarters, April, 1915." In that photo one of the younger German officers, Lieutenant Rumelin, is on one side of a wrought iron fence striking a domineering, imperial pose with an outstretched arm holding a long riding crop that extends over the eight Americans and one Belgian who are behind the fence in various positions of supposed subjugation. Stacy appears to be holding up his hands in surrender, Richards and Van Brée are crouching down and holding the bars as if in jail, and Dutton is trying to join in the fun but seems not sure how best to do so. Bowden is simply leaning against the fence smoking and looking bored, while Nelson and Gailor appear to be waving to the camera. By far the most creative expression comes from Stephens. He seems to be performing what the British call "cock a snoot" and the Americans call a five-finger salute, as he holds his thumb to his nose and extends all five fingers. Or, as others might interpret it, he is simply performing a half-hearted wave.

No matter what the poses, the air was one of jesting and joking.

Few of the men would be laughing as the true impact of life together in northern France became a reality.

The actual work of a CRB delegate in northern France was straightforward: ensure no imported food was appropriated by the army and that the food was distributed equally and fairly throughout the district. The process to do so, however, was complicated. Shipments had to be recorded and tracked, distribution needed to be calculated and administrated, orders had to be transmitted back and forth between communal committees and the Brussels office, local meetings had to be attended and recorded, and some semblance of inspection had to be achieved to assure the delegate that no abuses of the system were taking place.

A CRB office was established in each of the district centers, and that office handled all documents, reports, and correspondence. Assisting were one or two secretaries who were either German soldiers or carefully selected Frenchmen. From there, the CRB delegate would send out "circular and special letters to the French committees transmitting instructions from Brussels, with additional measures added at his own initiative to suit the special features of his district. He wrote calling attention to irregularities, authorizing changes when necessary, and occasionally responding to requests for information or for the settlement of local disputes on the part of the French committees. He furthermore used his office communication system to assemble statistics and information from the different parts of the district at the behest of the Commission for Relief in Belgium or the Comité Français in Brussels."

More important than the delegate's office work was his field work. Because northern France was in one of the two Army Zones, there was no CRB centralized Inspection and Control Department as there was in Belgium. As a result, this meant that each northern France delegate was obligated to do a tremendous amount of traveling and inspecting within his designated area.

Normally, such work and traveling would not have been much of a burden to the delegates, but adding a German accompanying officer changed everything.

NO JOB FOR THE FAINT OF HEART

Under the German agreement establishing relief in northern France, the accompanying officer had to live with the CRB delegate in a requisitioned house within the district. The two men—usually including a couple of support staff for the officer—would eat together, sleep in the same house, and travel together in the officer's Mercedes-Benz staff car. CRB delegates were not allowed to have conversations—business or personal—with any French person without the German officer being present. No personal or business mail could be sent by a delegate without first having it pass through the hands of his German officer. And, officially, there was never any free solo time allowed for the delegate.

This was no job for the faint of heart or those with a weak mental constitution. Legation Minister Whitlock explained, "These [accompanying officers] never leave the delegates day or night; it is an intolerable relation, and at the end of three weeks the delegates come back to Brussels so nervous and unstrung that they burst into tears."

Kittredge wrote, "In general it was the American delegate's duty to keep an eye upon the situation, to keep his ears open and his mouth shut. . . . He had first and last to get on well with the German officer. If he had the confidence of this officer, he enjoyed much greater liberty and was given much more information about what was actually going on than would otherwise have been possible and in general."

Most of the German officers ultimately became fodder for delegates' inside jokes and stories that rarely indicated how psychologically difficult the situation was between the Germans and Americans. Behind the officers' backs, the delegates called them "nurses," and one unnamed delegate called his officer "my man Friday, for we felt like Robinson Crusoe on his desert island."

The same delegate explained that "we could have no friends. . . . We were to superintend in all centres of distribution, but we were superintendents who were superintended—we were suspects. . . . We could never speak to a Frenchman freely or alone; the big ears of the German officer were always wide open. In the course of our rounds we passed the night in the same hotel with him, and sometimes in the same room; we took our meals at the same table; at the meetings of the French committees the German officer never left our side. We were as inseparable as a man and his shadow. We were young, and we were not there to grumble."

The strain of the job was so intense that it was quickly decided by the CRB Brussels office that all delegates working in northern France would come back to Brussels every Saturday for a meeting. They and their German officers would normally leave on Friday in time to be in Brussels by Saturday morning, then drive back Sunday evening or Monday morning.

These meetings became vital for two reasons. One was that they afforded direct and uncensored communications between the delegates and the CRB Brussels office, which would have been impossible if the delegates had stayed at their French posts. Second, and just as important, the Saturday gatherings helped relieve the personal pressure each delegate faced during the week. Kittredge was blunt in his history when he wrote, "The nervous strain of the work in France was so great that even with the weekly visits to Brussels most of the delegates in France found themselves physically unable to remain much longer than six months at a time in a French post. In fact quite a number had nervous breakdowns after only a month or two in France." (Kittredge used "nervous breakdown" more to describe physical or mental exhaustion than to indicate mental illness, as the words are widely used today.)

THE GERMAN "NURSES" GET A NAME CHANGE

In early 1916, the German *Begleitsoffiziers*, or accompanying officers, had their official title changed. The *Begleitsoffizier* would from then on be known as *Verpflegungsoffizier*, or officer dealing with food or matters of feeding. The name change was an important reflection of the evolving relationship between German nurse and American delegate and how each interacted with the food-relief process.

In Belgium, the CRB delegate was involved in both the administration and business sides of the shipping, supervising, and distribution of food. He had no German officer following him around, he could move about Belgium in relative freedom to supervise and inspect the operations of the CN relief committees, and he could investigate on his own initiative any complaints or accusations of abuse.

In northern France, the founding concept was that the German officer would be there only to accompany the CRB delegate, to help smooth his way, to act as protector from the local German authorities, and to observe his interactions with French residents to make sure they were always about the relief effort and nothing more.

The reality had become somewhat different. With the delegate's freedoms severely curtailed and his German "nurse" required to be with him at all times, the American wasn't able to inspect operations at will or conduct investigations without the permission of his German shadow. Such conditions led to the rapid turnover of delegates.

It followed then that with the German officers remaining in their positions and many delegates coming and going, the officers naturally became more active participants in the relief program. They had institutional understanding, which included relationships with all the various local relief workers and committees, personal knowledge of what had been done, and an awareness of what needed to be done to keep the food coming. The successive new CRB delegates would come into the situation with little if any preparation and would have to rely heavily on the German officers to get a full grasp of what the job entailed.

All of that meant the German officers ended up in nearly full command of the situation. That did not mean, however, the German nurses weren't doing a good job of following the relief's principles and guidelines, as defined by the military's agreements with the CRB. For the most part, the officers "took very seriously their obligation," Kittredge related. "It was their duty as soldiers to see that the other German authorities adhered to the convention approved by the supreme command, and the officers were very energetic in enforcing the assurances and guarantees given by the German army in these first conventions and in later supplementary agreements."

This left the CRB delegate in a somewhat paradoxical position. On one hand, because of the personal hardships attached to the job, it was acknowledged, "the [Brussels CRB] director sends only the best men to France." And yet, a "supreme insult" that was well-known inside the CRB declared that northern France delegates "are about as important as so many mosquitoes." Delegate Joe Green wrote in his typically blunt way that the Germans in northern France "really did most of the work and our men became in reality mere accompanying representatives."

The truth of the importance and impact of the CRB delegate in northern France would lie somewhere in between. One northern France delegate said, "Effort and accomplishment could not be gauged by ordinary standards."

Besides the personal tensions of living together, the CRB delegate and the German officer had to contend with international events that affected them both. The German initiation of submarine warfare without warning vessels in February 1915 had been denounced around the world. This was especially true in America, where public opinion was strongly against the lack of warning. One delegate stated that the German nurses "realized that American public opinion had condemned them and they were bitter with rage."

The Germans responded to such criticism by bringing up the fact that American companies were supplying both munitions and food to the Allies while not selling the same to Germany. On these two subjects, they would make "the most violent and blustering protests" to their CRB delegate.

Such tensions and opposing positions on sensitive subjects easily transferred to the work, where it seemed to be a constant struggle between American and German as to who was calling the shots and controlling the situation. "It's trench warfare," an unnamed associate once told the delegates of northern France, "and you are losing, and you will lose. Only you must lose as slowly as possible."

It took a special kind of individual to lose very slowly while making sure the French civilians kept eating and the German officer didn't blow up.

SIMPSON BEATS THE ODDS

One delegate who lasted longer than most (he stayed six months) was John Lowery Simpson, better known as "Pink." (A childhood classmate already had the obvious red-headed name, so Simpson got stuck with Pink.) A 1913 graduate of the University of California, Simpson became a lawyer and took a job in the legal department of California's Immigration and Housing Commission. In late 1915, he had just accepted, but not yet taken, a new position as an "economic expert" for the Federal Trade Commission (FTC) in Washington, D.C., when he was invited to join the CRB.

On February 1, 1916, only two weeks before his twenty-fifth birthday, he was appointed chief delegate of the Vervins District. In Simpson's CRB portrait photo, he appears to be a serious young man with his head cocked just so, hair parted sharply on the left, and a mustache neatly trimmed to not curl around the edges of his lips. But closer examination reveals an ever-so-slightly raised eyebrow that in Simpson's case hinted at his flippant, many times facetious, sense of humor.

Simpson's unique sense of humor and dramatic bent made him see the opening up of northern France to the CRB as "the vistas of a new adventure for American youth." He saw a major difference between occupied Belgium and occupied France. In Belgium, after the first few months of occupation, "there had been restored . . . some kind of social structure. There were central offices, ministers, civil authorities, negotiations, dinners—even tennis occasionally."

That was not the case in northern France. There was only "one dominating fact, insistent like tunnel pressure against the ears; a state of war," Pink maintained. "In Northern France there was no normality; there was no code of action; there was no 'way of doing things.' There was a state of war."

Figure 9.2. CRB delegate John L. "Pink" Simpson had a flippant, many times facetious, sense of humor. As one of the northern France delegates who was tethered to a German "nurse," Pink lasted in the position longer than most.
Public domain; author's archives.

Such conditions, Simpson suggested, were why northern France held a "fascination for the American youth: it was forbidden territory. Once past the line you stood where the army was supreme. . . . When one penetrated farther south one caught the grey sheen of moving troops; or one descried long supply trains—even occasional smoke of artillery fire."

When Simpson took over as chief delegate, he inherited from his predecessor, Dutton, the German nurse Captain Weber. Summing up in two sentences, Pink wrote, "The American was sent into Northern France to watch the food. The German officer was sent to watch the American."

Simpson and Weber would spend days on the road motoring through the district in the German's chauffeur-driven staff car. Wherever possible, Pink would push to visit not only the regional centers but also the individual communes of the district—a difficult task considering there were 431 communes in the Vervins District. Simpson would randomly choose communes in different corners of the district to try and get a sense of the entire district.

Figure 9.3. German Captain Weber was Pink Simpson's "nurse," or accompanying officer.
Public domain; Herbert Hoover Presidential Library Archives, West Branch, Iowa.

When he and Weber motored into a local commune, they would search out the communal representative and then begin the inspection. "A normal inspection," Simpson said, "consisted in looking over the books, viewing the storehouse for the food, ascertaining the quality of the protection from the army, inquiring into the manner of distribution, noticing the arrangements for baking, the quality of bread, etc."

And then there were the informal moments—some that became defining moments. Early on in their relationship, Simpson and Captain Weber came to a commune where they found German soldiers sleeping in a room that had access to the warehouse where the CRB-imported flour was stored. Simpson wrote in a detailed scene what happened next:

I was still new to the work. "This must of course be changed," I observed.

"Nothing of the sort," retorted the captain. "Your business is to see that no food is taken by the army. You have no proof that that has occurred here. I deny that you have the right to demand a change."

I finally closed a fruitless argument by stating that I intended to report the matter to Brussels.

"Very well," snorted the officer.

In the afternoon we passed by the place again. The officer absented himself for a few moments, and on returning announced: "On my own initiative I have ordered new arrangements made here. We shall examine them when next we pass in this vicinity. But you understand that it is I who have done this, that I deny absolutely your right to insist."

I grunted, and, still outraged, I privately recounted the whole incident to my Director at Brussels the following Saturday. "If such a principal is admitted," I protested, "the power of the Representative . . ."

"The power of the Representative!" The director smiled. "By the way, Simpson," he added. "I believe you said the Captain ordered the place to be put in shape, didn't you?"

"Yes, he did."

"Well, I guess that's what you wanted, wasn't it?" remarked the Director. And I am sure that his eye twinkled.

Simpson would fight back with his German nurse as often as he dared, reminding himself of what another had told him, that the best he could ever do was to "lose as slowly as possible."

A CREATIVE WORKAROUND

Some of the delegates in northern France began to understand what made their German nurses tick and what made them do what they did. They would share that information with their fellow delegates at the Saturday meetings in Brussels. Some obvious truths emerged—the German nurses were practically slaves to authority and chain of command. They also felt that they were the ones in charge, not the Americans. Their thinking was that northern France was German-conquered territory—it was their government that allowed the Americans to bring in relief; therefore, they were in command.

This meant they found it offensive when a delegate tried to give orders, even if those orders were reasonable and/or justified. They especially disliked when a delegate made formal complaints to the CRB Brussels office or, worse, to the German High Command in Charleville because that reflected badly on them as the officers in charge. With their great respect for authority, however, they did normally honor any requests or orders issued from the CRB office in Brussels, but they would have refused had the delegate asked for the same thing.

Those insights led to a devious delegate workaround. Kittredge, in his CRB history, noted, "Many of the representatives, therefore, gave up the useless procedure of arguing with their officer and accomplished what they wanted by the simple expedient of dictating letters to themselves while at Brussels over the week-end, giving themselves definite instructions that such and such classes of people should or should not be fed, that the reports should be handled in this or that manner, etc. They would then have these letters signed by the director of the Commission at Brussels. The following week the letter would be despatched [*sic*] to them through the German officers, as was the case with all mail. The German officer would receive the letter of instructions and, without saying anything to the delegate and often without handing him the letter, would proceed to carry the instructions into effect on his own initiative."

It was a case of American ingenuity outsmarting Prussian love of authority.

As the war dragged on, the conditions in northern France worsened for civilians. Hoover requested and received an increase in the monthly subsidy from 20 million francs to 35 million francs, and imports increased for November and December 1915 and January 1916.

However, due to the initial success of the Germans' unrestricted submarine warfare that began in February 1917, the CRB was barely able in the next five months to maintain import amounts that would sustain life. (See chapter 18 for what happened to northern France through the end of the war.)

10

Pressures from Von Bissing

The German governor general initially saw the humanitarian program as a way to gain greater control over his domain. As contemporary Dutch historian Dr. Johan den Hertog wrote, "Bissing's prime objective was to make Belgium a satellite state with a German leader—he naturally saw himself as a suitable candidate. This ideal was easily reconciled with the food aid. A turbulent, resentful Belgium would not want to be governed by Germans. So he was prepared to guarantee, up to a point, that CRB supplies as well as the domestic harvest would reach the local population."

During the first three months of CRB operations, von Bissing and his government had issued passes and allowed the delegates freedom to move about the country. But that attitude began to change as the relief work grew in scope, size, and overall importance. The Germans were concerned that this neutral organization was getting too powerful in a country that was supposed to be ruled absolutely by them.

Delegate Kittredge wrote, "The Germans naturally looked with no great favour on the idea of having a considerable number of Americans travelling about freely in a conquered territory so close to the theatre of military operations. The Commission, with its delegates in every province, was more than once suspected . . . of being a great espionage machine."

What made it worse was the fact that the delegates, who were some of the only nonmilitary personnel allowed to use automobiles, were heartily cheered by Belgians as they roared by in their motorcars. "It was undoubtedly galling to the Germans, who regarded themselves as absolute masters of the country, to see Americans, who were not in the least afraid of them and who were beyond their control, dashing about the country."

Figure 10.1. Baron Moritz Ferdinand von Bissing (right) became governor general of Belgium on December 3, 1914, replacing Baron Colmar von der Goltz (left). Von Bissing would rule Belgium ruthlessly.

Public domain; Hugh Gibson, *A Journal from Our Legation in Belgium* (New York: Doubleday, Page and Co., 1917).

THE US FLAG BECOMES AN ISSUE

Each car used by the delegates was adorned with a "CRB" in large letters on the front of the radiator or on the sides of the engine hood. At least one American flag, if not two, flew from the front fenders. Many Belgians who had rarely, if ever, seen an American flag suddenly knew it from afar and would stop to cheer and wave as the motorcars approached. To most Belgians, the American flag quickly came to represent not only food relief but also international acknowledgment of their plight and a kind of independence from—and rejection of—the hated German occupation. Brand Whitlock wrote that for Belgians the American flag "came to express their hopes, their ideals, their aspirations."

At one point in the late winter of 1914–1915, according to Whitlock, there were more than eight thousand American flags flying atop provincial warehouses, communal storehouses, mills, and the motorcars of the delegates.

Such prominence of the flag was more a natural outgrowth of how relief had begun than a planned action. As the first shipments of food had entered Belgium in 1914 and the first American delegates had followed in their wake, it was natural that American flags were used to indicate to both the Germans and the Belgians that the food in the barges and the men riding in the motorcars were part of a neutral humanitarian program. As the food went on to be delivered to provincial and commune warehouses, those facilities were also marked by American flags because the Americans felt the food was their responsibility until final distribution to individual civilians. (Later this concept was adjusted to responsibility until the food was turned over to the CN or provincial committees.)

Initially, the flags were accepted by all and honored by the Germans. But in early 1915, as the relief settled into a more long-term effort and Belgian civilians reacted so positively to the flag, the Germans began to resent its use. It reached a point where German officers would stop CRB cars and warn the delegate "there was but one flag in Belgium and that was the German flag." In meetings with von Bissing and Baron von der Lancken, Brand Whitlock was told that the American flag posed the possibility of spurring violence from German soldiers and must be taken down in all places.

In a move that would be highly criticized by many delegates, Whitlock ordered the Americans to remove the flags from their vehicles and any Belgian-controlled

Figure 10.2. The Belgians prominently displayed the American flag wherever possible, including this children's canteen in Brussels, until the Germans demanded that most US flags be taken down.

Public domain; Vernon Kellogg, *Fighting Starvation in Belgium* (New York: Doubleday, Page and Co., 1918).

facilities. By spring he would go on to negotiate with the Germans to have the flag removed from all but the provincial warehouses. Taking the place of the flag on the motorcars and elsewhere would be the CRB's own flag.

Whitlock wrote a long letter to newly appointed CRB Brussels Director Albert Connett about the situation. He felt strongly that the American flag should only be used by diplomatic personnel. In a surprisingly strong tone rarely used, he told Connett to tell all the delegates that "they are in no sense diplomatic officers and have no diplomatic functions to discharge. They are not here to protect anybody's interests nor are they to interfere in any way as between belligerents [Belgians and Germans] or to receive complaints of any sort except those relating to the food that has been sent for the relief of the civil population."

Whitlock's take on the use of the American flag and the delegates' duties was more in line with how Francqui, the CN, von Bissing, and the Germans felt than how Hoover, Gibson, and the delegates perceived them.

DELEGATES AND FREEDOM AT STAKE

While the flag issue was a small manifestation of German resentment of the presence of the Americans, in early February 1915, only two weeks after one of his staff officers was beaten by German sentries (see chapter 6), von Bissing decided it was time to restrict delegate movements and even limit the number of Americans allowed into Belgium.

This was a major move against the CRB, and to Hoover it was simply unacceptable. He was certain the CRB could not "discharge its obligations in Belgium without an adequate force of Americans to act as delegates in the provinces in close touch with the details of the work. These delegates could accomplish nothing without automobiles to carry them about their districts and passports permitting them to use the automobiles. It was necessary, in order to assure the success of the work, that the Commission representatives should enjoy complete liberty of movement and of action, and as great facilities of communication as were possible."

When von Bissing's new demands were issued, Hoover was in Brussels, having just come from Berlin. On February 11, 1915, Hoover went to see Governor General von Bissing in a somewhat unusual evening meeting. He stated later that Whitlock went along, but Whitlock did not mention it in his journal and even implied that Hoover had gone alone. (Whitlock's lack of focus about such a critical meeting was understandable—a few days before he had learned his younger brother Frank had died suddenly in Philadelphia.)

For Hoover, it was his first sit-down with the old Prussian cavalry officer. Hoover was not impressed: "Von Bissing was a small-sized man, and my impression was that without his uniform, high boots, and helmet he would have looked most insignificant. My impression of his mental processes would also be included in that term."

There's no record of what von Bissing thought of Hoover, although later the German reportedly said, "I fully trusted Mr. Hoover although I knew quite well that he was in constant touch with the French and British governments, and that he was at heart with our enemies."

At their first meeting, Hoover pleaded his case, but von Bissing remained firm. He angrily told the American that the delegates already had too much liberty of movement and that they were running all around the country to the great concern of the military. The CRB must change quickly and decrease its requests for passes because he was soon going to impose even more restrictions on the delegates.

"The Commission," he declared emphatically, "only needs a few men in the central warehouses, who should remain in these warehouses and not move about the country; the Belgians can attend to all the work of food distribution."

Hoover pointed out how the CRB had international responsibilities to both the Allied governments and the German government to ensure all the guarantees were followed and that the food continued to be distributed fairly and exclusively to Belgian civilians. The only way to do that was through complete freedom of movement so the delegates could inspect the entire scope and process of the humanitarian aid, as well as help speed along the shipments of food.

Von Bissing refused to accept any of Hoover's points and barely seemed to listen to what the American was saying. Part of the problem could have been the simple fact that they did not share a common language—von Bissing spoke German and French; Hoover spoke only English and had to converse through the awkwardness of translators.

"We did not get anywhere," Hoover said with great understatement. The next day he went to see Whitlock, who wrote that Hoover was still "boiling with rage" about the meeting and von Bissing's unwillingness to see the importance of the work and the need for unfettered independent delegates. To compound his frustration, Hoover had also been to see Dr. Marx, who was a German official in the bureau that issued passes. At one point during their conversation, the man had asked him point-blank: "What do you Americans get out of this, I should like to know?"

Hoover was furious. He constantly faced this same insinuation with many German officials—that the CRB and its delegates were in the relief business for monetary or political gain. This was probably due in part to the generally held opinion that America was a country of shopkeepers and businesspeople who were only interested in bettering their own bottom line.

"It is absolutely impossible," Hoover shot back, "for you Germans to understand that one does anything from pure humanitarian, disinterested motives, so I shall not attempt to explain it to you."

Hoover's next move was to write a detailed letter to von Bissing, in hopes that a dispassionate, logical explanation outlining the CRB's problems might have a better chance of success than a personal meeting. The day after his meeting with von Bissing, Hoover presented the letter to von der Lancken, who promised he would review it with the governor general.

In the extensive missive, Hoover outlined his position, the importance of relief, and the need for unfettered freedom of movement. He also wrote that if an agreement couldn't be reached, "we shall be compelled to withdraw and the flow of the stream of foodstuffs into Belgium from outside countries must necessarily cease."

Hoover would use the same threaten-to-leave tactic many times, on many different people and governments. He was confident that even if von Bissing didn't back off because of the threat, the German government in Berlin would.

On February 20, 1915, Hoover received von Bissing's reply. The German had written it only after his representatives had conferred with Dannie Heineman as to what the CRB wanted. Heineman was the American who had been so helpful in organizing early relief and had been the first CRB director in Brussels. However, by early 1915, Heineman had been removed as director because Hoover thought his efforts and sympathies were too closely aligned with the interests of Francqui and the CN and not enough with the CRB. Because von Bissing had a close association with Heineman, the German had had his staff work with Heineman and not the current Brussels director, Albert Connett. That meant the needs of the CRB were not properly conveyed to the Germans working on the issue.

Von Bissing started his reply by agreeing with Hoover that the work was important and that the Germans would support it. But then he had a long list of conditions that were to be met, including: the number of delegates must be restricted as much as possible; the current thirty to forty delegates would be cut to twenty-five by April 15; the frequent changes in delegates would be stopped as much as possible; delegates would be given passes for only their province and to Brussels; only four members of the Brussels office would be allowed to have passes for the entire country; and only six passes a month would be issued for trips to Holland.

A TURNING POINT FORCES ACTION

Upon reading the letter, Hoover said it was simply "reiterating a number of intolerable restrictions." He and the rest of the CRB were certain twenty-five men could not adequately supervise the work across the entire country. They also knew that if they agreed to such demands, it would be recognizing the Germans' right to control the CRB, something that was unacceptable to Hoover and to the British government.

This, Hoover knew, was a major turning point in his organization and in the life of the relief work. If he failed to win freedom of movement for his delegates, it would subjugate the entire humanitarian aid to German authority. That was intolerable to Hoover and unacceptable to the Allies, and it was a primary reason why he had threatened to pull out if the restrictions were not lifted.

If the British Foreign Office only knew about von Bissing's letter and demands, it would force the issue, in Hoover's favor he hoped. While that would temporarily mean hot water for Hoover, it would also justify his going over von Bissing's head and pleading the case to the German civilian government in Berlin, which had the power to override the governor general.

But how to alert the British Foreign Office to the situation? Hoover could not simply show the letter to the British because that would be a major breach of his adherence to strict neutrality and to international protocol during wartime.

In a not-too-surprising development, the British Foreign Office did find out about von Bissing's letter. Officially, there was never a full explanation of how that happened, although Hoover did point the finger of culpability at the British government's covert investigations of the CRB in Belgium. Throughout the war, Britain's military, which was opposed to the relief, had heated disagreements with its own civilian government, which generally supported relief. As a result, the military instigated investigations of the CRB in an effort to discredit the CRB. Hoover referred to that when he wrote, "The British Foreign Office, being informed of [von Bissing's letter and demands] through their Intelligence, promptly objected." It's just as likely, though, that von Bissing's letter, or the gist of it, was intentionally leaked to the British by someone in the CRB's London office.

No matter how the issue arose, the hot water came quickly; Hoover was called to the Foreign Office. He wrote Whitlock on March 6, "I have had a severe drilling this week, from the English Government with regard to our whole organization in Belgium." He also implied in his letter that Whitlock should try to change von Bissing's mind.

Hoover not only had to face von Bissing's objections, he had to contend with the lack of support for his position from Whitlock, Francqui, and even his own Brussels director, Connett. A well-known American engineer, Connett had started in February, and his belief about the need for delegates was more in line with Francqui's and even the Germans' than Hoover's. He was "unfavorably impressed with the youth of the delegates in Belgium" and did not see the necessity to have a large number of them roaming about Belgium.

When Hoover wrote Connett from London to convince him of his position and included a letter from Ambassador Page that stated the delegates in Belgium should be numerous and more actively involved in the distribution, Connett sent back a rather shocking reply on March 8, 1915. He wrote that he had initially intended to call the delegates together and instruct them to follow the new guidelines as outlined in Hoover's and Page's letters. "However," he then wrote, "after a night's sleep and a frank talk with Mr. Francqui, I changed my mind. We both are confident that the Ambassador's letter was inspired in London Wall Buildings [Hoover's office] and not in Grosvenor Gardens [Page's office]." (After such an insult—regardless of how true it might be—it's no wonder Connett was gone within a month.)

Facing pressures from all sides, Hoover decided it was time for strong action. On March 9, Hoover went over von Bissing's head and bypassed diplomat Whitlock. He wrote a telegram to Ambassador Gerard in Berlin outlining the situation and asking for help. "Do not believe that it can be in line with intention German Government toward us and trust you will take it up with them."

Hoover's line "trust you will take it up with them" was uncharacteristically diplomatic. That was out of necessity. While Hoover's end run around von Bissing and

Whitlock was highly undiplomatic, his interaction with Gerard had to be as diplomatic as possible. The fact remained that Hoover was still a private citizen, pleading the case of a private company to a diplomat whose country had no official function within the CRB and Belgium relief. The ministers of America, Spain, and Holland who had agreed to be patrons of the CRB had agreed to do so more as private citizens than as official representatives of their governments. Hoover had to walk a fine line of not pushing the ambassadors too far in his requests, or they might simply walk away or claim they no longer had time away from their other official duties to help the CRB. As for Whitlock, his case was different because he was inside Belgium—he had no choice but to be involved.

Hoover also had to tread more lightly with the US ambassador to Germany because he had not yet come to know Gerard well. So, in his telegram, he carefully outlined to Gerard what the bare minimum would be for the CRB to function properly. "Fundamental fact is that in order for us to give proper executive control to distribution of this foodstuff, to properly account to its donors, and above all to give credibility to our assurances to the Allied Governments as to their guarantees, it is absolutely necessary for us to have the right to at least fifty people, to put any such number of staff into Belgium as may be reasonable to meet our own emergencies. Their passes must be issued directly on certification of Mr. Whitlock and on liberal basis of movement." Hoover ended by asking Gerard to pass the telegram to Whitlock and Connett. He knew that Whitlock, Connett, and von Bissing would not take it well.

Much to the displeasure of the governor general, Hoover's end run worked—von Bissing's order limiting the movement and number of CRB personnel was rescinded. Von der Lancken told Whitlock on March 11, "Von Bissing is a touchy gentleman and was offended by Hoover going [over his head] to Berlin." But the governor general was a firm believer in chain of command, so he agreed to more delegates and greater freedom with passes.

As a result, the CRB Brussels office developed an extensive pass department that worked exclusively on ensuring speedy processing. One of the critical men in the department was Hermancito "Germàn" Bulle, the Mexican chargé d'affaires at Brussels, who was considered a CRB member from the beginning and became a unique diplomatic secretary representing the CRB to the German occupation government. He was a short, stocky, jolly man, always quick with a funny comment or smile, and was completely devoted to the relief work. Through Bulle's leadership and help, the department even took on the task of securing passes for members of the CN and provincial committees. (He would succumb to a stroke in Brussels on December 27, 1916, the only CRB delegate to die behind the lines.)

While passes would occasionally become an issue later, von Bissing's begrudging acceptance of what Hoover wanted in March 1915 effectively took care of the problem.

It would not be long, however, before the German turned his controlling sights on a new target within the humanitarian program.

VON BISSING TAKES ON THE CN

As spring 1915 turned into summer, the governor general grew more and more frustrated with Belgium relief efforts. He watched as the program, which had begun relatively modestly, grew into a huge operation that was taking on more and more significance in what he considered to be his fiefdom.

From the beginning, the CRB and the CN had grown organically, taking on greater power and decision-making as the massive humanitarian aid had developed. They had never considered consulting the Germans or asking permission for such incremental expansions of their authority. They simply did what was needed to keep the food coming and to distribute it equitably.

On June 26, 1915, von Bissing's frustration rose to the surface again. This time he tried to gain greater control over the CN. Making sure not to acknowledge the CN's authority by writing directly to Francqui, von Bissing wrote instead a long letter to Whitlock, the primary neutral patron of relief. He stated that it had become "clear that the sphere of the Comité's [CN's] activity has assumed an extension which had not been foreseen at the time of its creation." The time had come, he declared, that "the activity of the Comité be clearly delimited and that the mutual relations of the administration under my orders and of the sub-organization of the Comité be regulated." The Germans were going to take over.

He outlined how a member of his civil government would sit in on each of the Belgian provincial committee meetings and review all committee correspondence. In relating to local committees, the provincial committees would not be allowed to send any information, ask for any statistics, or make regulations without first consulting with the German civilian in charge. All policing powers that the CN had taken on regarding millers, bakers, and others in the distribution chain were "revoked since the administration under my orders is alone qualified to exact these measures."

Von Bissing did toss a bone to both the CN and CRB by stating that the two organizations "have the right to make inquiries and statements regarding the abuses committed by the millers, bakers, etc., but their right is limited to making these statements. They are allowed to communicate these afterwards to the competent [German] authorities," but that was as far as they could take such matters.

No matter how far apart the CRB and CN were in their internal squabbling about who was responsible for what, they could both easily agree that von Bissing's new regulations were totally unacceptable. Meetings in Brussels between Baron von der Lancken, Whitlock, and Villalobar were held to work through the issues.

At the same time, because von Bissing had written Whitlock, his letter was sent to the two relief patrons in London, Ambassador Page and Spanish Ambassador to Great Britain Alfonso Merry del Val. They, in turn, being accredited diplomats and following proper diplomatic procedures, forwarded the letter to the British Foreign Office for advice.

The process took nearly a month but on July 17, 1915, Foreign Secretary Sir Edward Grey replied to Page. He voiced the British government's strong objection to von Bissing's efforts to control relief and restated the conditions by which relief would be permitted. He explained that the British government believed in the "spirit of non-interference" with the CRB and the CN and that it would insist that "the German authorities shall also act [in the spirit of non-interference]. . . . It is on this spirit, and not on the strict belligerent rights of either government, that the whole work of relief is based, and the introduction into these discussions of any such claims of right cannot but be fatal to the continuance of that work."

In other words, the Germans had to lay off trying to control the CRB and CN or the food relief would be shut down.

The British government's objections were taken via Whitlock to von der Lancken, who held two long conferences with Whitlock and Villalobar. Nearly two weeks after Grey's letter had been written, Baron von der Lancken wrote to Whitlock on July 29, 1915, formally stating that the governor general agreed to the British conditions outlined by Grey. Von der Lancken wrote, "The Comité National and the Commission for Relief in Belgium shall be able to enjoy all liberty of action necessary for them to be in a position to fulfill the mission which has devolved upon them through the agreements entered into between the Governor-General and the representatives of the neutral Powers."

With von Bissing's acknowledgment of the integrity and authority of the CN and CRB, one would have thought any problems between the CN and CRB would have been shelved, at least for a moment or two.

Far from it, as the CRB found out immediately (see chapter 11).

11

Internal Strife and Battle for Control

As von Bissing's attempt to take over the CN was unfolding, so too were battles large and small between the CRB and CN over who controlled the relief. In the spring of 1915, the CN had quietly supported German insistence that the number of American flags be reduced, and the CN had overreacted to a CRB request to remove the word "American" from its "American Stores" (which sold sundry items not appropriate for mass distribution) by removing all CRB references throughout Belgium (quickly restored by order of the CRB).

THE ROLE OF THE DELEGATES

By June and July 1915, another issue came to the fore—delegate responsibilities—and it would reflect how Francqui and the CN wanted complete leadership. Delegates had already been an issue with von Bissing's February 1915 attempt to decrease their number and curtail their movements, and the CN had done nothing to aid Hoover in that fight. But the definition of a delegate's role was changing, primarily under pressure from Francqui, the CN, and some provincial committees. These Belgians wanted all delegates to assume passive, advisory roles rather than the irritatingly active, administrator-like roles that some were playing.

Efforts had been made by the CRB and CN to clarify the issue, but by the summer of 1915, the CN still saw some of the delegates as overstepping their bounds of responsibility. Conversely, Hoover and the CRB came to realize that the delegate tussles with Francqui and the CN were only "the first phase in a much more vital conflict affecting the whole matter of control of relief."

Hoover, in later writings, said little about this time and the infighting with the CN. It's left to the ever-frank Kittredge to state the case in his unofficial CRB history: "Many important decisions had been taken by the Comité National in Belgium without consulting the Commission or heeding its advice and counsel." Even with Hoover's reluctance to write about these CN troubles, he nonetheless was incredibly frustrated, as evidenced by what he ultimately did to counteract Francqui.

When the Chief came to Brussels in the middle of July to conclude the 1915 harvest agreements (see chapter 12), he brought with him two of his executive team, John Beaver White and Edgar Rickard, because he knew Francqui and the CN were working to undermine the CRB. What the three found, according to Kittredge, was that "Francqui's attitude was apparently not to be changed and that he intended that the Commission should no longer have any real authority in Belgium. Hoover recognised that this would make impossible the accomplishment of the purposes for which the Commission existed, that if it could not have an effective control in Belgium it would be perfectly useless as an organisation."

On July 20, 1915, Hoover and his team sat down with Francqui and the CN's executive committee for a major conference. The description of the meeting in the usually comprehensive book *Public Relations of the Commission for Relief in Belgium: Documents* neglects to mention any CN problems. The authors of the book give the section a muted, rather innocuous subtitle, "Adjustment of Functions of C.R.B. and C.N. July 1915."

The reality was a bit different. Hoover took the meeting by storm. The American played what he felt was his final, most dramatic card—threatening to pull the CRB out of all relief work. It was a tactic Hoover had used before and would continue to use during the next few years, but always when he felt the odds were stacked in his favor regarding the outcome.

In this case, the usually blunt Hoover didn't announce the CRB's departure, he simply asked the group "if the time had now arrived when the retirement of the Commission from the relief work in Belgium should be considered." Converting his frustrations to a perceived—but disingenuous—positive attitude, he listed four events and situations that had led him to that question.

1. Initially, because the military authorities had not allowed freedom of movement for Belgians, the CN and its committees needed the CRB to establish communications links within the distribution network. Now the situation was "improved" because of the "more liberal attitude of the military authorities in these particulars," and therefore the CRB wasn't needed that much anymore.
2. The financial situation had been resolved so "no further appeals for the charity of the world in support is necessary, or if necessary, they could be made by the C.N."
3. The Germans had kept to the agreements not to requisition any imported foodstuffs, so all the agreements in place should satisfy the Allied governments that the "whole line of guarantees can quite properly be transferred from the Commission for Relief in Belgium to the Comité National."

4. With the 1915 harvest agreement, the CRB's role in "conserving native food supplies has become less important." (See chapter 12 for details.)

Hoover summed up by saying the "sole object" of the CRB was to help the Belgians because they weren't free to help themselves. With the improving "political situation," he basically said the Belgians could get along without the CRB. The organization would retire gradually, with the plan of leaving by the middle of October, thereby completing one full year of service.

The Chief offered all this to Francqui, knowing quite well that the British would never agree to a CRB departure. Additionally, it could be easily argued that Hoover—with his sense of commitment, integrity, honor, and belief in the humanitarian work—would never have willingly left the Belgians and northern French and that his threat was never more than a bluff.

For Francqui—a man who led meetings like a dictator running a show he had scripted—it must have been difficult to sit through Hoover's presentation.

The official record says that Francqui and the CN's executives protested each of Hoover's reasons for pulling out and declared "it was impossible" that the CRB "should retire." The Belgians gave six points to why the CRB must stay. The last point summed up their official stand: "The Comité National is certain that it could not go on without (1) the political and moral support of the Commission; (2) that the executive work could not continue without the co-operation of the Commission; and (3) that the finance, purchase, and transport operations are impossible at the present time by Belgians alone.

"Therefore, the Comité National not only protests at the idea of withdrawal, but specifically requests the Commission to continue its activities without idea of cessation."

The turnaround was abrupt and startling to any who had been following the rising tide of CN challenges to the CRB. And one wonders why Francqui, when faced with what he had probably wished for, turned it down.

In all probability, it was because Francqui was more than anything a pragmatist, and he knew the Allied governments would not allow Hoover and the CRB to pull out or accept the CN taking over the CRB's responsibilities. He didn't necessarily want the CRB delegates gone; he just wanted them neutered. And he knew that with the newly formed Central Crop Commission (see chapter 12), he and the CN were making headway at diminishing the role of the CRB in everyday operations. He would continue to work behind the scenes to continue that movement.

Certainly none of the Americans in the meeting cared to question Francqui's reversal. The meeting then confirmed that the "ravitaillement [relief] and care of the destitute in Belgium shall continue as a joint undertaking." A long list detailed the administrative relationship between the two groups. The CRB would retain representation on the CN's executive committee, and the delegates would sit as members on the provincial and local committees.

A noticeable change was the timetable for when the CN took charge of imported foodstuffs. Initially, the CRB had retained control of the food until its distribution. But from the July 1915 meeting forward, the CN would take official charge of food shipments once they reached provincial warehouses (with mills being considered provincial warehouses).

Kittredge noted, however, that that change meant "the whole question of the activity of the provincial delegates was left unsettled, except that it was provided that they should co-operate as closely as possible with the provincial committees."

As a way of resolving that and other issues, a CRB internal memorandum regarding the organization and its delegates was prepared and circulated in-house. Much of it had to do with the CRB delegates' newly adjusted role and their work with the provincial committees. The E. E. Hunt concept of delegates taking executive action was definitely out. The memorandum stated clearly, "We are here to help, not to order." Kittredge noted, "The view of a number of the provincial delegates, that efficiency in the work could only be secured if the delegates were to be given authority to take executive action, was thus definitely overruled."

The delegates were instructed that there were three areas they were responsible for: providing help and general services to the provincial committees wherever possible; ensuring all guarantees were met as to German nonrequisition and the fair distribution of food to all; and maintaining transportation and statistics so that food could keep coming in and the CRB would be able to report on all operations.

As to relations with the provincial committees, the memorandum repeated that "the attitude of the delegates shall be entirely of the order of inspection and advice and not of executive action." As to relations with the Germans, the instructions were just as clear and vague: "The relation of the delegates to the local German authorities shall be purely one of a friendly intermediary."

While the memorandum did clarify much about the CRB's duties and its organization, according to Kittredge, it did something else as well: "This memorandum did, however, strengthen the hands of that group in the comité exécutif of the Comité National which objected to any sort of American interference in the actual work in Belgium. The conflict of authority and the incipient friction between the two organizations was therefore postponed rather than removed."

In the end, all the delegates could do was to feel a sense of relief that the major issues between the CRB and CN, and the CRB and the Germans, were seemingly resolved, at least for the moment. What the Americans had just experienced, however, was merely a skirmish with Francqui. The main battle would come in 1916.

FRANCQUI TAKES ON THE INSPECTION AND CONTROL DEPARTMENT

Petty issues and little grievances continued to plague relations between the CRB and CN through the rest of 1915 and well into 1916. During the summer of 1916,

Figure 11.1. Delegate Joseph Green was the head of the CRB's Inspection and Control Department. He faced constant harassment from Émile Francqui, who felt he was intruding in CN affairs.
Public domain; author's archives.

however, tension between the two groups dramatically increased after major moves by Francqui against the CRB's Inspection and Control Department.

The department was run by Joe Green, who had taken on the task in January 1916. The twenty-nine-year-old Princeton grad was an honest, albeit brusque and impatient, man who was not afraid of confrontation, regardless of whom he faced. He and his department had done an excellent job streamlining processes within provinces to ensure food went to only the right people, building a network of informers regarding black market activity to answer the numerous accusations of relief mismanagement by the British military, and keeping Francqui in check as best as possible.

By July 1916, however, Francqui was fed up with Green and his butting into areas that the Belgian thought were none of his business. He confronted the American on multiple fronts:

- Green was told no letters from him or his staff could be sent out without being first countersigned by Francqui. Later, he was notified that a stamp would be placed on his outgoing mail that instructed all replies should be sent to the CN—cutting him out of the communications loop.
- Francqui actually tore up one Green letter that requested an investigation by the Greater Brussels inspection service about a German violation of the relief agreements. Francqui told Green's CN counterpart, Van Gend, to inform Green that no such letters should be written in the future.

- The normal flow of reports to Green's department regarding all food regulation violations brought before the Belgian courts was suddenly funneled through Francqui's office, which suppressed some reports and altered others to remove certain facts Francqui did not want Green to see.
- Other official agencies in Belgium were instructed to reduce, if not completely cut off, information to Green.
- The professional investigators utilized by Green were told that all reports normally sent to Green and his department were to be sent only to the CN.

Green argued every point and fought every battle he felt he should, but there was no letup. Francqui and his associates kept trying to cut him out of the entire inspection and control operations.

In London, Hoover was "naturally very indignant," as Kittredge stated with uncharacteristic restraint. Still, the Chief wanted to try and work things out with Francqui before asking the British to get involved.

In the first week of October 1916, Hoover returned to Brussels and had numerous meetings with Francqui and others, to no avail. Kittredge termed them "rather inconclusive meetings" and summed up the situation: "The difficulties with the Comité National became more and more irritating."

After Hoover returned to London, Francqui made an incredibly bold move, basically shutting down the Inspection and Control Department by removing CRB files and documents and telling the Belgian staff to no longer report to Joe Green. Orders were also given to the Belgian prosecutor general to stop cooperating with the CRB regarding cases of relief mismanagement.

This was no passive resistance from the CN—which had been going on since the beginning of relief—this was an outright coup against Green and the CRB.

Hoover was incensed. In London, he immediately wrote a strongly worded letter to Lord Percy detailing Francqui's actions. In a calmer moment, he decided not to send it until first consulting with Page. The ambassador counseled Hoover to hold the Percy letter, and Page wrote to Percy asking that the British once again detail the relationship between the CRB and CN.

This led to more discussions, correspondence with those inside Belgium, and a Lord Grey letter, not publicly distributed, outlining the CRB–CN relationship and the British insistence that the CRB was running the show. Hoover held that letter in reserve.

On October 26, he made another trip to Brussels. Whitlock proclaimed, "Hoover comes tomorrow, with his faithful companion trouble." Three days after Hoover's arrival, Whitlock wrote that the Chief was "full of fight, and determined, doggedly determined to force the issue with Francqui."

Francqui was just as adamant as before. The CN was boss in Belgium, just as the CRB was boss outside Belgium. According to Kittredge, Francqui's attitude was "defiant and unyielding. . . . He declared that there could be no co-operation between the Comité National and the Commission. . . . All control in Belgium must be by the Comité National."

Francqui was taking such a tough, intractable stance because he had what he felt was a trump card. He had finally made a deal with the exiled Belgian government. Whitlock explained, "It appears . . . that Francqui and the Comité National have made their peace with the Belgian Government at Havre [France]. The Belgian Government recognizes Francqui and Company as its representatives in Belgium, and in return the Francqui and Company, who were becoming dangerous revolutionary rivals, agree to abdicate when the King comes back. Meanwhile Francqui assumes the powers and rank of a dictator, and has even told Hoover that the Comité National must be shown the respect due a government! The man indeed is quite blown with pride, and this morning told Hoover that the Belgians wished no more charity from America!"

Hoover finally gave Lord Grey's letter to Whitlock, who showed it to Francqui. The Belgian read the French translation "with a black visage." When he finished, he declared, "It is Hoover who wrote that, I know his style. . . That is the limit!" Francqui remained unmovable.

Hoover left Brussels once again frustrated but determined to somehow resolve the issue. Whitlock found his own opinion shifting: "The more one sees of Francqui, while admiring his brilliant mind, the less one respects him; the more one sees of Hoover, the more one respects and likes him."

From mid-November to mid-December 1916, there was a blizzard of letters back and forth between and among the Allied governments, the CRB, the American government, and the Belgian government. The British and French were firm in their position that the CRB was to be sole controlling entity in and out of Belgium and that without the CRB there would be no relief. Whitlock was getting tired of the whole thing, writing in his journal on December 20, 1916, "As to that quarrel between Francqui and Hoover—I wash my hands of it."

Not surprisingly after Francqui's strong stand, the Belgian government initially stood behind its man and his view of how and who should control the relief in Belgium.

When the Belgian government's support of Francqui was uncovered in December, Hoover once again played his we-will-leave card and proposed that the exiled government could take over the entire relief work by establishing its own buying and transport organization to work with the CN in Belgium. This idea was flatly rejected by the French for its northern France territory. Hoover responded by saying that he and the CRB could continue to provision northern France and leave Belgium to the Belgians.

Hoover's gambit once again worked. In the end, the pressures of the British and French, and the possibility of falling out of the good graces of neutral America, led the Belgian government to acquiesce to the belief that the CRB, in an equal partnership with the CN, should share control of the distribution within Belgium. A tentative agreement to that effect was drawn up for approval by all parties.

Back in Belgium, when Francqui heard the news of the Belgian government's shift and the agreement that had been drawn up, he immediately secured permission from the Germans to leave Belgium and go to Paris. There he spoke with leaders of the Belgian government. It was surely not a calm or quiet meeting. Ultimately, though, Francqui had to face the fact that his own government had come around to accepting the conditions dictated by the British Foreign Office and would not support his stand on the issue regarding control of the relief program.

HOOVER AND FRANCQUI'S CLANDESTINE SHOWDOWN

On December 28, 1916, Hoover was informed that Francqui had agreed to sign the document. That same day the two men met, even though Francqui's German pass had only been for the trip to Paris. According to Whitlock, Francqui "made a secret trip to London to see Hoover—was there four hours, Savoy Hotel, incognito, mysterious."

Kittredge, in his unpublished history of the CRB, described the twists and turns that took place in that important meeting at London's Savoy Hotel. Hoover added his own details in a letter to Whitlock the next day that appeared, in part, to be almost a stream-of-consciousness release of his frustration and anger. One sentence that explained a particularly thorny moment in the meeting went on for 160 words.

In the clandestine sit-down between Hoover and Francqui, the Belgian agreed to accept the document, which defined "the neutral and independent status of the Commission for Relief in Belgium and its relations to the Comité National." He did say there were certain "changes in form" that he and the Belgian government wanted to make. "Hoover immediately accepted the whole of the alterations and told Francqui that the intent in drafting the whole contract was to restore the relations between the two organisations to their original basis."

Francqui said he had been prepared to do that all along. "If this contract had been proposed any time," the Belgian reportedly declared, he would have been "glad to have accepted it, and there [would have] been no occasion for all the difficulties during the last three months."

Hoover was taken aback. Knowing he had gotten what he needed and wanted, Hoover chose *not* to take the moral high ground and let the statement go, as Whitlock and Lord Percy would have counseled. He flatly rejected Francqui's remark (stimulating his later 160-word sentence to Whitlock) and told the Belgian that his "attitude in Brussels in October and November had shown that he wished to exclude the Commission for Relief in Belgium from any real co-operation in the work in Belgium; that his whole attitude totally ignored the fundamental fact that the relief was founded and was permitted to continue by the Governments concerned only as an organisation under the control of independent neutrals."

After that release of pent-up frustration, Hoover stated more calmly that "I did not wish to go into history and therefore, as we were now in accord, the matter ended with the execution of this memorandum."

To Francqui it wasn't that simple. He made a surprise move—he said he was resigning from the CN.

Hoover—finding himself on the other side of what had become *his* special maneuver—"protested vigorously to this, stating that since [Francqui] was entirely in accord with the contract there could be no reason for his withdrawal, that Hoover and the whole Commission were convinced that he was indispensable to the Belgian people in his position at the head of the Comité National."

Francqui insisted he was resigning.

Hoover insisted on knowing why.

According to Hoover, the Belgian finally said, "The reason was that he had found himself out of tune with myself during the past three months . . . that the American interest and my own connection had to be maintained at any cost; and that he did not wish to jeopardise the relief by remaining in a position where there was such possibility of breakage."

Not to be outdone, Hoover said Francqui's resignation "made my own position untenable, for, if he resigned because we disagreed on important policy and I could not come to his view that was one thing, and understandable, but to agree on policy and resign because he could not get on with me was another and a reflection on me."

If Francqui insisted on resigning, so would Hoover.

In any other situation—and with no lives hanging in the balance—the scene would have been laughable.

Francqui stared at the American for a long moment. He told Hoover, you use a "sledge hammer to kill gnats."

"I would use a pile-driver to kill a malarial mosquito," Hoover replied.

Another long pause.

"We thereupon agreed to go on," Hoover wrote Whitlock, "both of us to continue as before as the heads of our respective organisations, and that the entire matter would be considered as a bad dream and excised from our recollections."

In a parting shot, Francqui "expressed the fear that a document of this kind being circulated amongst the junior members of the C.R.B. might lead them into arrogance towards the local Belgians and the production of disagreeable incidents." He requested that the agreement not be widely circulated. Hoover agreed and assured him, "We had no intention of handing clubs to irresponsible men." And, he reminded him, the earlier agreements outlining the CRB–CN relationship of October 1914, July 1915, and February 1916 had never been in "common circulation."

The extensive document, officially dated December 30, 1916, was signed by Hoover on that day and by Francqui in early January and approved by the British, French, and Belgian governments.

There is very little about the yearlong CN–CRB conflict in any official CRB or Hoover-penned books. Many of the most important letters and documents relating to the issue, including the Hoover-to-Whitlock letter dated December 29, 1916, are not in the otherwise comprehensive, document-heavy *Public Relations of The Commission for Relief in Belgium: Documents*. Without Kittredge's generally detailed *The History of the Commission for Relief in Belgium, 1914–1917*, the entire story of Hoover and Francqui's most confrontational issue would be barely known.

Kittredge, in his retelling of the situation, did give Francqui and the Belgians their due. "It was, of course, quite impossible for anyone in Belgium to realise the conditions which the Commission had to face outside of Belgium, and therefore the attitude of Francqui is better explained. It was no more than natural, too, that the leaders of the Belgian committees should want to keep as much of the relief work as possible in their own hands, and should be jealous of the part played by any outsider, even if the intentions and purposes of the latter were as altruistic and straightforward as those of Hoover and his associates."

The CRB and CN were finally on agreed-upon solid ground. The work could proceed in a more harmonious fashion, and the Belgian people would be better for it.

12

Critical Crop Negotiations

Once the realization hit in early 1915 that the war would last more than a year, all those involved in the relief program understood the importance of one key question: who owned the coming harvest? The negotiations around that issue would be long and at times arduous.

BELGIUM'S 1915 AND 1916 HARVESTS

Initially, Governor General von Bissing had thought little about the subject beyond his belief that Belgium was under his absolute control; therefore, any crops grown in Belgium would be the property of the German Empire.

But in early 1915, the British announced that food imports into Belgium would not be continued if the Germans did not agree that the upcoming Belgian harvest would be used to feed only the Belgians.

Hoover, working through multiple diplomatic channels and multiple individuals, put pressure on von Bissing to give the harvest to the Belgians. As the months slipped by without any German assurances, the British took a stronger stand. In May, Foreign Office liaison Lord Percy wrote Hoover that relief would be shut down by the middle of August if the Germans did not agree to give up all rights to the harvest.

Francqui weighed in on the issue but definitely not in the way that most would have thought. His contention—spelled out in a letter to Hoover on May 6—was that the Germans would probably not give up requisitioning the harvest. But that, he wrote, should not stop the British from allowing relief to continue because the original agreements regarding nonrequisition applied only to imported foodstuffs, not to native crops. Therefore, Francqui believed, the British "had no right to make new conditions for the continuance of the relief work."

Hoover told Francqui that this argument basically justified the Germans' claim to take the harvest for themselves, thus giving up the harvest before an argument could be made to keep it. As Kittredge noted dryly, "At first in the matter of harvest negotiations Hoover and Francqui were working rather at cross purposes."

What followed was a series of meetings and negotiations in Brussels in June 1915 between Hoover, Francqui, the patron ministers, and representatives of the German government, most notably Baron von der Lancken. The gatherings covered multiple topics, including who would receive the 1915 Belgian harvest.

The differences between the two sides were manifest in what the British envisioned versus what the Germans finally established.

The British stated in a July 7 letter from the Marquis of Crewe to Ambassador Page that the first stipulation to any crop agreement was "that the purchase and distribution of the harvest in Belgium shall be under the management of the Commission for Relief in Belgium and the Comité National, in the same manner as the imported foodstuffs."

That stipulation was slightly strengthened and repeated by Sir Edward Grey in another letter on July 17.

And yet, in a decree from von Bissing on July 23 that finally acknowledged the 1915 harvest would be given only to the Belgians, the governor general wrote unequivocally, "I assign to the Comité National de Secours et d'Alimentation the sole right to purchase for cash, the requisitioned stocks and whatever bread grains remain."

Hoover, undoubtedly, saw Francqui's editing pen on von Bissing's words that the CN had "sole right to purchase." Francqui would have probably rebuffed Hoover's objections by simply stating that Belgian crops in Belgium deserved to be handled by Belgians.

The only way that von Bissing's arrangement was at all palatable to Hoover and the British was that von Bissing had created the Central Harvest Commission (later known as the Central Crop Commission) to handle the harvest, and the CRB had representation on it.

Regardless of Hoover's feelings, the important fact was that the 1915 harvest was finally earmarked for Belgians. Hoover later found out that von Bissing had come around, once again, because of pressure from the German civilian government in Berlin, which had been prompted by Ambassador Gerard, who was becoming an indispensable weapon in Hoover's diplomatic arsenal.

A direct benefit of the agreement was that during the peak months of harvesting, the CRB could decrease the amount of imports, but it wasn't by much. The CRB still had to import fifty-four thousand tons each month to maintain the bread ration in Belgium, not to mention the new amount of foodstuffs needed to feed more than two million northern French, which had been taken on in April. The most important benefit to the harvest agreement, however, was that it led the British to allow continued CRB imports into Belgium until the 1916 harvest—contingent, of course, on the honoring of all relief agreements. One more year of humanitarian work was tentatively secured. (The 1915 harvest in northern France was ultimately negotiated to go to the French as well.)

Even with the agreement in place, sporadic German requisitioning of native foodstuffs happened. Relatively minor abuses ultimately led to a December 1915 agreement, signed by von Bissing, that repeated the Germans would not take Belgian food.

In spring 1916, however, Hoover was forced once again to ask Ambassador Gerard to talk to the German civilian government about von Bissing not living up to the December agreement. Gerard spoke with German minister of foreign affairs Gottlieb von Jagow, who promised to look into it. A short time later there was a marked improvement in von Bissing's attitude toward the relief work.

Hoover took Gerard's information and pressed the issue by asking Whitlock to demand the Germans stop any exports of food from Belgium, no matter how small, and any requisitioning of native food. He even supplied Whitlock with some of the accusations that the British military had brought against the CRB regarding those issues. Whitlock, joined by Villalobar, worked with von der Lancken to secure such an agreement.

On April 14, 1916, Governor General von Bissing signed a long document that agreed to both terms. This gave many in the British Foreign Office greater confidence that the CRB was maintaining the integrity of relief. Because of this document, it became a relatively easy task to get von Bissing to agree that the 1916 Belgian harvest would be solely for the use of Belgians. He did so on July 8, 1916.

THE 1916 NORTHERN FRANCE NEGOTIATIONS

Not as easy to secure was the 1916 harvest for northern France. In many ways, those crops were more important than the Belgian harvest because the civilians of northern France were in the Operations and French Etape area of the Army Zone, where life was much more controlled and harsher than in Belgium.

Compounding the situation was a change in who controlled the German government. Since the start of the war, the Berlin civilian government, led by Chancellor Theobald von Bethmann-Hollweg, had been able to rein in the more aggressive German militarists in many policies, strategies, and tactics. But in August 1916, as the war dragged on much longer than expected, Field Marshal Paul von Hindenburg became chief of the General Staff. A successful commander who wanted to end the war decisively by using more aggressive measures, von Hindenburg was very popular with the German public. The Kaiser—no doubt feeling as if von Hindenburg could succeed—relinquished more of his wartime powers to von Hindenburg. Von Hindenburg, along with his deputy, Erich Ludendorff, ended up leading a de facto military dictatorship. Over time, von Bethmann-Hollweg and his moderate policies would be pushed aside by the aggressive military leadership.

By early 1916, conditions in northern France were far worse than in Belgium. In Lille, for example, Hoover learned from community leaders that general and elderly mortality had increased by 30 percent over the year before, and births in 1915 were only 40 percent of what they had been in 1914. The Lille committee's general secretary had written a plea for help, saying, "Salvation can only come to us through the Commission for Relief in Belgium." It was critical that the civilians should get as much of the 1916 harvest as possible.

In relatively rapid succession, events took place that at first improved the situation but then threatened it:

- April 1, Hoover wrote German Major von Kessler explaining the conditions in northern France and stating that without German nonrequisition guarantees of native food, the Allies might decide the CRB was "degenerating into a replacement by importation" operation and would end the relief.
- April 5, Hoover wrote the British outlining the situation in northern France and asked for an increase in imports.
- During April, the Germans agreed to provide the northern French with a ration of potatoes.
- April 11, the British agreed to increase northern France imports from 29,700 tons a month to 36,800 tons a month.
- May 10, the Germans agreed to allow dairy cows into northern France to provide milk for children.
- June 13, the French insisted that the Germans turn over to civilians the entire 1916 harvest in northern France.
- July 7, the British backed up the French and insisted the whole harvest must go to the people, or imports would not be allowed.
- In July, the Germans refused to commit to giving all of the 1916 harvest to the northern French.

The situation was far more complex than most would assume. The critical crop, wheat, had four separate "classes" that reflected where and how it was produced: (1) land planted by, and harvested by, the Germans, (2) abandoned land that the Germans hired French laborers to cultivate, (3) land the Germans plowed and seeded but the French either helped work or owned, (4) land exclusively cultivated by the French. Who was entitled to what from where?

Additionally, the farming area, as Hoover pointed out to the Allied governments, was so close to the front that it was impractical and unrealistic to expect civilians to put themselves in harm's way to harvest the crops. It would be more practical to have the Germans collect the entire harvest and then get them to remit a portion to the CRB for distribution.

By early August, with no resolution in sight, Hoover headed to German military headquarters in Charleville, France. He joined Vernon Kellogg, who was already there negotiating as the CRB's Brussels director. They had multiple conferences with both the German liaison officers to the CRB, von Kessler and Captain Wengersky, and with German Quartermaster General Traugott von Sauberzweig. According to

Kellogg, the quartermaster general was second only in the military hierarchy to the chief of staff of the armies. Von Sauberzweig had another distinction as well—he had been the military governor of Brussels who many considered responsible for the October 1915 execution of British nurse Edith Cavell.

Negotiations went nowhere, primarily because von Sauberzweig, as Hoover wrote, "was obstinate, arrogant, and generally overbearing." Hoover suggested, in a hope of excluding the quartermaster general, that the negotiations be taken to Berlin. The German agreed.

Unfortunately, von Sauberzweig was already going to Berlin to attend an important meeting.

HOOVER FIGHTS FOR THE LIFE OF THE CRB

When the group arrived in Berlin, events happened differently than Hoover and Kellogg had hoped. Their arrival coincided with von Sauberzweig's meeting—a high-level conference regarding the handling of the civilian populations in all the German-held territories. The Americans were not allowed to attend but learned that the CRB was the focus of intense conversation about whether or not it should be allowed to continue. And von Sauberzweig was the highest-ranking military man at the conference. Because the military was in the process of usurping the civilian government's power, attendees would look to the quartermaster general for a decision.

Suddenly, a discussion about crops in northern France had turned into a battle for the life of the CRB—and Hoover could not even participate.

At 4:00 p.m., during a break in the meeting, Major von Kessler and the quartermaster general came out to the hotel lobby to talk with Hoover and Kellogg. Both Germans were upset. Von Sauberzweig immediately ordered a whiskey and soda and downed it while von Kessler related in English what had happened (later recorded by Kellogg).

As a supporter of the CRB, von Kessler was upset because it looked bad for the future of the CRB, especially in light of a British Foreign Office dispatch that had been recently published in all the German newspapers. The British government had demanded that the Germans turn over to civilians not only the entire 1916 northern France harvest but also all the harvests in other occupied territories as well, just as it had agreed to do with the Belgian harvest.

"Extremely violent speeches" about the CRB's relief work had been made by numerous people, most notably the military men, von Kessler said. There were demands that the humanitarian program be stopped and alerts be sent to the worldwide press laying the blame for the cessation on the English blockade. The speakers reportedly stated it was "no worse for Belgians and French to starve than for Germans to starve." (Food was already getting scarce in Germany, and sporadic food riots would not be far behind. By the end of the war, many German civilians would struggle to find adequate supplies of food.)

At this point, with such bad news hanging in the air, Hoover's and Kellogg's retellings of the event diverge but ultimately reach the same ending.

Kellogg's account, which included Captain Wengersky in the hotel meeting, stated that "just one ray of light came to us in this dark hour." That opening was that one of the Germans (probably von Kessler) made the remark that "if the request for a larger allocation of the native products to the civilian population had come simply from the Commission, something might have been done, but with England demanding it—'No, a thousand times No.'"

Kellogg stated, "This was our cue. We repudiated England! What England demanded was its affair. Let the Germans fight it out with England. What the Commission pleaded for was its own affair—the affair of saving the lives of human beings; of keeping body and soul together for ten million people, known to the world as Belgians and French, but known to the Commission as human beings, men, women, and children, especially children, crying for help!"

Hoover's account is even more dramatic. He stated that at the worst moment, "there came one of those unforgettable episodes" that would change the course of millions of lives.

According to Hoover, during von Kessler's retelling of the meeting, the quartermaster general had been conspicuously quiet, downing multiple whiskey and sodas. Hoover knew that the German was opposed to the CRB, so why was he upset?

It was then that von Kessler explained. He "apologetically mentioned that the General was greatly broken up by the news he had just received that his son had been permanently blinded in a gas attack on the Western Front."

Hoover and Kellogg expressed their sympathy.

Taking another drink, von Sauberzweig then began a discourse on the war, as Kellogg and von Kessler translated for Hoover. "He said that civilians were messing into it too much and that it was no longer a soldier's war with manly weapons. Civilians had made these poison gases. They were engaged in many activities which they should keep out of."

The general veered off to angrily describe how women and children in Germany were starving because of the British blockade. At one point, he made what seemed an offhanded remark, "and then, there was the case of that Cavell woman."

Reference to such a highly charged topic was a surprise. Hoover felt the German wanted to talk about the execution of the British nurse, Edith Cavell, who had been allowed to remain in German-occupied Belgium because she had treated soldiers from both sides, but was caught working in the underground and had faced a firing squad for her crimes. The person who had signed off on her execution was General von Sauberzweig.

Hoover and Kellogg asked what the German meant by his remark. According to Hoover, the German said, "She had organized an espionage group of a thousand Belgian women. He said he had warned them. He had punished some of them mildly. They would not stop. He was compelled as a soldier to make an example and stop it. He had her tried, she confessed, and as a soldier he was compelled to execute her to protect the German army."

In fulfilling his duty by signing her execution orders, though, "he had been 'painted as a monster all over the world.' He said he was 'called a murderer; a second Duke of Alva.' The neutral peoples think 'I am the most infamous of men.'"

Hoover saw an opening. He recognized someone who "obviously did not like the kind of publicity he had received in the neutral world." This was a problem that matched Hoover's strength and knowledge—public opinion. He was a master of realizing how important PR was to any endeavor, whether it be relief or redemption. Feeling as if there was little left to lose, Hoover turned to Kellogg and told him to translate exactly what he was about to say. Kellogg agreed.

"I said that the conclusion of the German authorities [to get rid of the CRB] would mean death for millions of people, mostly children; that as he was the responsible officer he would be portrayed to the world as a monster infinitely bigger and blacker than the picture they drew of him after the Cavell incident."

Hoover started to pick up steam, probably sensing he was on the right track with this troubled man. He pushed the point so strongly that Kellogg stopped translating and said it was too much.

Von Kessler jumped in, saying he would translate. "He did so with no reservations."

Hoover continued to pound the point home, that to kill the CRB would be far worse in the eyes of the world than executing Cavell. Would von Sauberzweig want that on his conscience? The general, who had been silent but listening, suddenly remarked that Hoover might be onto something.

Both stories could have been, and probably are, true. Kellogg, with his sense of propriety, could have chosen to refrain from telling the von Sauberzweig story because it was too personal; Hoover, with his strong feelings toward the British, might have decided not to relate how the CRB publicly rejected the British to the Germans.

Hoover concluded his retelling with: "Whether it was the threat, the whisky, or his grief, or the human appeal that had moved him, I do not know. He directed von Kessler to inform Minister Lewald [the German interior minister] that he thought the negotiation ought to continue. He would be obliged if the Minister would take the matter in hand and settle it."

According to Hoover, the group broke up and Hoover, Kellogg, and von Kessler went directly to Lewald's office, where they quickly established a statement of agreement and wrote it up. They took the letter to Ambassador Gerard, who told them they should take the document and get out of Berlin immediately, "within the hour, lest the generals reverse the civilians again."

Kellogg's account explains that because the Americans were not allowed in the conference, they worked before resumption of the meeting on individuals representing the Foreign Office, Department of the Interior, and von Bissing's Belgian government. Kellogg wrote, "We argued here and pleaded there. And it all had to be done before that fateful conference of the day's length should dissolve."

"The long story must be cut short," Kellogg concluded. "We succeeded! The Commission was allowed to continue its work."

No matter the tale told, the result was the same—a statement of agreement was reached, and Hoover went back to London to sell it to the British (they accepted it), while Kellogg went back to Charleville to "hasten the formulation and the agreements."

As Kellogg stated simply, "The crisis was past."

By the end of August, the Germans had agreed to provide twice the proportion of the harvest as had been provided in 1915. As Kittredge explained, von Kessler estimated that it would amount to four-fifths of the 1916 harvest "as the year was a bad one and the harvest had been poor." Kellogg would estimate the same amount to be only approximately one-half—rather than four-fifths—of the French crop in northern France.

Either way, the northern French and the Belgian civilians living in the Army Zone were going to get something. By September, the agreements had been formalized, and the Germans, British, and French had put their stamp of approval on them.

One critical behind-the-scenes condition had been added to help the Germans save face from the earlier British demands about the harvest in the worldwide press. Hoover referred to it in a letter to his CRB director in Paris, Louis Chevrillon. "One important condition of this arrangement is . . . that there shall be no attempt to put it over the Germans by

Figure 12.1. Major von Kessler was one of the German liaison officers between the German General Staff and the CRB. He would act as translator between Hoover and German Quartermaster General Traugott von Sauberzweig during a fight for the life of the CRB.

Public domain; Herbert Hoover Presidential Library Archives, West Branch, Iowa.

the Allied Governments in this matter. The British Government is willing enough to suppress any exultation. . . . It is certain enough that the agreement is the result of pressure and it is undesirable at this stage to rub it in."

A sad footnote to the event, and to the CRB, was what happened to Major von Kessler. He had been a strong supporter of the CRB, a major broker in the deal, and the official German signer of the 1916 harvest agreement. In September, he was suddenly transferred (another name for demoted) from his liaison position in Charleville to Romania and, as Kittredge stated, "consequently the Commission lost his powerful and intelligent support."

With von Hindenburg and Ludendorff settling into their increasing military power position, von Kessler's transfer was probably retribution for what the generals perceived to be a bad deal for Germany.

Ultimately, the Germans never did live up fully to the agreement, citing the bad harvest and destruction of crops from the Battle of the Somme as reasons for providing only a portion of food they had promised. Kittredge concluded, "The Commission made repeated efforts to induce the Germans to live up to their promises, but those efforts were more or less resultless."

The northern French and Belgians in the Army Zone would have to make do with what little they received from the Germans and the steady contributions from the CRB. The CRB did its best to increase imports to account for lack of German food delivered from the harvest.

Each year, through the end of the war, it would become harder and harder to get the Germans to agree to sharing the harvest with civilians.

13

Accusations: Hoover as Traitor, Delegates as Spies

In late October 1914, as Hoover began organizing the newly formed CRB from London, he was well aware of multiple other relief groups for Belgium that had sprung up spontaneously in America. He firmly believed that the best chance of success in creating and implementing the massive aid necessary was if only one organization was in charge (see chapter 3).

A strong CRB office in New York City would go a long way toward consolidating the CRB's position as sole provider of Belgium relief. To run such a critical office, Hoover chose one of his closest friends and associates, Lindon W. Bates Sr., an internationally known engineer, who had had a hand in the building of the transcontinental railways and the Panama Canal.

By early 1915, Bates had developed an influential New York office, which was a powerful advocate for the work being done—not only by Hoover and the CRB in Belgium but also by himself and the New York office. The entire Bates family had become involved. His wife, Josephine, and his sons, Rox and Lindell, did various jobs for the CRB. His elder son, Rox (Lindon Bates Jr.), decided to go to Europe to work directly with Hoover and the CRB; he booked passage on the *Lusitania*.

AN OLD FRIEND TURNS FOE

When news came that their son had been lost during the May 7, 1915, sinking of the *Lusitania*, the Bates family was nearly inconsolable, especially the father. Unfortunately, despite the Hoover family's love and support, at some point in the grieving process, Bates turned on his old friend.

But the schism between Hoover and Bates had begun to appear even before Rox's death. It was noticeable in their underlying strategies for charitable giving,

Figure 13.1. Lindon Bates Sr. was a well-known mining engineer and a personal friend of Hoover's who became director of the CRB's New York City office. The death of his son on the *Lusitania* would contribute to his turning against Hoover.
Public domain; Herbert Hoover Presidential Library Archives, West Branch, Iowa.

in their different approaches to publicity, and, finally, in their perceptions of who was in charge.

To resolve those problems, Hoover had asked Captain Lucey to join the New York office to try to work with Bates. The friction between the two men was such that Lucey left soon after arriving. In April 1915, Hoover tried again, sending over Colonel Hunsiker, one of the CRB's founding directors. He, too, "encountered difficulty through Mr. Bates' opposition to his arrangements" and did not last long.

By the end of May—a few weeks after the *Lusitania* had sunk—some of Hoover's most trusted advisers in London were calling for the reorganization of the New York office because of Bates's reluctance to follow all of Hoover's instructions.

Bates's vision was more and more at odds with Hoover's. Once Hoover had secured permanent financing, Bates believed that requests for donations should stop by June 1, 1915. Hoover cabled back, "Many reasons why cannot abandon benevolent side." He argued that the financial arrangements did not cover all sides of relief, most notably the destitute.

This led to a disagreement about the public relations message that should be projected. Initially, the PR message Hoover and the CRB had told was that the humanitarian aid was all about *saving a nation* in the midst of a crisis. Once it was accepted that relief would be needed for a long war and relatively stable funding had been established, Hoover realized the PR message had to shift to *saving the destitute*. Changing times dictated a changing PR message to sustain donations.

Bates disagreed and would not reposition his office's PR messaging. Because the New York office had become such a strong presence in America, Bates felt it was on par with the London office and that he and Hoover were on an equal footing when it came to running the entire CRB.

On August 28, 1915, the highly popular *Saturday Evening Post* published a major feature article that declared the CRB had risen rapidly to be "one of the most efficient business machines of the world . . . due primarily to the genius of Lindon W. Bates."

Hoover, in a fit of frustration, cabled an outright command on September 22: "For political reasons do not wish one more word publicly or public appeals to emanate from your office. Applies here as well and includes your news sheet."

On October 1, Hoover received a reply. Bates would comply but only "temporarily." Acting like Hoover's equal, Bates added that he expected reciprocal respect—Hoover should not release anything regarding American issues from his office without consulting Bates first.

It was time to confront Bates; Hoover booked passage to America. When Hoover reached New York on Sunday, October 24, 1915, he found a cable at his hotel from eight of his most trusted advisers. It congratulated the Chief on the first full year since the October 22, 1914, founding of the CRB, but it also demanded that Bates be replaced.

After sitting down with Bates, Hoover learned that things were much worse than he had imagined. When Bates had heard Hoover was coming to America, he was sure it was to try to remove him from office. So, without consulting anyone, he had secretly traveled to Washington, D.C., and visited the State Department, the Justice Department, and Senator Henry Cabot Lodge, who sat on the Committee of Foreign Affairs and was a fierce opponent of President Wilson.

Bates had taken with him a huge Hoover file, which laid out accusations that Hoover was un-neutral and had committed treasonous acts by violating the Logan Act of 1799. He listed specific incidents and situations and declared he was doing all this because he "felt that his duty as a patriotic American necessitated his intervention with the American government."

The Logan Act stated that any unauthorized American citizen who "directly or indirectly commences or carries on any correspondence or intercourse with any foreign government or any officer or agent thereof, with intent to influence the measures or conduct of any foreign government or of any officer or agent thereof, in relation to any disputes or controversies with the United States, or to defeat the measures of the United States, shall be fined under this title or imprisoned not more than three years, or both."

Hoover, sitting in the NYC office with Bates and reading the file that Bates had taken to Washington, was at first somewhat amused, but as he read more he turned horrified, then angry. He was particularly upset that Bates had quoted from their private correspondence and that he had not consulted with anyone before his trip to the capital. He was convinced that Bates was doing it for revenge against Hoover's moves to relegate him to a secondary position in the CRB and for publicity—publicity that would destroy Hoover's image, tarnish the CRB, and elevate Bates in the public eye for rooting out such a scandal.

Hoover was sure Bates had lost his mind, noting, "Mr. Bates was so tense I immediately came to the conclusion that his mind was deranged." But Hoover was also profoundly rattled that he had been so mistaken about Bates and his loyalty. More importantly, Hoover had to do something to stop whatever negative reactions to Bates's accusations were taking place in Washington. He spent the next couple of days consulting with numerous prominent men in the city, including presidential adviser Colonel House.

HOOVER HEADS TO WASHINGTON, D.C.

On October 28, 1915, Hoover took a train to Washington and met with two senior officials at the State Department. He was told the department was concerned that the CRB was setting precedents that would later jeopardize America's campaign for neutral rights in wartime. Senator Lodge had added his criticism by writing the State Department that Hoover had clearly violated the Logan Act. According to the senator, sending charity from American citizens was one thing, but distributing money supplied by belligerent governments was another.

Personally, Hoover had dismissed the Logan Act accusations "because our negotiations were not on behalf of the United States but on behalf of a private, neutral organization sponsored by neutral Ambassadors and Ministers. However, it seemed that Senator [Henry Cabot] Lodge, a violent critic of President Wilson and the State Department, was developing a sensational story."

The State Department requested that Hoover defend himself in writing. He responded with three separate letters of explanation. In them, he spoke of the "extraordinary esteem and privilege" that he and the other CRB personnel received from other countries. He flatly refused to accept the idea that the CRB had established any kind of precedents that would hurt America, saying the CRB was no different than the Red Cross and other humanitarian agencies. He declared that he and his associates were not guilty of a single "atom of moral turpitude." He ended by holding up the CRB as one great bright spot in the war, a bright spot that counterbalanced the criticisms that America was only interested in profiting from the war.

Hoover's words worked their magic. The State Department determined that there was nothing to Bates's accusations and that they had been made more for publicity than to elicit a government response.

Back in New York City, Hoover was relieved. But rumors were circulating in Washington that he should resign to clear away the entire messy situation. Hoover decided he needed to call in support. British associate William Goode, who was then in New York, cabled Ambassador Page, outlining the situation and asking for immediate help on Hoover's behalf.

Page jumped in as always. He cabled the State Department on November 2 his enthusiastic support for Hoover as the only one who could handle the job. "The Commission for Relief in Belgium is Hoover," he declared, "and absolutely depends on Hoover who has personally made agreements with the Governments concerned and has carried these delicate negotiations through only because of his high character and standing and unusual ability. If he is driven to resign the Commission will instantly fall to pieces. . . . I believe that no other man in sight could have done this task and I know that no other can now carry it on."

The same day, Hoover received an unexpected invitation from President Wilson to visit the White House the next day. That night Hoover had dinner with Colonel House, who prepared him for the upcoming meeting. At the end of the meal, Hoover and John Beaver White took the overnight train to the capital.

Much to Hoover's great relief, the 10:30 a.m. meeting went better than expected. The president greeted him warmly and complimented him on the fine work he was doing to help the Belgians. He also said that Hoover's recent troubles had come to his attention but that the State Department had found no basis for the accusations.

Hoover told the president he was currently asking some prominent men in New York to join an executive committee, but they "were a little loath to come into a quarrel and suggested it would be of the greatest possible service to us if [Wilson] would add his personal request to my own urging."

Wilson agreed and went further by asking if it might be helpful for the administration to make a public statement "as to their unqualified approval of all the work of the Commission and of its actions." Hoover jumped at the offer, suggesting it be sent out immediately "as it would probably head off any attack" by Bates or others.

Wilson was true to his word, and that day the administration's press release touting the CRB was picked up by numerous American newspapers. The administration stated it was "highly pleased" with the CRB and that its work had been done "to the entire satisfaction" of all belligerents. It had been the source of no "international complications" whatsoever but instead had produced "international good will and disinterested service."

The president also wrote letters to seven men asking that they help Hoover and gave them to Hoover to deliver.

Hoover left Washington that day and arrived in New York that night but did not stay. He caught a midnight train for Boston to face another potential detractor. The next day he sat down with Senator Lodge. He wanted to show the powerful politician that he was ready to address any charges. At the end of the meeting, Lodge's concerns were completely alleviated.

The senator sent a letter to the State Department detailing his meeting with Hoover and reporting that "he has satisfied me on the points which disturbed me when I wrote to you."

Regarding the Logan Act, Lodge was frank: "They have undoubtedly violated the Logan Act, but that is a domestic matter, the violations are technical, and considering the nature of the work I cannot conceive that any point should be made in regard to it." He concluded with a strong statement: "I am very glad now to be in a position to defend the Commission if any point is raised in Congress, for their work has been the finest thing ever done by a neutral in war and I wanted to be able to sustain them to the limit. That was why the attack of Mr. Bates disturbed me so."

As he had done with Lloyd George in early 1915, Hoover had once again convinced another powerful, skeptical man of the rightness of his cause.

On November 5, Hoover was back in New York and convened the first meeting of a newly installed New York executive committee from those who had heeded Wilson's letters. The group immediately disbanded the old New York executive committee (on which Bates and two of his loyalists had sat) and elected John Beaver White to run the New York office.

The new direction for the New York office would be to begin a clothing campaign in America to raise money and donations for clothes to be sent to Belgium and northern France. While the Allies had established steady funding to provide food, there was no money for clothing, which would become a critical necessity in the coming winter. The executive committee would quickly take this new directive and from it "an energetic campaign was made by the reorganized committees formed in the different states and cities of America."

Finally, Bates himself informed the committee that his relationship with the CRB was over—he would retire from the field. No sensational articles appeared regarding Bates's accusations.

For Hoover, it had been an emotional roller coaster. He and Lou had known the Bates family for decades and considered them some of their finest friends. And yet Bates had attacked the CRB and Hoover's reputation—two of the most important components of Hoover's professional life.

On November 9, 1915, Hoover, Lou, and the two boys sailed for England aboard the *New Amsterdam* with what must have been a tremendous sense of relief.

Only a few days later, however, Hoover's rare sense of equilibrium was once again upset when he received onboard an urgent communiqué from Brussels. It was "a tense demand that I come at once to Belgium because several of our Americans were about to be expelled for espionage."

CHARGES OF ESPIONAGE

During Hoover's American trip to deal with Bates, the conclusion of an international story was playing out in Brussels that would have ramifications for the CRB.

Forty-nine-year-old English nurse Edith Louisa Cavell had been teaching nurses in a Brussels clinic when the war began. The Germans had allowed her to remain in Belgium because she had compassionately served the wounded from both sides. As the occupation wore on, however, she began secretly hiding Allied soldiers and young Belgian men and helping them escape to Holland. The network, which ultimately took her name, became so large that the Germans uncovered it and arrested her on August 5, 1915. On October 7 and 8, a German tribunal was held for her and thirty-four others. At dawn on October 12, she and a Belgian, Philippe Baucq, were executed by firing squad.

Hugh Gibson and Spanish minister Villalobar had spent the night before arguing with von der Lancken to save Cavell's life. Yet it was Brand Whitlock who immediately took a leave of absence because of the mental strain he had suffered from the trial and execution. He and his wife went back to America while Gibson, the legation secretary, became the chargé d'affaires, or temporary minister. It was Gibson who sent Hoover the November 12 coded message through the American embassy in London that a handful of CRB delegates had been charged with espionage.

Figure 13.2. Thirty-one-year-old Hugh Gibson was the secretary of the US Legation in Belgium when the war broke out. He was a strong supporter of the CRB and in late 1915 helped Hoover fight spy charges leveled against some CRB delegates.

Public domain; author's archives.

Hoover was only three days into his transatlantic crossing. With multiple challenges and crises waiting for him upon his arrival back in London, Hoover was not able to reach Brussels for two weeks.

In the meantime, Gibson had a flurry of formal and informal meetings with anyone who he thought might give him insight into how to proceed. One such person was Villalobar, who was the consummate diplomat, polished and sophisticated, yet brutal at times with a temper that was legendary (possibly because of some physical challenges he had to endure). Villalobar's counsel was especially important because he was close to von der Lancken, who, as the head of the German's political department and righthand man to von Bissing, was the point person for the espionage charges.

Villalobar helped Gibson determine that von Bissing had received information from his extensive spy network in Belgium and Holland that certain CRB delegates were guilty of crimes against the German Empire. Von der Lancken told Gibson that four Americans and a Belgian (three in Belgium, two in Holland) were accused of espionage and that the three Americans working in Belgium were to be expelled immediately. These transgressions were unacceptable, von der Lancken said, and were even causing von Bissing to consider throwing out the entire CRB.

While Gibson failed to get specific information about the charges, he did find out who the men were and received assurances they would not be removed until Hoover had a chance to reach Brussels. The three American delegates working in Belgium were Joe Green, Lewis Richards, and J. B. Van Schaick, and the two men in the Rotterdam office were American Carl Young, director of the Rotterdam office, and Belgian Jean van den Branden, who was the CN liaison in the transshipping center.

The five accused had little in common and had given no suspicions to their bosses of working for the Allies. They were sure—as was Gibson—that the charges against them were simply misinterpreted bits and pieces overheard by agents of the German counterespionage network.

Hoover arrived in Brussels on Saturday evening, November 27, 1915, and huddled together with Gibson to discuss strategy. Sunday began a few days of whirlwind activity. "There have been conferences day and night with all sorts of people and we keep them on the jump," Gibson wrote.

On December 1, Hoover, von der Lancken, and Gibson met in the German's office. Gibson wrote a memorandum that recorded who said what to whom.

Hoover, following his usual style, came out swinging. He and his CRB colleagues were "very much disheartened by the general attitude of the German officials in Belgium toward the Commission." He compared von Bissing's harsh supervision of the CRB in Belgium with the German military's less abrasive handling of the CRB in northern France.

Von der Lancken interrupted. "You formally informed me that if any time a member of the Commission should become persona non grata to the German authorities, he would be removed from the country." The German concluded firmly, "You placed no conditions on that promise, so you cannot now, as a matter of right, ask for any information about the accusations."

"That might be a technical interpretation of an isolated statement," Hoover admitted, but he shot back quickly that his comment had been predicated on the assumption no injustice should be done to the Commission. Removal without valid reasons was just such an injustice, Hoover insisted.

With both Hoover and Gibson arguing that they had a right to know the charges, von der Lancken finally admitted, "I have proof that there exists a system of some sort by which Green, Richards, and Van Schaick were gathering and forwarding, or perhaps causing to be forwarded to Holland, information hurtful to Germany's military interests."

"This information," von der Lancken added, "was received and made use of by Mr. Young, manager of the Rotterdam office of the CRB and Mr. van den Branden."

That was not the end of it. "I have positive proof," he declared, "that two English spies had called upon Mr. Young and had asked to be sent into Belgium to carry on their work under the cover of the Commission."

Hoover vowed to personally investigate the charges immediately. Von der Lancken said he would await Hoover's findings.

Gibson, for his part, went further than Whitlock would have done if he had been there. "In accord with Hoover I have precipitated 'a kill or cure situation.'" That meant Gibson officially told von der Lancken that the United States "threatened to withdraw" its patronage of the CRB and allow it to end if the charges weren't dropped and relations improved between the CRB and the German general government in Belgium. He had no diplomatic authority to have made such a threat.

As for Hoover, he had to accomplish two goals: get the spy charges dropped and somehow resolve the long-term issues with the German general government in Belgium.

Even before the von der Lancken meeting, Hoover had taken steps to resolve the government relationship problem. Prior to the spy charges, the work of the CRB had been initially supervised within von Bissing's civil government by Max von Sandt, who was head of the civil administration. In June 1915, much of that responsibility had been transferred to the *Politische Abteilung*, or Political Department, which was run by von der Lancken. Hoover felt the supervision of the CRB by these two departments was hindering the relief work and must be changed.

The action he took he had used before—he went over von Bissing's head. Before meeting with von der Lancken, Hoover had contacted the two main CRB men in Charleville, Vernon Kellogg (then outgoing CRB director in Brussels who was at the time in Charleville) and Caspar Whitney (CRB general representative to northern France), and asked that they come to Brussels and bring the two German officers in charge of supervising the CRB in northern France (von Kessler and Wengersky).

The group (including a Captain Uhl) arrived on December 2, a day after the von der Lancken meeting, and sat down with Hoover. The military men were able to give the American more details about the spy charges. Supposedly, Green, Richards, and Van Schaick had transmitted verbally to Young in Rotterdam details about the September German offensive on the Western Front. Additionally, it was discovered that a Major Winchell was an Allied agent approved by Young as a new CRB delegate.

Hoover couldn't answer all the charges, but he did know a few things. He knew that Green and Van Schaick had both joined the CRB after the Germans' September offensive, negating that German claim. As for Winchell, it was a comical story. He was a major in the nonmilitary Salvation Army, and it had been a bad joke in the Rotterdam office that he was part of the Salvation Army's intelligence service. The joke had somehow reached the ears of a German agent who had passed it along as a serious matter.

Regarding the long-term issues of supervision, the German military men were able to get von Bissing to create a special department to supervise the CRB and the CN. A handful of representatives from various departments would sit on the committee and would include a member of the German General Staff. Captain Uhl was to be that member because, according to von Kessler, "he was a good American resident of Santa Barbara, California."

Hoover couldn't have been more pleased.

As for the remaining spy charges, the Chief motored off on the morning of December 6 headed for Rotterdam, determined to face each man in the office and find out who had instigated such nonsense. When he reached Rotterdam, he quickly uncovered what he called a "Benedict" in the office. Hoover, who never identified the man, later wrote that he had "set up an espionage job for himself with the German intelligence agents in that city. The youngster was a second-generation German, spoke German, and had seemed to us a perfect associate for handling our routine relations with the German authorities in Holland."

Unfortunately, the man had an overly inflated sense of himself and was known to be a busybody who talked to anyone about what he heard and saw in the office. It remains unproved that he worked for German intelligence, but somewhere along the line, one of his listeners had obviously been an espionage agent who passed on whatever rumors the man was touting as facts.

Regarding the charges against Green, Richards, and Van Schaick, they all stemmed from Benedict's probing "for their opinions of the Germans, thereupon reporting their chatter to the German authorities." He had also related the Major Winchell story.

Hoover quickly secured certified statements from all parties disclaiming all the German charges. With the documents safely in hand, he raced back to Brussels, making the entire round trip in only a day and a half.

His packet of statements took care of all spy charges. As for the three delegates, Van Schaick was sent to the London office, Richards remained where he was in Brussels, and Green left his position in Mons on December 15 to begin work as a delegate for the Agglomêration Bruxelloise (metropolitan Brussels). Later, Green would head up the Inspection and Control Department, where he would continue to do good work that would raise the hackles of both the Germans and Émile Francqui.

During the remainder of the time American CRB delegates spent in Belgium, there would be no other major spy charges leveled against any of them.

14

A Breaking Point

The life of the CRB was one of never-ending challenges, obstacles, and full-blown crises. Most times, Hoover weathered them like a stoic fisherman in an unrelenting storm, head down, working on, expecting at any time to be capsized. During the last few months of 1915 and the first few months of 1916, however, the problems and challenges piled on and never seemed to get fully resolved.

The major concern was imports, which had initially been approved by the British for 80,000 tons a month for Belgium. In April 1915, an additional 15,000–18,000 tons were allowed in for northern France, and those had risen to a total of 35,000 tons a month by the end of the year, meaning the CRB was importing more than 115,000 tons a month to provide for nearly ten million civilians.

Over the course of 1915, items such as meats, potatoes, and fats (e.g., lard) were approved and began to supplement the principal imports of wheat, maize, rice, beans, and peas. Nevertheless, the CRB and CN were having trouble maintaining 1,800 calories per person per day (normal intake for adults ranged from 2,000 to 3,000 calories a day).

With Francqui repeatedly calling for more food, Hoover formally requested on December 21, 1915, that the British Foreign Office approve an increase for Belgium from 80,000 tons a month to 126,400 tons and for northern France from 35,000 tons to 48,000 tons.

"VARIOUS EMBARRASSMENTS" BECOME "WHOLLY INTOLERABLE"

Hoover would not officially hear Britain's response until February 23, 1916, but when he did, the news was devastating. Not only were the increases denied, but both current figures were reduced: Belgium imports decreased by 12,000 tons to 68,000 tons and northern France imports by 5,000 tons to 30,000 tons. Hoover believed it was because the Foreign Office had received "pressure from the militarists in Britain and France."

"It was a great shock to us—and to the people of Northern France," Hoover said. He knew the reductions were "far below the level at which we could maintain public health. The effect was a program 50 per cent short of the minimum needs of fats and proteins."

The Chief had nearly reached his limit. "We had no taste for being an instrument of slow starvation, and by the end of February, 1916, we—who had, after all, taken on our heavy burdens voluntarily—became, to use a British expression, 'about fed up' with these obstructionist attitudes."

As this critical piece of humanitarian relief was seemingly crumbling away, Hoover had to put up with something nearly as distasteful. A Belgian delegation of CN President Francqui, CN executive Baron Jean Lambert, and Spanish Minister Villalobar showed up in London. The three were officially there to present to the British letters of nonrequisition guarantees from von Bissing, although there was no need because Hoover had already transmitted the basics to the Foreign Office earlier.

The group was also there for two other clandestine reasons. The first was a far-fetched scheme of peace that they hoped might lead to a Treaty of Brussels (nothing came of it). The second was to implement a plan to remove the CRB from Belgium by having the CRB handle all operations outside Belgium and the CN handle all operations inside.

As if that wasn't enough, Hoover had been facing since the start of the new year a serious illness. He had ear abscesses—an exceedingly painful and dangerous ailment normally seen in infants and children. Many times started by an untreated throat or ear infection, an ear abscess could lead to death in a world that did not yet have pharmaceutical antibiotics. Hoover was told by his London doctors that he should stop all work for three months at least and to immediately take to his bed. He spent a few weeks in bed at the start of the year but refused to stop working.

So, after suffering through ear abscesses, the many months of problems and challenges that never seemed to get fully resolved, and the rejection of his request for import increases, Hoover took the invasion of the three envoys from Brussels as the last straw.

"By the end of February, 1916, the various embarrassments besetting the Commission were becoming wholly intolerable to my colleagues and to me." He wrote of how the work was taking its toll on the CRB delegates and staff and "required working twelve hours a day, seven days a week, and it brought many personal dangers as well as constant, bitter, and unnecessary discouragements."

Before he took decisive action—and maybe to help him think through the situation—he wrote out nine points where events and/or individuals had become "intolerable." Some were major developments; others were personal situations.

The first two involved the refusal of the Belgian and French governments to allow their vessels to be used for shipping CRB food (never resolved).

The third was Hoover's feeling that Whitlock was "was too sensitive a person to be American minister amidst such suffering and tragedy. He shrank from battles with von Bissing and resented the constant pressures for action applied by us and by his First Secretary, Hugh Gibson." Hoover was especially angry and frustrated at what he felt was Whitlock's recent decision, predicated on a German demand, to remove Gibson from his post in Brussels. (Gibson ended up working for Ambassador Page in London.)

The fourth point was a major one: the Germans, through von Bissing, had not upheld their December 1915 nonrequisition agreement of Belgian native food. "Although the civil authorities in Berlin and their military authorities in Northern France were co-operative, in Belgium itself we were subjected to a great deal of Governor General von Bissing's arrogance and anti-Americanism."

That had led to point five, that the British, acting also for the French, had reduced the food imports allowed into Belgium and northern France.

The sixth point was about the general conflicts between the CRB and the CN, which Hoover put diplomatically: "There was an inherent conflict between the responsibilities imposed upon the C.R.B. by the Allies and the very natural feelings of the Belgians in Belgium." (See chapter 11.)

The seventh and eighth points involved the British military's continual harassment of the CRB in its efforts to discredit the organization and end relief. Specifically, the seventh point, as Hoover stated it, was that "the British Military Intelligence was constantly feeding the Foreign Office stories of trivial or mythical infractions or violations of the guarantees by the Germans, and we were constantly being hectored and harassed as if we had some evil intent."

The eighth point was personal. The chief of British Naval Intelligence, Captain Hall, whose boss was Winston Churchill, had called Hoover into his office a month before. He asked multiple questions about the German military operations in the areas served by the CRB. Hoover refused to answer on the grounds that he and the CRB must remain absolutely neutral. "He pressed me, arguing that inasmuch as the Relief was being supported by the British and French Governments, it was my duty to aid their interests." Hoover refused again, saying his duty was to the Belgians and northern French who would starve without the CRB.

The harassment didn't stop there. Hoover included in his eighth point that a few weeks later a naval intelligence agent had begun calling on Hoover's friends and associates "making extensive inquiries about my private business, my character, and had even inquired about if it was possible that I could be a German spy." (This issue would not go away and, in fact, would ultimately lead to Hoover reluctantly facing a judicial inquiry before a British judge in chambers; he would be exonerated of any wrongdoing.)

The ninth and last point of Hoover's list was the fact that Francqui, Lambert, and Villalobar had come to London to undermine the CRB. With all these issues fresh in his mind, Hoover decided it was time to act decisively.

He wrote a long letter to Ambassador Page saying that he felt it was time the CRB resign and turn over the reins to the CN. He sent a copy of the letter to each of the patron ministers and, in a critical statement at the end of his letter, asked Page to pass it on to the "interested governments and ascertain whether they would be prepared to transfer the guarantees and responsibilities to the Comité National in such a manner as to ensure the continued feeding of and relief of the Belgian civil population."

Even though Hoover worked directly with the British nearly every day—most notably Lord Eustace Percy, the official liaison between the CRB and the British—he probably felt the impact of his letter would be stronger by having been forwarded to the British through Ambassador Page than sent by him, an American citizen with no official title.

Hoover's last statement of the letter regarding transference of all guarantees and responsibilities to the CN was his way of ensuring his resignation would not be accepted. He was sure the British, in particular, would not agree to turning over the CRB's operations to the CN. Additionally, most of those who knew Hoover well would never have thought he meant to follow through with the resignation. This threat was a tactic that he had used before. It was meant primarily to force a resolution of the multiple issues that were hobbling him and his organization. After nearly a year and a half of work, Hoover was simply too honorable and too committed to the relief to actually go through with full departure.

But few on the other side of the resignation letter would have tested Hoover on that. Especially those closest to the work, such as Francqui. Hoover had written his Page letter on February 24, 1916, and had presented a copy to Francqui on the following evening.

Francqui no doubt saw that any power position he might have had in privately presenting his plan to the British (which he had not yet done) was suddenly undercut by Hoover's dramatic action. The proud Belgian was quick to respond with a letter that must have been difficult to write. The day after receiving Hoover's letter, he all but admitted defeat when he wrote to Ambassador Page on February 26, "You know . . . that without the active leadership of Mr. Hoover it would have been absolutely impossible for us to continue the provisioning and assistance of the Belgians; also you will not be astonished when I insist, not only in my own personal name, but also in the name of my colleagues and in that of all my fellow-countrymen, that Your Excellency should use your kind influence of Mr. Hoover that he should abandon the idea set out in his letter of the 24th."

The Belgian also showed he could be just as disingenuous as Hoover when he wrote to Page, "The harmony which has never ceased to exist between the C.R.B. and the organization that I direct in Belgium is today too intimate to allow of any blow being struck at either without the risk of destroying the whole organization of both. Also, I feel obliged to inform Your Excellency that it would be impossible for me to continue for one moment without the co-operation of Mr. Hoover to carry on the work which he and I have assumed." The man who had come to London to get rid of Hoover and the CRB was now saying he couldn't do the work without them.

The British reacted just as swiftly. They first dealt with Villalobar, who had inappropriately discussed the CRB and CN relationship with Prime Minister Asquith at a private dinner. Sir Edward Grey, the foreign secretary, wrote to Villalobar stating strongly that Hoover was "the only person directly and personally responsible for the manner in which the whole work, both inside and outside Belgium is carried on." The "inside and outside" qualifier was a huge statement of support for Hoover and one that would have galled Villalobar.

Grey didn't leave it at that, knowing full well how Villalobar felt about Hoover. He told the Spaniard in diplomatic terms that he and the others should play nice, understand just how heavy the burden was for Hoover and the CRB, and "in every possible way lighten that burden by making [the CRB's] responsibility as easy to discharge as possible."

It took Grey two weeks longer to officially reply to Page's forwarding of Hoover's resignation letter, but his response on March 13, 1916, was no less vehement than his letter to Villalobar. "I must state clearly that His Majesty's Government can only allow the work of relief to continue if the entire responsibility for it both inside and outside Belgium is borne by neutrals who, having complete freedom to come and go, and having no official position limiting their personal liability, can in fact be held responsible for the carrying out of the various conditions upon which His Majesty's Government has insisted. The American Commission is the only organization which fulfills these requirements, and His Majesty's Government therefore feel obliged to insist that either the whole work should cease or the American Commission shall continue to direct it as heretofore.

"I shall be glad if you will convey these observations to Mr. Hoover, and ask him to reconsider his views in the light of these contributions."

That was followed by another letter from Grey to Page restating the continued cooperation of the British government and the Commission. "I therefore beg that you will be so good as to make it clear to Mr. Hoover and those associated with him in this great humanitarian work that it is the desire and intention of His Majesty's Government that various public departments connected with the work should co-operate with the Commission in the closest way.

"I am happy to be able to say that the Commission continues to enjoy the complete confidence of His Majesty's Government, and I should like to add my own personal tribute to the admirable organisation which they have evolved, and to the tireless energy of all its members, who are so devotedly carrying out their difficult task."

The Germans were nearly as supportive. When Ambassador Gerard passed on Hoover's desire to resign and turn the whole operation over to the Belgians, the German minister of foreign affairs, Gottlieb von Jagow, reacted strongly, stating that his country would not agree to the Belgians controlling relief. Further, he expressed the complete confidence of the Berlin government and the military General Staff in Hoover and the CRB to run the humanitarian operation.

THE THREAT OF RESIGNATION WORKS

As Ambassador Gerard was talking with von Jagow about Hoover's possible resignation, he also took a moment to bring up another issue. He informed von Jagow that von Bissing was not living up to the agreement of December 1915 about requisitioning Belgian native food. Von Jagow promised to look into it, and a short time later there was a change in von Bissing's attitude, which ultimately led to von Bissing signing a nonrequisition agreement on April 14, 1916.

After all the responses to Hoover's threatened resignation had come in, the Chief must have had a huge feeling of vindication. He summed up the situation by simply saying, "After prayerful conferences with my colleagues and after having received many promises of better co-operation, we agreed to carry on, with the hope that we had cleared the air."

Realizing, however, this advantage would not remain in place too long, Hoover decided to ask for an increase in imports, in the hope that the devastating decrease that the British had imposed in February might be reversed.

On April 5, Hoover asked Lord Percy to increase CRB imports from the February-established 68,150 tons per month to 75,500 tons per months—which was still below the 80,000 tons per month agreed to when relief had first started. He also asked that the northern France imports be increased from 29,700 tons a month to 36,800 tons.

Hoover's strategy and timing were pitch-perfect. On May 10, 1916, the British agreed to the 75,500 tons per month for Belgium and the 36,800 tons per month for northern France. On June 14, they also agreed to lift an embargo they had imposed on clothing imports.

Even as Hoover was receiving gratifying confirmations that all the governments wanted him and his organization to remain, and renewed statements of cooperation from Francqui and von Bissing, British Intelligence kept bringing to the Foreign Office a steady stream of reports about supposed "leakages" of food from the system into German hands or into the black market. Hoover wrote, "The requests that we continue and the promises of better co-operation did not include the British Admiralty, who now seemed to renew their determination to wipe us out."

15

The German Deportations

The path that led to the Germans' mass deportation of Belgian and northern French civilians in late 1916 and 1917 was not created from a carefully crafted policy. Starting in 1915, small incidents and tentative actions grew and multiplied until a military plan was formulated for countrywide deportations.

Overall, the concept was that civilians would be shipped to Germany to replace workers who could then become soldiers. To most of the world, these mass deportations would become one of the most inhumane actions taken against noncombatants during the war. (German deportations also took place in other countries.)

THE UNEMPLOYED AS THE STARTING POINT

The German invasion and occupation had thrown many Belgians out of work. These unemployed, or *chômeurs*, were a substantial portion of the population. In prewar Belgium, the total number of civilian workers was nearly 1.8 million. With the start of the occupation—and the shuttering of most industries and commerce—the first enrollment of classified unemployed across the country totaled 760,000, and when dependents of those unemployed were added on, the total came to nearly 1.4 million people.

Added to these *chômeurs* were Belgians who could have worked for the Germans but refused. They saw any work performed for the Germans as war work directly against their country, the Allies, and the stipulations of The Hague Conventions of 1899 and 1907. Those multilateral treaties (which dealt with the conduct and laws of war) had declared people in occupied territory could not be forced to do work that would help the conqueror's war aims. While most Belgians employed in essential services such as transportation, water, and power did return to work after the invasion, resentment was building and would soon lead to action by some.

Figure 15.1. The CRB did its part to help the Belgian unemployed by hiring thousands of people as everything from translators and auto mechanics to stenographers and accountants. Here, Belgian women typists are kept busy by never-ending CRB correspondence, documents, and reports.

Public domain; Hoover Institution Archives, Stanford University, Stanford, California.

The CRB did its part to aid the unemployed. It ultimately hired thousands of Belgians in ancillary relief work, including chauffeurs and mechanics for the delegates' cars, stenographers, typists, translators, and general office personnel.

Initially, the *chômeurs* were not an issue with the Germans because they were included in the total population covered by the food relief. In fact, one of the major tenets of the CRB was that no one could be denied food because of employment status. The concept was that all Belgians must be allowed access to relief, at which point those who could pay would pay, and those who couldn't would receive charity.

Through 1914, the Germans generally went along with the unemployed being part of food relief. They also issued statements assuring the Belgians and the world that Belgian men of military age and the unemployed would not be singled out for forced labor or for the nearly inconceivable idea of deportation.

But time, a stalemated war, and the realities of the military's need for bodies were strong inducements to change German minds.

In 1915, the situation began to change. Governor General von Bissing attempted to prod Belgians back to their jobs or to work for the Germans. The first moves were not to *force* Belgians to work; they were to entice *volunteers*. Some skilled workmen were offered wages as a high as £2 per day (equivalent to $200 in 2020 US dollars).

The German offers to work, however, fell mainly on patriotically deaf ears. Most preferred to live either on Belgian half wages or on the monetary assistance of the CN and the food assistance of the CN and the CRB. Across Belgium and northern France, few accepted the German offers, as many began what some termed the "strike of folded arms."

While this labor resistance was tolerated for a while, by the spring of 1915, the Germans were losing what little patience they had had, especially when the unemployed were living off the food relief and the Germans had to bring in men to do their work.

Belgian playwright Émile Cammaerts wrote, "It became more and more evident that Germany, whose man-power was steadily decreasing, would no longer tolerate the resistance of the Belgian workers, and would even attempt to enroll in her army of labour all the able-bodied men of the conquered provinces."

On one side of the issue were the German militarists, who saw nothing wrong with forced labor. On the other side was the German civilian government in Berlin, which seemed reluctant—most probably over a concern that worldwide opinion would be strongly against any such action.

Numerous skirmishes between the Germans and Belgian workers escalated tensions, including an April 1915 small strike in the town of Luttre, a larger May–June 1915 rail workers' strike in the city of Malines, and the February 1916 demands placed on a small group of men in the Walloon village of Rockefort in southeast Belgium.

The Americans were in a tough position. The Germans were officially breaking no relief guarantees when they tried to force the unemployed to work—or even to deport them. But the moral issue still remained that the Germans' actions were barbaric and inhumane. Hoover knew that a direct, moral challenge from the CRB might lead the Germans to shut down the food relief, so he worked the edges of the issue, trying to convince the Germans that coercion and deportation were not in the true interests of Germany.

He was about to be proven wrong, by his own men.

THE FIRST ATTEMPT AT MASS DEPORTATION

With what appeared to be no thought-out, long-term strategy for getting the unemployed working again, the Germans conducted in spring 1916 the first mass deportation in northern France, where they had the most control. They chose the highly congested and industrialized metropolitan area that included the cities of Lille, Roubaix, and Tourcoing. Eighty percent of the working population was comprised of laborers, most of whom had been employed in textile mills before the war.

Many of those people had been extremely hungry a year before, prior to the CRB taking on northern France. The first shipments of food had begun arriving in April 1915 and had continued since then. The food supplied, however, was minimal compared to what had been consumed before the war, and hunger was a constant companion to many. In fact, in March 1916, an event occurred that alarmed the German military—approximately two hundred people had rioted in Roubaix, breaking into a few grocery stores and stealing whatever food was found.

That riot added fuel to a fire of articles in the German press calling for the Belgians and northern French to work for their occupiers. And the sentiment quickly became stronger—if inducements did not succeed, forced labor would be acceptable to many Germans.

The German military agreed and came up with a plan. Approximately fifty thousand *chômeurs* in Lille, Roubaix, and Tourcoing would be relocated to the agricultural areas around Vervins and Charleville to work the fields. The benefits would be twofold: decreased unemployment and increased agricultural productivity. A small salary would be paid to each person, and any deportees not employed in the fields would labor in German "saw-mills, roadways and other trench industries," which were jobs that German soldiers and some Russian prisoners had been doing.

The CRB was officially notified of the German plan in mid-April 1916 by Captain Wengersky, who told CRB Brussels director William Poland that the General Staff's intention was to "evacuate" the 50,000 French to agricultural areas. Poland was assured that "volunteers would be asked for, whole families would be transported together when practicable, the main object was to obtain laborers, and, in general, laborers only would be selected."

Poland was a civil engineer and expert at managing international railroads. He had been with the CRB less than a year, but he knew—and Hoover had drilled it into the heads of all CRB personnel—that the linchpin of the entire food relief program was absolute neutrality, no matter what the situation. To protest could be construed as an un-neutral act that could justify the Germans kicking the CRB out of northern France, if not Belgium as well. Poland diplomatically replied that "while in principle we could not object to the moving of the population . . . we anticipated that such a movement could be carried out only with disturbance and suffering."

The city of Lille added its vehement objections, but to no avail.

The Germans first called for volunteers. The vast majority of workers in the area were urban dwellers who knew little, if anything, about field work. They were also patriotic, and most felt that working in any capacity for the Germans was an insult to their native land. Out of the fifty thousand workers the Germans hoped to relocate, they received only thirty to forty volunteers.

On April 22, 1916—the day before Easter in a heavily Catholic country—the German High Command gave the order to begin forced deportations in Lille. Officially, only the unemployed were to be taken.

The Lille military commander seemed to see it otherwise. He ordered all residents to be in their homes from 6:00 p.m. until 8:00 a.m., with "candles or other lights in the halls and with their luggage ready for transport. German troops would go through the house and select the people to be sent off."

Eyewitnesses to the deportations included CRB delegates Laurence C. "Duke" Wellington and Gardner Richardson. Wellington wrote an extensive report on the entire issue that was circulated heavily by Hoover. Duke wrote that a regiment was deployed to a particular quarter of the city, and "machine guns were placed in the streets, and six, eight, or ten fully armed soldiers entered each house to remove all inhabitants capable of doing field labor."

Each officer, Wellington said, "had orders to deliver a given number of souls at a designated point, and they were herded through the streets on foot or in cars like so many beasts, being made to wait hours in the cold. Any reluctant attitude was treated with the bayonet point."

While the stated goal was to take only the unemployed, the reality was that boys of fifteen and men as old as sixty-five were chosen, regardless of employment status. Worst of all, however, was that women and young girls were also taken. "Girls of good family, women up to the age of fifty . . . were taken from all parts of the cities without any discrimination or consideration as to what class of society they were from. Girls who had known nothing but the protection of refined homes were thrown together with prostitutes or men of low life."

Wellington and Richardson were powerless to do anything as they watched the scene unfold. The only action they could take was to report what they saw to Poland at the next Saturday meeting in Brussels. They did so on April 29, 1916.

Poland was horrified at what he heard, which contradicted what Wengersky had assured him would happen. The CRB director was determined to do something but didn't know what. Neutrality was one thing, but as Kittredge related, the Lille deportations forced the CRB to get involved "in the maelstrom of the controversies of the war and compelled it to take a definite stand against action taken by the Germans toward the French population."

In an incredible coincidence during the CRB staff meeting, Poland received a phone call from the German Army headquarters in Charleville. He was told that Ambassador Gerard was then in Charleville to talk with the Kaiser regarding the diplomatic crisis around the torpedoing of a French ship, the *Sussex*. While in Charleville, Gerard had asked to see the CRB delegates of northern France, so Major-General Zoellner, chief of staff of the quartermaster general in Charleville, had agreed to set up a meeting. Because the northern France delegates were then in Brussels, a special train was arranged to immediately take Poland, the delegates, and their German accompanying "nurses" down to Charleville.

When they arrived in Charleville, the Americans discovered they were only there as "ornaments" at a tea party "in connection with the demonstration the Germans were giving to the Ambassador of how *they* cared for the [French] people," according to Kittredge. In attendance were Ambassador Gerard, Major-General Zoellner, German CRB liaisons Captain Wengersky and Captain Otto Karl zur Strassen, numerous German barons, lesser German officers, the northern France CRB delegates, and accompanying officers Captain Weber and lieutenants (and brothers) Paul and Friedrich Neuerbourg.

No matter how frivolous the event was meant to be, Poland did not let the opportunity pass, as his "sympathetic nature, revolting at the [Lille deportation] tale, impelled him to do something." In great understatement, Poland noted in his official report, "The proper opportunity occurring, I begged leave to call General Zoellner's attention to the distressing conditions which had arisen in Lille, as a result of the evacuation movement."

A much less constrained description—and probably a more accurate accounting—by Kittredge relates Poland's action in a slightly different way. "A bombshell bursting in the room would have hardly produced more astonishment than the raising of this question in the midst of what was ostensibly a quiet social tea. Mr. Poland described to the Ambassador and to General Zoellner the distressing conditions which had arisen in Lille as a result of the evacuation and proceeded to protest most energetically against the whole proceedings." Poland then turned to Wellington and Richardson, who both confirmed what Poland had said.

Captain Wengersky and Captain zur Strassen countered by maintaining the deportations had been carried out in a "proper and satisfactory manner" and that "the French people were very happy to be taken from Lille to the quiet, peaceful, rural districts of the departments of the Aisne, Marne and the Ardennes."

Major-General Zoellner, Poland reported, "expressed himself as much surprised and stated that the condition described was not intended in his order."

That was when Lieutenant Paul Neuerbourg spoke up. Kittredge wrote that he "proved himself . . . to be a man in the best sense of the word. He confirmed everything Mr. Poland had said and agreed with Mr. Poland that it had been a very great mistake on the part of the German army to carry out the new deportation." It was a highly risky and courageous act by an obviously principled man.

Stunned silence must have followed such a statement from an officer far down the command chain. Ambassador Gerard, Poland said, "was much affected by the statements." Major-General Zoellner promised there would be an immediate investigation and that the commander of the Lille District would be ordered to appear in Charleville to explain what had happened.

After the tea party, action was swift. Orders were telegraphed to Lille halting the deportations immediately.

Nonetheless, in the eight days the deportations took place, nearly twenty thousand men, women, and children were taken. A month later, Wellington reported that around three hundred to four hundred people had been returned because they were sick, but the fate of the rest remained a great unknown. He explained that the Germans refused to allow the CRB delegates to investigate. (Most deportees did return after the harvest season.)

The story of the Lille deportations became sensational news around the world once the details were smuggled out of northern France. The world was shocked by the Germans' plan and horrified by how it had been implemented. The British Press Bureau released a dramatic eyewitness account by a Lille resident, while the French government published an official version of the event. Most of the Allied press played on the more dramatic, sensational sides of how the Germans had taken young women and children and placed them in compromising, if not dangerous, situations.

In May 1916, the Germans made assurances to the nations of the world that such deportations would never be repeated.

Before the year was out, however, they would renege on that promise in a way that would far surpass what had happened in Lille.

THE "SLAVE RAIDS" BEGIN

In August 1916, there was a major power shift in Germany that would impact the war and the relief program. The relatively moderate civilian leadership of Chancellor von Bethmann-Hollweg was replaced by the more aggressive military leadership of Paul von Hindenburg and Erich Ludendorff. Then in early September 1916, another change happened when Hindenburg demanded full mobilization of Germany, meaning conscription. Many Germans did not like that idea, and there were calls in the German press for complete utilization of manpower in the occupied territories before full conscription should be enacted.

On October 3, 1916, the German General Headquarters issued a decree announcing mass deportations with no destination given, no work identified, and little or no regard for employment status. The decree stated that the "voluntary or involuntary" unemployed "may be compelled to work even outside the place where they are living." Anyone who resisted could face up to three years in prison and a fine of 10,000 marks. Reportedly, the German General Staff had prepared a deportation plan for all the occupied territories within the German Empire. For Belgium, the plan called for 350,000 to 500,000 men to be deported, which meant almost one in four would be taken.

This was no sporadic effort in a specific place to get the unemployed to work for the Germans. This was mass deportations of all men on a countrywide scale. At stake were approximately 1.6 million Belgian men—employed and unemployed—between the ages of seventeen and fifty-five.

Following the decree, in late autumn 1916, CRB delegate Joe Green watched and reported in restrained anger the brutal taking of men from the small town of Virton, in Luxembourg Province.

Before the war, the Belgian town of Virton was a thriving administrative and commercial center. A Walloon, or French-speaking, municipality of 3,500 residents, Virton was located less than five miles (eight km) north of the French border. During the 1914 invasion, the area saw more than two hundred men, women, and children dragged from their homes and executed in one of the worst massacres of the time.

Nearly two and a half years of occupation had passed when the deportations, commonly referred to as "slave raids," came to the region. The posted *affiche* ordered all men between eighteen and fifty-five from the town and surrounding villages to appear the next day at Virton's Saint Joseph's College. The men were to be there at 7:00 a.m. with blankets and three days' rations. Nothing was said about what would happen to them or where they would go.

"No one slept throughout the night," wrote Green. "The women were busy mending and packing clothes and blankets. The men were settling their affairs. The notaries' offices were crowded with men making their wills. The priests and the burgomasters [mayors] and the leading citizens moved all night from house to house, giving words of encouragement and advice, and promising to look after the wives and children left behind."

The next day dawned heavy, with low-lying pewter clouds and snow that changed back and forth to rain as it fell quietly. The sense of foreboding was heightened by the dull sound of the big guns thundering off in the distance toward Verdun.

Those who did not obey the *affiche* were taken from their homes by German soldiers wielding rifles with fixed bayonets. Protests, explanations, and pleadings were lost on the soldiers, who responded with rough handling and rifle butts. Women and children stood by helplessly as they watched their husbands, fathers, or brothers forced into the street. They joined others—the ones who had heeded the *affiche*—trudging toward Saint Joseph's College.

By 7:00 a.m., the streets around the college were clogged with people. Green was watching as "the men, each with his sack on his back, were herded like cattle, village by village. The women and children, kept at a distance, stood in compact masses, wailing, moaning, wringing their hands. Order was kept by the Uhlans, especially brought from France for the purpose." German *uhlans* were lance-carrying cavalry who had become infamous from their brutality during the invasion—and for their aggressive crowd control.

In Virton, the men who were corralled outside Saint Joseph's College were called in groups by village. As they stepped forward, they were shoved and shouted at by the soldiers and formed into a single line that led through the gate into the courtyard of the college. There the Belgians found a long table and four German officers—the men who would decide their fate.

No time was given for any meaningful review of the health, employment status, or general fitness of each man. "Scarcely any questions were asked. There was no time for questions. The examinations averaged less than ten seconds per man." Each man showed his identity card, which had his name, age, and profession. He then waited for the last officer to make his pronouncement, a one-word command in German: *links*, left, or *rechts*, right.

Left was freedom. Right was forced deportation.

Green watched as "those who passed to the right disappeared, waving a last farewell" as an "agonized shriek went up from some woman in the crowd." And as more men disappeared, the crowd become more agitated. Women kept trying to break through the barricade of soldiers to "say one last word to a husband or a son."

The horrifying scene continued to unfold as Green bore witness. The women were "pushed back roughly into the crowd, often with kicks and blows. In a short time all the women in the front rows of the crowd were being beaten by the soldiers, both with fists and with the butts of guns. . . . Finally an officer came out of the court[yard] and put an end to the worst of the brutality."

As the rain and snow continued to fall, the men marked for deportation were herded by soldiers with fixed bayonets to the train station. Cattle cars were waiting, and the men were shoved in. Each car had a recommended capacity of only eight horses or forty men, yet the Germans were known to force up to sixty men into one car. By nightfall the Virton train, packed with its human cargo, was gone. As the train pulled away from the station, the men had no doubt been singing, like many before them, the Belgian and French national anthems, "La Brabançonne" and "La Marseillaise."

In the end, about a third of the men from Virton were taken and, as Green wrote, "almost none under the age of 25 . . . escaped." The nearby village of Ethe was hit the hardest—only seventeen "able-bodied men remaining out of a population of 1,500."

Green was horrified by what he saw that day in Virton. He wrote his parents about the deportations, dropping any pretense of neutrality: "They are carried out with the last degree of brutality. They are utterly unwarranted by the situation in Belgium and they may simply be regarded as the latest and worst manifestations of that systemized German barbarity which must be crushed."

Fellow CRB delegates were seeing and experiencing the same thing, as they stood helplessly on the front lines of the deportations. All they could do was file reports and hope the brutal slave raids were somehow stopped.

Legation Minister Whitlock wrote, "The delegates were instructed to be present [at the deportations] and to render any service they could, and Mr. [William Hallam] Tuck and Mr. [John A.] Gade, delegates of the C.R.B. in the province of Hainaut, went over to the commune of St. Ghislain on the morning of October twenty-ninth to witness the selections, to prevent the seizure of the employees of the C.N. and the C.R.B., and to distribute food to those who were deported." They came back, Whitlock wrote, "sick with horror and full of rage."

In Whitlock's official report on the deportations, he wrote: "Appalling stories have been related by Belgians coming to the Legation. . . . Even if a modicum of all that is told is true, there still remains enough to stamp this deed as one of the foulest that history records."

Hoover and the CRB were drawn deeper into the issue as the Germans began deporting Belgians who were employed as critical support staff for the relief. In total, more than one thousand Belgian CRB employees were taken.

Hoover was about to face a nearly impossible decision.

A DEADLY ETHICAL DILEMMA

The deportations did not escape the notice of the outside world. Shortly after the deportations began, the first accounts filtered out of the occupied territories to the rest of the world. People around the globe were horrified at the stories of families ripped apart and cattle cars crammed with defiant men yelling, "We will not sign!" or singing the Belgian and French national anthems. Worldwide condemnation filled nearly every newspaper and magazine, and protest rallies were held.

In America, organized gatherings took place in multiple cities, including Boston and New York City. The *New York Times* reported that on Friday evening, December 15, 1916, Carnegie Hall was "packed to capacity" with more than three thousand people there to protest "against the crimes of the Imperial German Government in its treatment of the Belgian people." A letter from Teddy Roosevelt was read to loud applause, especially when it came to the statement that "as long as neutrals keep silent, or speak apologetically, or take refuge in the futilities of the professional pacifists, there will be no cessation in these brutalities."

On December 5, 1916, the British, French, Russian, and Italian governments joined the chorus of protests. A strongly worded joint press release spoke directly about the CRB and the possibility of the relief being shut down.

It was at this time that Hoover faced one of his toughest CRB decisions. As a neutral providing food to belligerents behind the lines, Hoover had no legal right to question the forced labor of civilians. As a Quaker and a man of integrity, honesty, and conscience, he could not ignore the situation.

"Should we risk the lives of ten million people," he wrote, "with a declaration to the Germans that we would terminate the Relief if the deportations were not stopped? We had tried every measure of persuasion and every measure of pressure of neutral opinion. Nothing less than such an absolute declaration on our part would stand any chance of success, but what if it failed?"

Threatening to pull out had become a Hoover maneuver that had worked successfully multiple times. Every other time, though, he had read the situation correctly, understanding that the other side would back down.

This time, Hoover saw how steadfast the Germans were against tremendous worldwide pressure. As a result, he asked the opinion of the two CRB patron ministers in London, Ambassador Page and Spanish Ambassador Merry del Val. They both were against any CRB pullout threat and recommended Hoover ask Lord Grey, the British foreign secretary. Lord Grey counseled Hoover not to make such a threat and said the CRB would still have the backing of the British government.

Hoover finally made his choice; he did not threaten to leave. He did, however, remain committed to putting indirect pressure whenever he could on the Germans to stop the deportations.

The Chief's decision was a tough pill for the young, idealistic CRB delegates to swallow. For at least one, such a course of action was unacceptable. William Hallam Tuck, after witnessing the deportations, felt he could no longer remain neutral in the

Figure 15.2. After witnessing the German deportations of Belgians, William Hallam Tuck could not remain neutral, as the CRB required. Following his conscience, he left the CRB and enlisted in the British Army.
Public domain; author's archives.

company of those who had brought on such inhumanity. On December 21, he left Belgium and joined the British Army. Many of the other delegates thought about doing the same, but all remained at their posts.

Despite the international outcry and official government protests, the German military refused to change its policy. It even turned its back on the objections of some of its own people. In the German Reichstag, on December 2, 1916, deputies of the minority Independent Socialist Democratic Party stood in the great chamber and protested the deportations. Nothing swayed the German military. Ludendorff stated that the outcry from the rest of the world showed only a "very childish judgment of the war."

Meanwhile, the Belgians were fighting back as best they could.

A BELGIAN MORAL VOICE RISES AGAIN

The Belgians did not take the deportations quietly, despite the fact they lived under German rule. Towns and cities across the country officially protested with letters to von Bissing that were written and signed by numerous local dignitaries. Countless burgomasters and committee members refused to hand over lists of the unemployed that would have helped the Germans. And some Belgian men, deciding not to chance a cattle car to Germany, attempted the dangerous clandestine border crossing into Holland so they could join the fight.

Besides individual efforts, there was one mighty voice that could not, and would not, be silenced. It was the moral voice of the country, and it sprang from the tall, reed-thin man of the red cloth—Cardinal Mercier. Ever since penning a patriotic December 1914 pastoral letter that had circulated around the world, the cardinal had shown no reluctance to reacting strongly to any perceived German injustices against the Belgians. Nearly everything Mercier did either frustrated or angered the German governor general.

Von Bissing used house arrest as a way of keeping Mercier contained, and he tried hard to stop the circulation of any letters or statements from the cardinal, but they always seemed to find their way out to the rest of the country and the world. The solution of imprisonment or execution (such as what others suffered for lesser crimes) was unthinkable to the German, who believed in the importance of the Catholic Church in helping to keep civilian order.

Figure 15.3. To many Belgians, Cardinal Désiré Félicien François Joseph Mercier was the moral voice of the country. He passionately argued for the return of deported Belgians and ultimately won.

Public domain; Hugh Gibson, *A Journal from Our Legation in Belgium* (New York: Doubleday, Page and Co., 1917).

On the deportations, Mercier wrote numerous letters of protest to von Bissing. He also penned one missive to the world that was smuggled out of Belgium. It was widely circulated and helped stimulate unofficial and official condemnation. While the pope and countries around the globe did stand up and protest, nothing shook the German military's resolve.

That was not all the cardinal did. In December 1916, he established a committee to collect appeals for those who felt they had been unjustly taken. On January 24, 1917, the cardinal made his first official appeal for 698 men to the interim governor general, Baron von Huene (von Bissing had taken ill and was recuperating in Germany). That was quickly followed in the next month by six more letters that included appeals from more than 2,500 men.

As the cardinal was doing all that he could to get back at least some of the deported, he was visited on February 11, 1917, by Spanish minister Villalobar and Belgian statesman Michel Levie. They had a plan to gather the most notable men in Belgium to sign an appeal that would be taken to Berlin by von der Lancken and presented directly to the Kaiser. Mercier agreed immediately, not only to sign the document but to write it as well.

The cardinal wielded as his sword what he knew best, religion. "Your Imperial Majesty prides yourself on your loyalty to your faith. May we not then be allowed to remind you of the simple and yet striking words of the Gospel, 'Do unto others that which you would have done to yourself'? . . . We venture to hope that your Majesty will be guided by but one sentiment—that of humanity."

Dated February 14, 1917, the document was signed by prominent Belgians and was delivered not only to the Kaiser but also to von Bissing, who had returned to Belgium and must have been furious at the audacity of those who went over his head to petition the Kaiser. However, that anger might have been tempered by von Bissing's reportedly less-than-enthusiastic support for the deportations.

On Friday, March 9, 1917, Baron von der Lancken verbally told the president of the Belgian senate, Baron de Favereau, the Kaiser's answer. No doubt contrary to what his generals wanted, the Kaiser ordered that all those who had been mistakenly deported as unemployed be returned and that the deportations be suspended. On March 14, the imperial decree was officially announced in Brussels.

It was a great, but not complete, victory. Only those who had been taken by mistake—meaning men who had jobs when deported—would be returned. Nothing was said about the majority who were unemployed and had been taken forcibly, or of the reported 10,000 to 13,000 who had signed contracts to work for the Germans (whether because they wanted to or because they felt signing would get their families better treatment).

Still, it was a significant victory. After more than a year, and more than 120,000 ripped from their families (58,500 Belgians from the occupation zone and 62,155 Belgians and northern French from the German Army Zone), the slave raids were over. And some of the men were coming home.

DEPORTEES RETURN BARELY ALIVE

True to the Kaiser's word, train cars of Belgian men began to return home in February and March 1917. Their condition spoke of harsh treatment and severe deprivation.

"I saw trainloads of them arriving in the Antwerp station," CRB delegate William Percy said. "They were creatures imagined by El Greco—skeletons, with blue flesh clinging to their bones, too weak to stand alone, too ill to be hungry any longer."

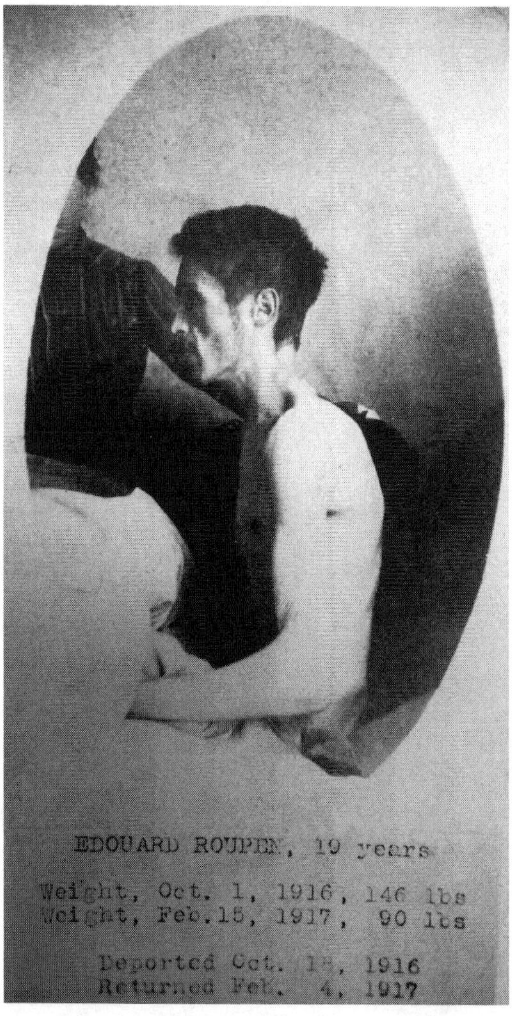

EDOUARD ROUPEN, 19 years
Weight, Oct. 1, 1916, 146 lbs
Weight, Feb.15, 1917, 90 lbs
Deported Oct. 1916
Returned Feb. 4, 1917

Figure 15.4. Deported by the Germans on October 1, 1916, nineteen-year-old Edouard Roupen weighed a healthy 146 pounds. When he was shipped back home in early February 1917, he weighed 90 pounds.

Public domain; Herbert Hoover Presidential Library Archives, West Branch, Iowa.

Writing much later, during World War II, Percy commented, "This was only a miniature venture into slavery, a preliminary to the epic conquest and enslavement of whole peoples in 1940, but it seemed hideous and unprecedented to us in 1917." He neglected to mention that "left" or "right" became words that defined the brutality of the forced deportations. None who were taken in World War I Belgium, however, could have guessed that those two words would foretell even greater terror only twenty-four years later as they became forever linked with the horrors of World War II's Holocaust.

Prentiss Gray also wrote on March 1, 1917, about a trainload that came into Antwerp. "They had been *en route* twenty-four hours and during that time fifty-two had died. Every man was carried from the train on a stretcher to the hospital, broken wrecks of humanity." Gray followed the ambulances to the hospital and spoke to some of the men. Admitting some of the stories they told might be "overdrawn," Gray stated strongly, though, that "there were unmistakable signs in their physical condition of suffering beyond human endurance. Evidence there was plenty in frozen feet and hands, great red welts on their emaciated bodies, pneumonia and tuberculosis ran riot among them."

Many of the deported would not get back to Belgium until the war was over. Others never made it home.

16

The Human Toll

What were the physical and emotional effects of living under the harsh German occupation? That question pertained not only to Belgian and northern French civilians but also to the CRB delegates who lived and worked behind the lines.

When it came to the lives of civilians, Hoover wanted the world to fully grasp what they were going through as a way of stimulating donations and as a way of sustaining worldwide public opinion, which would ensure the food relief would continue to receive necessary governmental supports and subsidies from both warring sides.

To do so, Hoover periodically sent into Belgium outside experts to provide scientific verification of deteriorating health conditions, and he had his CRB delegates monitor and file numerous reports about local communities and individuals. He then presented many of those documents and countless news and feature articles to the worldwide press in hopes of creating both empathy and sympathy for the innocent civilians trapped in the middle of the war.

"SLOWLY BLEEDING TO DEATH"

One major Hoover-supported article written for American readers by delegate Robinson Smith was blatant in its intent by being titled, "How Does It Feel?" Smith wrote that if an American wanted to experience a little of what the Belgians were feeling, "all he has to do is skip his dinner. That will make him feel exactly as millions of Belgians are feeling at the present hour. They have each day something to eat, but it is not enough. They have their litre of soup and their half-pound of bread and some potatoes and rice, but when five o'clock comes, they are hungry; some of them very hungry."

But according to Smith, skipping dinner didn't tell the whole story. "It is only when you have come to know this people, that you can realize the terror of their plight. When you picture Belgium, think not only of the black lines before the soup-kitchens, of the black groups of men without work in the squares by day, of the villages pitch-black by night; think too of the tens of thousands of the once well-to-do, who now have lost or are losing all that they have hitherto enjoyed. Surely and with almost mathematical progress poverty is penetrating into every home of the land, and all that [middle] class[,] who in America form the suburbs[,] can now count the months that their little capital will hold out."

His conclusion was simple but powerful, "Belgium is like a person slowly bleeding to death, and only the care of the whole world can save her."

Smith, who worked in Mons and covered the Hainaut Province (the country's largest in size and population with 1.3 million people), put the relief effort's ultimate goal in perspective when he stated, "It is not starvation the Commission wishes to forestall, but an approach to starvation."

That was echoed by an old peasant woman Smith met on his travels around the province. The CRB delegate asked her if anyone had died of starvation in her commune. She answered straightforwardly, "No, we have too much to die, and not enough to live."

Such a thin line meant that everyday life became focused more on simply surviving than living. The poorer residents in small villages and towns were the hardest hit by the lack of food, and some of those barely found the will to survive.

This was evidenced in reports filed by CRB delegate Maurice Pate, who lived in the Belgian town of Tournai and covered the same Hainaut Province that Smith did. At twenty-one, Maurice Pate was tall, gangly, one of the youngest CRB delegates, and his French was weak. But he was also known as a diligent worker and an astute observer who could turn good thoughts into action.

By autumn 1916, Pate had become well acquainted with his job and the Tournai District of the province. In August, he had completed touring forty-five of the eighty-two communes within his region. His traveling was so extensive that one week in September, he and his Belgian chauffeur, Julian van Mohl, logged more than six hundred miles (965 km) in the motorcar (made more incredible by the fact that top speed on the cobblestoned roads was about forty-five miles per hour).

In late February/early March 1916, Pate visited numerous families in his region and wrote an extensive report detailing the food situation of three of them. His full description of the families illustrates the kind of life many poor Belgians had to endure. Following is his write-up on one of the families:

Family A: There are 7 persons in the family. The father and eldest son work 4 days per week in a mine at Quaregnon [5 miles southwest of Mons], earning Frs. 4.40 a day.

At home are the mother, 2 young children and a third adopted infant, a child of a lost relative.

The resources for the family of 7 are thus Frs. 35 a week or Frs. 5 per day. The food consumed by the family is exclusively that obtained at the C.R.B. magasin [warehouse] viz: the following quantities per day:

300 grams of bread.
8 grams of rice.
12 grams of lard and bacon.
10 grams of cerealine and other foodstuffs by occasion.
The 2 miners receive a supplementary ration of 100 grams of bread a day.

This particular region is almost entirely lacking in native foodstuffs [known, instead, as a coal mining area]. There are no more potatoes to be found and the cattle beet at 50 francs a hundred kilos is, with its little nutritional value, regarded as a luxury for the small purse.

In the case of the family in question, for breakfast, they eat one small slice of bread together with a cup of black brew made of burnt grain. During the day, the father and son, who leave the house at 4:30 in the morning, are at their work in the coalmine. Each takes with him 350 grams of bread, or 3 large slices. This, spread with white sour milk cheese, form their sole [nutrition] during the day's work. The men return home at 4 in the afternoon. The family, after their light breakfast, eat nothing during the day, because of the fact that the mother and children must sacrifice their ration to the men to give them the necessary strength to go to work. At 4:30 the family eat together a bowl of rice with a quantity of bread. To save themselves from the pains of hunger, they all go to bed about 6 o'clock.

On examination of the pantry it was found that there remained none of the lard which was distributed 4 days ago, and of which there will not be another distribution for one month. There were no other foodstuffs of any kind in the house except a small quantity of rice and 1 [kilogram] loaf of Holland bread. Were it not for this latter, which is distributed from time to time in the commune, the family would have been entirely without bread.

As I was about to leave the house, a woman of very respectable and neat appearance, a miner's wife, came in to borrow from her neighbor a small amount of bread, which she promised to return upon receiving a ration tomorrow. She had been obliged to give to her husband, when he descended the mine the same morning, what little was left in the house. The 2 children, both under three years of age, had been without bread during the entire day. The woman, distracted between furnishing the food which is absolutely necessary to her husband, as the family's 'bread winner' and in answering the cries of the children, had sacrificed herself to an extent which was very apparent in her physical appearance. She was depressed and morally exhausted. She said that she could not keep much longer under the present strain, and even had a great difficulty to keep [from throwing] herself into the canal.

The family of 7 persons above mentioned, never eats meat, except for an occasional Sunday, when a small quantity is purchased for the men.

*In the examination of the house, a fact which struck me very forcibly, was the insanitory [*sic*] condition due to lack of soap because of the present price of this article. They told me there was not a gram in the house. The fact of not being able to keep themselves clean, it is evident, has a very deteriorating and discouraging moral affect.*

Many of the people Pate saw, and tens of thousands more, had lived like that for more than two years and would continue to do so until the end of the war.

None of the CRB delegates had to face the hunger and privations that many of the poorest in Belgium and northern France experienced daily. In fact, most of the young Americans were wined and dined across the country by the wealthy in chateaux that were luxurious and serviced by numerous household staff (some of whom still dressed in traditional livery). Such stark and brutal contrasts played mental havoc on many of the young CRB men, who struggled to reconcile those two different worlds that they traversed every day.

THE EMOTIONAL TOLL ON THE DELEGATES

Few of the delegates publicly acknowledged the internal, emotional stress the job created within them. E. E. Hunt was one of the few who did so, and as a trained and experienced journalist, he brought a literary bent to his efforts.

"The conditions of war soon grow to seem normal," he wrote in his book, *War Bread*, "but there is an emotional and physical strain about them which eats at one's heart.

"Belgium was like a military prison and an asylum for the insane, rolled into one. Always, just under the surface of life, one felt the tearless, voiceless, tragic resistance of an unconquerable people."

Such emotion, while beautifully expressed, could still indicate a depth of feeling and internalization that could result in a strong and at times disabling effect.

As delegate Kittredge related in his history of the CRB, the stress experienced by many delegates in northern France led to "quite a number [who] had nervous breakdowns after only a month or two in France." (Kittredge's expression of "nervous breakdown" was used more to describe a state of mental and physical exhaustion than what is widely used today to indicate mental illness.)

These were young, and in many cases inexperienced, men facing battle-hardened German officers who scorned and mocked them, buttoned-down Belgian businessmen who mistrusted them, and half-starved women and children who looked at them as saviors. Every day the Americans awoke to a place where few spoke English, news of family and friends was rare, and the work was a tedious mixture of bills of lading, stocktaking, endless meetings, and incessant demands for written reports. Such mundane days could be suddenly, unexpectedly shattered by desperate Belgians making personal appeals—which the delegates could not help—or witnessing some form of German brutality—which the delegates were powerless to stop.

Everywhere the Americans looked, there was little that cheered them. In the cities, towns, and villages, the people were muted, subdued in their dress and emotions, and ever watchful for the German soldier, secret policeman, or spy who might be observing a little too closely or listening a little too intently to their innocent conversations. And many times the Belgian weather seemed to match the worst moods—dark, cloudy, cold, and rainy.

"Until late in the spring [of 1915]," Hunt said, "when a special censorship for the Commission members was arranged with the Germans, we received no letters or newspapers from any one outside of Belgium. We had no new books. We knew little about the progress of the war. Home was almost a myth."

It was a country that in many ways appeared normal from afar, but on closer inspection was revealed to be an emotional prison that wore one down day by day. In such a stifling world, Hunt noted, "breathing spells were not many, and we sometimes longed for escape from Belgium as a convict longs to break prison."

As the months went by, the strain of the work would show itself, especially during the Thursday Brussels meeting of all the delegates when they could finally talk honestly among themselves. Those weekly meetings were important release valves, as were the evenings that were spent together in collegiate camaraderie prior to the meetings.

"When we spent the night in Brussels," Hunt recalled, "Amos D. Johnson's house at 12 Galerie de Waterloo roared with our fun and the recitation of each others' Odysseys: how [Carlton Bowden] and [Frank Gailor] refused to salute the German colonel at Longwy and how the colonel almost died of apoplexy in consequence; how Robinson Smith, translator of *Don Quixote*, gently but firmly refused a gold watch tendered him by the Provincial Committee of Hainaut, until the Committee had adopted his scheme of bread locaux communaux; how [C. H. Carstairs] was soon to marry a Belgian girl, and how other delegates were suspected of being matrimonially minded . . . how somebody tried to ram a Zeppelin shed, and should have been shot in consequence . . . of one of our fellow-citizens who said to Cardinal Mercier, 'You're a Catholic, ain't you? . . . Well, I'm a Presbyterian myself; but I ain't got no prejudices' . . . the competence or incompetence of our respective chauffeurs and automobiles, and the greatness of Hoover."

Such a spirit of camaraderie was critical to the morale of the delegates, and yet the Thursday delegate meetings were discontinued in February 1915 by new director Albert N. Connett. Kittredge minced no words when he stated that Connett "soon grew impatient with the attitude of some of the delegates and was frankly bored by the discussions at the delegates' meetings. After attending one, he decided it was useless to hold any further meetings and no more were held during the time that he was in Belgium." (Connett lasted only until April, after which the meetings were reinstated.)

Tempering the February 1915 loss of the Thursday meetings were Brussels office luncheons, where food was brought in and any delegate in the vicinity could join in. Kittredge explained that a lunchroom had been established in the Brussels office in January 1915 and "it soon became a gathering place, at luncheon time, for the heads of departments and provincial delegates." This was where the delegates could have "bicker sessions" and laugh and argue. "It was there that Hugh Gibson would delight the company with his inimitable witticisms and caustic comments upon the general situation and particularly upon the German administration. It was there that the developments in Belgium were discussed from day to day and the problems of the Commission informally thrashed out."

But that wasn't all that the luncheons served to do. They also were where the delegates came to know one another "in a companionship which made of the body a real fraternity, a group of men actuated by unwavering loyalty to their chief and by self-sacrificing devotion to the interests of the people whom they had come to Belgium to aid."

By far, though, the most important release for delegates was the occasional permission to leave Belgium for some much-needed R&R in Holland. This was Hoover's doing, according to Hunt, as he had "arranged a series of vacations for delegates, because the men could not stay long in the work and remain well in body and spirit."

"Crossing the border to Holland was like a spiritual experience," Hunt explained. "The sudden sense of freedom was as strange and real as mountain air after a long stay in the city, and one's heart sang like a lark, merely to be quit of Belgium."

Many of the delegates beyond the headquarters in Brussels worked either alone or with only one other man. Most of them found their own unique ways or places of escaping, even momentarily, the pressures of the job and the prison they lived in.

One of Hunt's special places was the old Premonstratensian Abbey of Tongerloo (now spelled Tongerlo), twenty-six miles (forty-two km) southeast of Antwerp, where he would "try to forget everyday affairs. The avenues of venerable linden trees, the gaunt halls, the white-gowned canons and gray-gowned acolytes and novices, the sanctity and repose of the place were irresistibly soothing."

There were also the short, sporadic times spent at the numerous Belgian country chateaux that had been flung open by their owners to the Americans. They were homes like the Bunges' Chateau Oude Gracht on the Hoogboom estate, where the men could play tennis, take long walks in the woods, and have evenings of music in the salon, quiet reading in the well-stocked library, or a fiercely competitive game of billiards upstairs with Edouard Bunge and daughter Erica.

Hunt would often go to Chateau Oude Gracht to relax. On one visit in the spring of 1915, "I ran out of the chateau for a lonely, happy, night walk. . . . A lake behind the castle lay mirror-still, and I stopped beside it." But even in that serene place, there was no peace, for he could hear the "guns—the everlasting guns. Seventy-five miles away, along the Yser, in the spring dusk, men were killing and being killed. Each explosion could be heard: a toneless stab in one's head, not like a sound, but like a wound; a thrust that twisted and tortured into one's consciousness and could not be forgotten."

ONE DELEGATE'S SOLITARY JOURNEY

Nothing could better illustrate the CRB delegate's precarious position—both physically and emotionally—within Belgium and northern France than the story of Robert Warren, a CRB delegate from the second wave of Oxford Rhodes Scholars, who was arrested in late April 1915 at the border of Holland and Belgium.

Warren was the victim of a German system in which the local military command seemed at times to act independently of higher authority and could steamroll some-

Figure 16.1. The story of what happened to Robert Warren, twenty-one, showed how isolated and ultimately alone many CRB delegates were in a world totally controlled by the Germans.

Public domain; Herbert Hoover Presidential Library Archives, West Branch, Iowa.

one into oblivion, even when the person was a citizen of a neutral country serving with the acceptance of the German occupation government. Warren's story shows just how isolated and ultimately alone these young men could become in a world totally controlled by the Germans.

Warren was only twenty-one and had attended Yankton College, a small liberal arts school that had been founded in 1881 as the first institution of higher learning in the Dakota Territory. Clean-shaven with dark, wavy hair and prominent ears, Warren had the studious, serious look of a student, which was accentuated by heavy eyebrows and a tight, small mouth. In his official CRB photo, his stare seems intense and focused on trying to project his maturity and honesty.

Since early December 1914, Warren had been a delegate working in Hainaut Province and living in Mons. In mid-April 1915, he decided to return to his studies at Oxford and was in Brussels preparing to leave Belgium for good. It was then that CRB delegate administrator and fellow Oxford student Perrin Galpin told him that delegates were needed in northern France.

Warren immediately volunteered to postpone his return to Oxford and serve in the new area. Because the CRB director in Brussels, Oscar Crosby, felt the London office had to approve the reassignment, and that could take a week or more, Warren asked if he could use the travel pass already issued to him and spend his waiting time in Holland. Crosby agreed, and Warren left on April 16. He had no trouble getting through the border.

The delegate stayed for a week at the Hotel Weimar in Rotterdam. He visited the CRB office, where he told Director Carl Young of his situation and how he was awaiting word from Brussels to either go back to Oxford or return to Belgium for posting in northern France. While at the office, he collected fifty letters from friends and family and several packages that were delayed Christmas presents. He also visited numerous cafés, took in two moving-picture shows, and spent time reading, walking along the many tree-lined canals, and waiting for news from Brussels. He rarely talked with anyone other than CRB men, although he did share a word or two with people in cafés, on train station platforms, or in railcar compartments. Such mundane details of his time in Rotterdam did not seem important at the time.

On Friday morning, April 23, a week after he had left Brussels, Warren received a telegram from Crosby saying that if he still wanted reassignment to northern France, he was approved by London and should return to Brussels. "I'll go," he telegraphed back, then went straight to the German Consulate office in Rotterdam and received a pass to travel to Brussels. The rest of the day was spent writing letters to friends and family about his change of plans.

He left for Brussels Saturday morning, first taking a train from Rotterdam to the Dutch border town of Roosendaal, where there was a perfunctory Dutch customs checkpoint. He then boarded another train to the Belgian border town of Esschen, where the German military took over examining those who wanted to enter occupied Belgium.

"On arriving at Esschen, I went into the station to have my baggage examined. I paid duty on some tobacco and on opening my two valises for a second examination, was taken into custody by an officer and led to a small room for personal examination."

At that time, all his papers and documents were taken, after which he was asked to sign a statement that his papers were authentic. He did. He was then personally searched, which came up with only one inappropriate item—his hotel room key that he had forgotten to return. The Germans kept that, along with all his documents, which included his passports (one CRB, one US), German travel pass, and identity papers stating that he worked for the CRB.

Up to that point, nothing had happened that was too much out of the norm for CRB delegates dealing with German harassment at borders and sentry posts. Usually, however, once a delegate's papers were thoroughly studied, the German in charge would let the delegate proceed with his trip.

Warren wasn't so lucky. Suddenly, the German officer handling the exam turned mean. He accused the young delegate of saying good-bye to someone at the station that morning. That person was overheard saying he was going on to Flushing, the Dutch town where ferries came and went from England. The implication was that Warren had been dealing with a spy, which meant he was a spy as well—a serious offense.

Staying outwardly calm, Warren now knew the cause of his troubles—one of the thousands of German counterespionage agents who was scattered throughout Holland and Belgium had probably followed him during his stay in Rotterdam, had seen or overheard things he felt were suspicious, and had talked to the German authorities. As long as Warren kept his head, he was sure he could straighten things out. He knew he had done nothing wrong.

He quickly denied the accusation, then added that even if he had, it would have been nothing of importance. Saying good-bye to someone at a train station was not a crime.

"Speak the truth!" the officer shot back in German. He told Warren that they knew all that he had said and done while in Holland, so he might as well tell the truth.

Warren again denied the charge. At that point, the interview turned into a full-blown interrogation. "I was closely questioned regarding date and place of birth, family connections, residence, time spent at Oxford, reason for coming to Belgium, date, length of time spent here, number of trips taken to Holland from Belgium, passes used, routes taken, purpose of trips." His answers were all written down, and he was told to sign the resulting statement. He did.

Warren then turned on his accuser. "I officially requested he inform the American ambassador at Brussels, Mr. Brand Whitlock, that I had been arrested. It was my right as an American citizen."

The German refused, stating that the American was a prisoner, and prisoners had no rights.

"I officially requested he contact the Commission for Relief in Belgium and told him that in my documents I had a letter, signed by CRB executive Captain Lucey and stamped with the CRB seal, that stated I was a member."

The German refused again.

Nothing Warren said made a difference. Soon, he was taken to the waiting room of the train station and placed under guard for the night. As he sat in the empty room, waiting for dawn, he wondered how long it would take for someone to start looking for him. Director Crosby in Brussels was so busy it might be days before he even realized Warren hadn't shown up. Director Young in Rotterdam had already moved on to a hundred other jobs after saying good-bye to Warren. No one he could think of was actively thinking of him and his whereabouts.

As he tried to sleep on the hard wooden benches, he took stock of his situation—he was twenty-one, a prisoner of the German Empire, and no one knew where he was. He was truly on his own and had no idea how he was going to get out of his predicament.

Morning brought no resolution. The same officer escorted him by train to Antwerp, where they went straight to the offices of the German political department. There, numerous conferences were held with various people and Warren was repeatedly asked the same kinds of questions he had been asked back in Esschen.

"I urgently requested they tell Mr. Whitlock, or some officer of the Commission, in Brussels or Antwerp, of my arrest."

Again the requests were refused.

The Germans said someone would have to go to Holland to investigate the entire matter. Warren gave them the address of the CRB office in Rotterdam and the personal address of Young, the director, repeating his plea to tell someone at the CRB what was happening. Warren was then escorted by armed guard to Antwerp prison and placed in cell sixteen.

"I was permitted to speak to no one except prison officials." With nothing else to do but stare at the walls and wonder what was going to happen, Warren wrote two letters, one to E. E. Hunt in Antwerp and one to Crosby in Brussels. He convinced a prison guard to take them and hoped they'd be posted. He would have written another letter to Harry Diederich, the American consul general in Antwerp, but he didn't know the man's address.

The young CRB delegate spent the rest of Sunday afternoon and evening in his cell.

Monday came and went with no news.

Tuesday the same, with no word as to what was happening.

He wondered how long the letters might take to reach their destinations and how long it would take for someone to get him out of there. As each day passed, he wondered if he might never get out.

His thoughts would have darkened even more if he had known neither of his letters ever got through.

Finally, on Wednesday morning, April 28, at nine o'clock, he was taken back to the German political department and stood before a new officer.

To Warren's great relief, also in the room was Diederich, the American consul general, who told him that an unofficial, unnamed source (probably a sympathetic Belgian from the prison staff) had told him on Monday about Warren's situation. It had taken more than a day to start the process of getting him released.

Warren was escorted to an Antwerp hotel for lunch and kept there under guard until 5:30 p.m. But he was still not out of the woods. He was then taken back to the political department, where he once again faced the German officer from Esschen, who had either made the trip to Holland or had received more information regarding Warren's case.

The German stated that the proprietor of a café in Rotterdam, a certain Mueller, had said he had observed Warren having multiple conversations with a certain person in his café in the evening and then seeing the same person off at a train station on Saturday.

Warren—standing there in the same suit, shirt, and tie he had put on four days before—had no idea when this ordeal would ever end. He once again wearily denied all charges.

"I told him I knew of no Mueller, nor the café he mentioned. I admitted to the bare possibility that I had exchanged words with someone at the Rotterdam station Saturday, but, I swore he was someone I didn't know, had never seen before, and that whatever I might have said was nothing more than ordinary small talk."

The officer also produced a handful of letters addressed to Warren that he had somehow gotten from the CRB Rotterdam office. They had been opened and read. All of them were personal letters from friends and family in America.

"I protested against this action, but no attention was paid to my protest."

A statement was drawn up recounting all of what had been said. Warren signed it.

And with that, just as it had begun, the whole ordeal was suddenly over, with no words of explanation or words of apology. "I was released in the presence of the American consul at 8 p.m. Wednesday, April 28th."

Even though Warren had initially agreed to be a delegate in northern France, he never made it there. He returned to Oxford. No reason was ever given for why he didn't go into northern France. It could be that the London office had already filled all the new posts by the time Warren was freed from jail. Or maybe Warren was simply fed up with the Germans after what they had just done to him.

The whole experience must have been a frightening one—to know that he had done no wrong, that he had certain legal rights as a neutral in occupied Belgium, and yet the local Germans in command had taken total control of his life. Warren must have also thought how easily the entire incident could have gone the other way and he'd still be in jail.

Either way, he and all the other American CRB delegates knew one thing for certain—Warren had been treated far better than any Belgian would have been in the same situation.

17

The Last Days of Americans in Belgium

By late December 1916, the weather turned foul across much of Belgium and northern France. The normal winter rains came not with their soothing, gentle touch but with a vengeance that took many by surprise. It was as if the clouds were sick of the war and wanted to flush it all away. In the south, the flooding was so bad that trains from Brussels to Tournai stopped running for a few days. CRB delegate Maurice Pate reported, "On account of heavy rains the country is under water in many places."

By January 1917, the rains had subsided, but then a killer cold swept in. Soon, daytime temperatures were hovering between 0 and 10 degrees Fahrenheit, and the vital canals—the primary roadways of relief from Rotterdam—began to freeze. Pate wrote, "The most important question of the moment is the freezing of the canals. Water transport is now stopped and all CRB goods must be brought in by rail." This necessitated the creation of "an entirely new system of making food shipments by rail, and with the present demand for rolling stock every place in Europe this was a rather difficult task."

On February 4, Pate observed in Tournai, where the Mons-Condé Canal met a larger river, sixty Belgians laboring to free several trapped CRB barges that were filled with much-needed wheat. The men cut a path through the ice twenty feet wide and a mile long to get the barges back from the canal to the river so they could return to Mons for unloading.

The situation was critical in Rotterdam as well, as much of the harbor froze over. Prentiss Gray reported that Rotterdam's "shipping organization, which has taken more than two years to build up, has been disrupted and disorganized in a day."

Replacing the ice-bound barges were railcars, or at least that had been the contingency plan for frozen canals drawn up with the Germans in 1916. However, that plan was mostly scuttled by British attacks along the Somme front that started on January 11 and continued into March, which drew most German railcars to the

Figure 17.1. In late January and early February 1917, arctic weather froze Rotterdam harbor and most of the Belgian canals, which were the primary roadways of food relief. This photo shows men in Rotterdam harbor trying to break up the ice.
Public domain; Herbert Hoover Presidential Library Archives, West Branch, Iowa.

Army zones. Even so, the CRB pulled together enough train cars that the food found its way into Belgium.

By late February, the arctic cold broke, and by the first of March, barges from Rotterdam began moving once again toward Belgium and northern France. Nevertheless, CRB imports would not rebound to their previous levels primarily because something much bigger than frozen canals had appeared and would create much more havoc to relief efforts.

From the last few months of 1916 into early 1917, many of the CRB delegates were sure America would enter the war, the only questions worth debating in their "bicker" sessions were how and when. So many German provocations had passed without Wilson calling for war that the men wondered what it would take to make the reluctant president act.

Two separate issues, coming back-to-back, would finally be the tipping point not only for Wilson but for most Americans—resumption of Germany's unrestricted submarine warfare and the Zimmermann Telegram.

UNRESTRICTED U-BOAT WARFARE RESUMES

At 10 a.m. on February 1, 1917, Brand Whitlock attended a meeting in Baron von der Lancken's office. The German had summoned Whitlock and the two other CRB patron ministers—Spanish minister Marquis de Villalobar and Dutch minister Maurice van Vollenhoven. Von der Lancken addressed the three ministers solemnly, explaining that the day before, on January 31, German foreign secretary Arthur Zimmermann had informed US Ambassador Gerard in Berlin that Germany had established a war zone and blockade along the coasts of England, France, Spain, and Italy. Any ships—neutral or belligerent—caught in the war zone would be sunk without warning. Germany's unrestricted submarine warfare had begun again (after being halted by the Kaiser in 1915 with the sinking of the *Lusitania*).

Von der Lancken said the Germans still wanted the humanitarian program to continue. A statement was read that "the Imperial Government has not the slightest intention of hindering the work of the *ravitaillement* [food supplying] of Belgium." But the Germans demanded that the CRB keep its ships outside the war zone and strongly recommended that the CRB "divert by an immediate notice all ships *en route* toward those waters situated outside the forbidden zone." He then handed out copies of a map that showed the new war zone areas.

Whitlock was sure the Germans' aggressive military strategy would draw America into war. Returning to the legation, he worked all afternoon on a telegram to President Wilson, sent it off, then waited. He knew it could take days, if not longer, before a reply came.

Back in America, Wilson's official response to Germany's action was to take the first significant step toward a declaration of war—he severed diplomatic ties on February 3. He was making good on a pledge made after the March 1916 sinking of a French passenger vessel, the *Sussex*, in the English Channel. At that time, he had warned the Germans that he would cut diplomatic ties unless they stopped attacking all passenger ships and allowed the crews of enemy vessels to get off safely before sinking them.

Wilson's action left Whitlock and the CRB in a very precarious position, trapped behind German lines, still as neutrals but no longer with official diplomatic protection.

At the same time, Hoover was in America, primarily to secure a $150 million loan from American banks that would be guaranteed by the British, French, and Belgian governments. All had gone well with the negotiations, and on January 31, 1917, he had even met with President Wilson, who had "expressed his great interest in our work and his good wishes on the success of our loan."

Once Wilson severed diplomatic ties, however, the loan was suspended and never reinstituted. More importantly, Hoover knew that Germany's decision to unleash its U-boats and establish a naval war zone would probably have a devasting impact on relief shipping. He was painfully aware that during the year before—even without such a brutal strategy in place and despite safe-conduct passes and pronounced CRB vessel signage—eleven ships of the CRB had been damaged or sunk by torpedoes or mines. This represented one-fifth of the CRB's fifty- to sixty-vessel fleet.

As Hoover had suspected, the immediate effects of the Germans' actions were quick and crippling to relief shipping:

- Shipping owned by neutral countries (which made up a large portion of CRB vessels) pulled out of CRB operations and sat in safe harbors to see what would happen.
- Of seventeen CRB vessels at sea, two were sunk by U-boats, two made it to Rotterdam, and thirteen ended up stuck in English ports.
- Hoover ordered an immediate stop to all CRB buying, loading, and shipping relief supplies until safe passage could be secured for all CRB ships.

Compounding the CRB problems were two facts: One, Hoover was trapped in America because all passenger services were halted across the Atlantic. "I could not reach Europe, which I urgently needed to do."

Two, Hoover was at the mercy of a communications system that was breaking down more and more. If Hoover wanted to contact Brussels, in many cases that meant first sending a cable to London, which then relayed it via cable to Rotterdam, which then sent the message by courier service through the border into Belgium. Censors between each leg could slow down a message while the Germans could—and did—close the border on a whim or hold up any cables they wanted to. Even in the best of scenarios, a message could take days to reach its destination and by then be long out of touch with how events had changed in the meantime.

Like a field general separated from the battlefield and his commanders, Hoover struggled to maintain an understanding of what was happening in London, Rotterdam, and Belgium so he could send critical instructions that were relevant and useful.

Initially, Hoover quickly sent a message to Brussels CRB Director Warren Gregory requesting a count of the quantity of food stocks on hand and instructing the delegates to stay at their posts for as long as possible. He cabled London Director William Poland to consult with the relief's patron ministers in London (Page and Merry del Val) and with the British Foreign Office, then send any "conclusions reached."

The Chief also maintained strong contact with all those he knew in the US government to ensure he was consulted about any relief-related decisions and communications. Those people, in return, kept in close communication with Hoover because he was the expert on relief, and the government wanted to somehow continue the program even though the move toward war was escalating.

On February 3, Hoover showed how strong those connections were when he was able to arrange for a cable from US Secretary of State Lansing to Ambassador Page that, according to Hoover, gave "the Secretary's view and my view at that moment and my instructions to our staff." The cable carried a clear and powerful message that Page should "express to the British Government the strong feeling of this country and of the Government that the relief of the Belgian and occupied French population must in any event continue, for this country will wish to show no less interest in this great work of humanity than has been shown during the last two years by the British and French Governments, [even] should it become impossible for the Americans to remain in Belgium and in control."

It also stated that Hoover felt it would be best, if necessary, that the Dutch take over the CRB's duties. (This cut out completely the Spanish and Villalobar, who very much wanted to take over for the Americans. Such a replacement plan had been developed by Hoover years before, in May 1915, during the crisis created by the sinking of the *Lusitania*.) The cable then included direct instructions from Hoover to Poland and Kellogg that began: "Think it extremely desirable for all members in Belgium to remain at their posts even after the departure of diplomatic and consular staff, if Germans will guarantee their freedom to depart if situation becomes entirely untenable."

In a few days, Hoover was informed that food stocks in Belgium totaled 227,000 tons of grain, 9,000 tons of meats and fats, and 12 tons of sundries, while Rotterdam was holding 64,000 tons of supplies, and northern France had warehoused 3,000 tons of grain, 8,200 tons of meats and fats, and 5,000 tons of sundries. That meant the CRB and the CN had enough supplies to continue operations for sixty days, which, it was hoped, would get the relief through the immediate crisis.

Hoover had four major issues to resolve simultaneously:

1. Get the British to drop the requirement that all CRB ships had to stop at British ports for inspection.
2. Get the Germans to assure the safety of all properly marked CRB ships.
3. Get the CRB ships in British ports safely to Rotterdam.
4. Find a way to continue the relief with or without American delegates.

With US diplomatic ties cut and Hoover trapped in America, he had to rely on others for much of the negotiations with the Germans. He turned to one of his least favorite people, Villalobar, and asked him to take up the issues with the Germans. The Spanish minister quickly agreed and headed for Berlin. Hoover also maintained contact with Whitlock in hopes the minister could help as well, despite the severed diplomatic relations and Whitlock's personality that Hoover felt "shrank from the rough stuff of dealing with the Germans."

In a few weeks, after confusing and sometimes contradictory communications, the problems began to be resolved. While the ships stuck in British ports had to sell their cargoes where they were, the British did agree to let ships be inspected in other British ports, such as Halifax, rather than in the British Isles. And the Germans did agree to a new safe route for CRB ships.

Overall, the result was that relief could continue. On February 24, Hoover instructed CRB ships in America to begin sailing again for Rotterdam. Sadly, on March 8, a German U-boat sunk another CRB ship, the *Storstad*, which resulted in the loss of two crew members. It was only on March 13 that the Germans officially issued orders to their submarine commanders regarding the CRB and the new route. The loss of CRB ships would become an all-too-frequent event in the coming months.

Out of the four major problems Hoover faced in early February, the last one still remained—find a way to continue the relief with or without American delegates if America entered the war.

CONFUSION IN BELGIUM

With America and Germany officially not speaking, any communications between the two countries had to formally go through intermediaries, such as representatives from neutral nations (such as Holland and Spain). When it came to CRB-related matters, communications between the two countries were handled primarily through the CRB's Spanish patron ministers—Merry del Val in London and Villalobar in Brussels—and, at times, those communications could have great difficulty getting in and out of Belgium.

During the next few weeks in Brussels, discussions raged back and forth—principally among and between Whitlock, von der Lancken, Villalobar, and the American CRB principals, Gregory and Kellogg (who went back and forth from Brussels to Rotterdam). Francqui, for the most part, stood anxiously in the wings, at times consulting, demanding, and pleading with the various diplomatic principals in the hope that relief would somehow continue.

Making matters far worse was the fact that communications with Washington and with the CRB London office were spotty in frequency and completeness, and in some cases they were contradictory.

Because it was still unclear how America could sever diplomatic ties with Germany and still maintain support for the CRB, positions shifted nearly daily: Should Whitlock take down the US flag at the legation and remove it from his car? (He did both immediately without being ordered to do so.) Would the State Department change its mind again and order Whitlock home? If Whitlock and the CRB delegates did stay, in what capacity would the Germans allow it?

Compounding the issue—and surprising most—von Bissing announced that the relief could continue but with only five or six delegates; all other delegates had to leave. When the news reached Ambassador Page in London and Hoover in America, each reacted differently, causing a dizzying array of responses, replies, and reactions that created days of utter confusion. The most notable included:

1. Page immediately cabled the State Department proposing the US government officially and publicly announce the immediate withdrawal of the CRB and all its delegates.
2. Sensing von Bissing was acting on his own, Hoover requested the Spanish ask the Berlin German government if that was what it truly wanted.
3. Hoover sent a message to Brussels instructing the Americans to privately threaten a complete pullout, sensing von Bissing would back down.

4. The American press got wind of Page's cable to the State Department and confronted Hoover before he had heard from the Spanish; he had to confirm his pullout order.
5. That news caused the British and French governments to publicly blame the Germans for the end of relief.
6. The Spanish quietly confirmed to Hoover that von Bissing was acting on his own and that the Berlin government did not want the CRB to leave.
7. Once Hoover knew that, he sent word to Brussels for all delegates to stay at their posts.

While Hoover's initial pullout instruction might have sounded like what Page had proposed, it was totally different. Page wanted a very public withdrawal; Hoover wanted only to privately bluff von Bissing.

By the end of February 1917, the situation was settling down a bit. It was decided that the CRB delegates in Belgium and northern France would ultimately leave, and negotiations were beginning to determine who would replace them (see chapter 18 for details). Whitlock and the US Legation staff would stay on and leave with the last of the CRB delegates.

Suddenly, however, the game changed completely.

THE ZIMMERMANN TELEGRAM

Because of the poor and sporadic communications with the outside world, it was a few days into March before Whitlock heard the monumental news of what later would become known in America as the Zimmermann Telegram.

Sent on January 16, the secret telegram was decoded by the British soon after and made public by the American government on February 28. The message was from German foreign secretary Arthur Zimmermann to the German ambassador to Mexico. Sent before the Germans had announced the restarting of unrestricted submarine warfare, it was an incredibly audacious proposal. The telegram read:

We intend to begin on the first of February unrestricted submarine warfare. We shall endeavor in spite of this to keep the United States of America neutral. In the event of this not succeeding, we make Mexico a proposal of alliance on the following basis: make war together, make peace together, generous financial support and an understanding on our part that Mexico is to reconquer the lost territory in Texas, New Mexico, and Arizona. The settlement in detail is left to you. You will inform the President [of Mexico] of the above most secretly as soon as the outbreak of war with the United States of America is certain and add the suggestion that he should, on his own initiative, invite Japan to immediate adherence and at the same time mediate between Japan and ourselves. Please call the President's attention to the fact that the ruthless employment of our submarines now offers the prospect of compelling England in a few months to make peace.

Signed, Zimmermann

The American public was outraged. Whitlock wrote later that he was told, "The country is aflame, all parties standing solidly by the President, even [peace advocate, William Jennings] Bryan, ready for war!"

The feeling was different in Belgium. Whitlock recorded, "Everybody laughing at the frightful blunder the Germans made in proposing to Mexico to become an ally."

By this time, most of the international diplomats in Brussels agreed that war between America and Germany was inevitable. Once again there were countless meetings, spotty communications, contradictory instructions, and fearful uncertainty.

Back in Washington, decisions had still not been made regarding whether the American CRB delegates were going and who would replace them.

Whitlock, after recommending that men of other nationalities immediately begin replacing the Americans, was losing his patience and blaming the situation more and more on Hoover. On March 13, he wrote, "I gave this advice [of replacing the Americans immediately with other neutrals] as strongly as I knew how to state it. Very well. I have done my duty, and the Department has again allowed itself to be dominated by Hoover. . . . Hoover, though three thousand miles away, thinks he

Figure 17.2. Brand Whitlock was minister of the US Legation in Brussels and had to navigate the confusing last days of Americans in Belgium after America entered the war.

Public domain; Robert Arrowsmith papers, Hoover Institution Archives, Stanford University, Stanford, California.

knows more than Gregory, or Kellogg, or I, or any one who is here, and seems able to impose his brutal will on the [State] Department!"

Whitlock would have been happy to hear that on the day he wrote that journal entry, Hoover had sailed from America, ending what Whitlock considered to be Hoover's in-person stranglehold on the State Department. (It would take Hoover longer than usual to reach London because the only passage he could secure was on an old freighter bound for Cádiz, Spain.)

Outside Belgium, events were transpiring that would move America closer to war. By the last weeks of March, four more American merchant ships had been sunk by the Germans, pushing Wilson closer to war. On March 23, at the instructions of the president, the State Department ordered the withdrawal of all the Americans from Belgium and northern France.

The message reached Belgium on March 25, via Villalobar, who brought it to Whitlock. Gregory was also at the legation as the dispatch, which had been in Spanish, was translated and read. President Wilson instructed Whitlock "to leave Belgium immediately accompanied by the personnel of the Legation, by the American consular officers and by the American members of the Commission for Relief in Belgium."

The direct, explicit instructions were a "distinct relief" to both Whitlock and Gregory. Gregory said he would immediately send the Spanish and Dutch delegates he had met earlier to the provinces and recall all the Americans to Brussels (he had recalled the delegates in northern French much earlier).

FINAL FAREWELLS

The Germans agreed to give all the Americans—legation staff and CRB delegates—safe conduct passes out of Belgium. On the evening of March 29, seven delegates who had received passes earlier left Brussels on a train heading for Switzerland. The rest of the Americans were scheduled to depart on April 2 on a train quickly dubbed the American Special.

The next few days were filled with packing and farewells, both personal and official. On Saturday morning, March 31, Francqui and the CN held a *grand déjeuner*, or great breakfast, at the Taverne Royale for the departing CRB delegates. There was an abundance of food, drink, and toasts and the putting aside of petty infighting to celebrate what the two great organizations had achieved in a time of war. Francqui made what Whitlock reported was a "touching speech," after which the US minister returned the favor.

Whitlock—who had initially come to the quiet post of Belgium simply to write novels but who had had to face the toughest of diplomatic and humanitarian challenges—took a last look at the city he had come to love. The frigid temperatures and snow had given way to early spring rains and "pale, melancholy days." The entire city seemed to have changed. "The shops were closed, the people were in rags, the lines at the soup kitchens trailed their squalid miseries farther and farther down the street; the doors of the *ouvroirs,* those posts of charity where sewing was given out, were besieged by throngs of pale and patient women."

Brussels had been muted and muzzled for more than two years by the German occupation. In the last days of March, the city became even quieter and more morose as it mourned the upcoming departure of the CRB and the US Legation.

In contrast, the youthful delegates were whirlwinds of activity as they tried to finish up any outstanding business and say their farewells to Belgian friends and co-workers. They knew the clock was ticking, and they were determined to do as much as possible before showing up at the train station.

Milton Brown's activities reflected the frantic nature of their last days. On Sunday, April 1, the day before the train's departure, he worked at the office until 6:30 p.m. He then rushed home for a quick break before returning and working from 9:30 p.m. until 2:30 a.m. Monday. He once again raced home, this time to pack, which he had not even started. By 6 a.m., he had finished packing and grabbed a quick forty-five-minute nap before hurrying back to the office. Before leaving the house for the last time, he left instructions with one of the servants to get his bags to the train station as soon as possible.

That morning at the office, Brown received what he had been longing to get for months—a purchase order from the CN for clothing materials that totaled a staggering 25 million francs. His plan was to take that order, go to London, and then prepare a report for the British that would get them to accept and place the order.

For the American delegate, that last day, April 2, "was perfectly frightful with work—one long strain of nerves and energy up to the very last minute to finish my work. We had been told to leave the office at 4:30 in the afternoon, at twenty-five minutes to five I finished dictating my last letter. I rushed upstairs to say goodbye to the stenographers and clerks; all the Americans had left; it was a gloomy place! I went down again and signed my last letters. In saying goodbye to my three stenographers tears were in the eyes of each of them and one of them broke down completely."

It was a highly emotional moment, but Brown had been through "so much work and nervous strain during those last few days that my nerves were taut to the point where they could not give way." He wouldn't dare let himself feel what he knew was inside.

Whitlock's last day was a bit different. He received a spontaneous invitation to lunch with Baron von Bissing at the German's residence outside of Brussels. The old Prussian officer had been ill and had just recently returned from a convalescent leave. Whitlock hurried out to see him, had a quick lunch, and said farewell to the man who had created so much havoc and misery in the life of Belgium and the CRB. It would be the last time Whitlock would ever see him. Within a few days, von Bissing would resign as governor general and would die on April 18, 1917, at the age of seventy-three. He would be replaced by Ludwig von Falkenhausen.

Whitlock sped back to the city to attend a major farewell luncheon hosted by the burgomaster of Brussels, Baron Charles Lemonnier, before hurrying off to the legation. In the late afternoon, Villalobar came to take the Whitlocks in his motorcar to the Gare du Nord train station. Following close behind were various vehicles carrying the Whitlocks' fifteen trunks, which were surpassed only by the twenty trunks of legation secretary Ruddock, his wife, and their two children. Also part of the legation staff's luggage were two huge diplomatic pouches that contained the legation's complete records and the code for encrypted communications.

The Place Rogier, the square at the front of the train station, was packed with a huge crowd that flowed into the station and filled it to capacity, despite a German proclamation prohibiting any demonstrations regarding the American departure.

Partially out of respect and partially because of the fear of German reaction to any outbursts or public displays, which had been outlawed, the large crowd was silent. Whitlock and the others got out of their cars and made their way through the crowd to the station as men pulled off their hats and many women cried.

Inside, with German guards and officers watching the proceedings, there was little in the way of emotional outbursts. According to Whitlock, approximately ninety people boarded the special train, including twenty legation staff, fifteen from the US consuls who had been stationed across Belgium, eighteen members of the Chinese legation, approximately forty members of the CRB, and a few accompanying German officers.

Staying behind with the approval of the German civil government were Prentiss Gray (along with his wife and child), who had volunteered to aid the transition to Dutch and Spanish delegates; six American delegates who had to be "quarantined" in Brussels for a few weeks because they had been recently close to the front (Charles H. Carstairs, James Dangerfield Jr., Maurice Pate, Carlos H. Stone, Francis Wickes, and Julius Van Hee); and three American accountants/auditors who had been serving in Brussels (Francis D. Neville, Oliver W. De Gruchy, and James A. St. Amour—the three accountants were never considered members of the CRB, despite their diligent work side by side with the CRB men; they should have been).

When the American Special pulled out of the station, Brown stood shoulder to shoulder with his fellow delegates looking out the windows. "I shall never, never forget the sight as the train began to pull out," he wrote later to his fiancée, Erica Bunge. "Nor shall I ever forget the feeling of utter despair that rushed through me as I realized that we were actually leaving Belgium. I stood it until, passing a side street a half kilometer or so out from the station I saw a street crowd massed against the fence to see us pass, their hats and handkerchiefs waving frantically. That last real view of the Belgians for whom we had been giving the little we could to help, that final farewell was too much and I broke down and sobbed like a child; and two men beside me did the same. I felt as though my heart were breaking—to be going out like that and leaving you and your countrymen to God-knows-what! I think it was the bitterest moment of my life."

Brown would have felt even worse if he knew how the not-yet-reported food imports had decreased dramatically in recent months. For Belgium the monthly imports, which had totaled an acceptable 64,873 tons in December 1916 and 60,794 tons in January 1917, had plummeted to less than half that, to 29,502 tons in February and 27,651 tons in March. For northern France, the statistics were just as bad: December and January had seen respectable tonnages of 34,115 and 27,803 tons, but February and March were less than half that, at 11,246 and 14,548 tons.

The humanitarian relief was in dire straits just as the Americans were leaving Belgium and northern France.

Negotiations in Brussels, Berlin, London, and Washington led to the belligerents agreeing that the Americans under Hoover's direction could continue relief efforts outside of Belgium (financing, purchasing, and shipping). The CRB offices in New York, London, and Rotterdam would remain and function as they always had.

Hoover, who had answered President Wilson's request and returned to America to become the director of the US Food Administration to organize the country's food resources, retained the title of CRB chairman but gave London director William Poland the new title of director for Europe. Poland took on the everyday supervision of the Commission that Hoover had previously done.

As for the Brussels CRB office, that was another matter. It was decided that when Gray and the other Americans left, Belgians would take their place and the CRB director would be Fernand Baetens. While Baetens had run the shipping department, he had become much more than that. Kittredge noted that Baetens "had been far more than shipping director; he had been the esteemed and indispensable adviser of all the American directors of the Commission." Two other non-Americans would be critical to the Brussels office: Rene Jensen, who was a Dane and had served as a CRB courier since early 1915, was the office's new secretary; Belgian Armand Dulait, who had run the automobile department since its inception, would remain so. Rounding out the office personnel were numerous Belgian clerks, stenographers, and assistants.

On April 23, Gray sent a detailed letter explaining the reorganization and Baetens's promotion. The letter went to the three primary people of relief in Brussels—Francqui, Villalobar, and the Dutch minister, van Vollenhoven. They quickly responded with their enthusiastic approval and once again thanked the Americans of the CRB for what they had done.

By May 1, 1917, the situation had settled into relative calm. Seven Dutch and five Spanish delegates were in place and more would arrive in the coming weeks. The executive decisions regarding the new delegates would be shared by a joint venture of the Spanish and Dutch named the Comité Hispano-Hollandais. Kittredge wrote, "Delegates had gone to the districts of Northern France and the period of transition from the old regime, that of the Commission for Relief in Belgium, to the new, that of the Comité Hispano-Hollandais, was over."

That day, Prentiss Gray, his family, and the last of the Americans left Brussels on a train bound for Switzerland. Gray's last note on the trip was one of relief. "And so we have come to Switzerland where we can breathe free air, and where people smile."

Tracy Kittredge, the author of the unofficial history of the CRB, ended a section he termed "the final parting" by writing, "So came to an end the American occupation of Belgium. The romance and uniqueness of the experiences of the delegates cannot be adequately portrayed here. In the history of the world no group of men had probably ever held a similar position. They had served the people of Belgium loyally and well and had succeeded in mitigating the harshness of the German regime. Now that they were no longer neutral they turned their work over to the new delegates of Dutch and Spanish nationality and withdrew with the consciousness of having lived up to their obligations—and with the knowledge that though they had left the scene of their endeavours, their work would be continued, and that the American participation in the relief would still go on outside Belgium. Some of the delegates went into the London, Rotterdam and New York offices and thus remained in the service of the Commission. These offices continued throughout 1917 and 1918 to keep the stream of supplies flowing into Belgium in the face of ever increasing difficulties."

Milton Brown summed up many of the delegates' feelings about their CRB experience when he wrote that it was "the greatest thing that ever has, or ever can, come into my life and I am very, very glad that this wonderful privilege has been mine." He explained to Erica Bunge—and told to Hoover on April 21, 1917—that the year he spent as a CRB delegate in Belgium was a "tremendous privilege rather than an experience—a privilege of doing something for others, of working hard uncommercially, of giving something for which we were not paid in money; a privilege I never hope to have duplicated."

Epilogue

AMERICA'S ENTRY INTO THE WAR

For more than two and a half years, President Wilson had kept America out of war, believing neutrality was the best path to take. Generally, American sentiment had initially been with the president. Public opinion began shifting toward war, however, after major events, including German "atrocities" (real and alleged) during the invasion of Belgium and France (1914); the sinking of the *Lusitania* and the attack on the *Sussex* (1915 and 1916, respectively); America's selling of war supplies to the Allies; the Germans' reinstitution of unrestricted submarine warfare (February 1, 1917); and the release of the Zimmermann Telegram (February 28, 1917).

Additionally, America's shift toward war was inadvertently aided by the Commission for Relief in Belgium.

Hoover's firm belief that public opinion was critical to the survival of the CRB led him and the CRB to provide newspapers and magazines with a constant stream of news about the relief efforts in Belgium and northern France. The resulting nearly continuous press coverage kept the dual stories of civilian suffering and the Germans' harsh occupation in the minds of many Americans.

Hoover also understood that a fully engaged public was best in supporting a cause. To convert Americans from mere readers of relief to active participants, he had created two pathways. The first was periodic national and international calls for donations—money, foodstuffs, and clothes. The second path was to establish US state and local CRB committees that actively engaged communities in their own backyards. Hoover knew that a person who gave to a cause and/or worked for that cause would naturally follow its progress closely.

By the very nature of the relief coverage and how it changed over time—reflecting greater civilian suffering and a harsher German regime—"neutral" Americans who were fully engaged in the topic of food relief couldn't help but be pulled away from strict neutrality.

It's also quite probable that the horrific deportation of Belgian and northern French civilians might not have been so widely exposed and reported if the CRB delegates had not been actively engaged in the occupied territories and had not witnessed the "slave raids." Certainly, knowledge of general civilian suffering—which the Germans actively worked to suppress from the world—would not have filtered out of Belgium and northern France as much as it did. Numerous magazine articles by delegates (some approved by Hoover, others not) and E. E. Hunt's 1916 book, *War Bread*, did their small part in swaying public opinion toward the Allied side.

Even with such coverage, Americans were still divided for years, as simply illustrated by two song titles that were popular in 1915 and 1916, respectively: "I Didn't Raise My Boy to Be a Soldier" and "You'd Better Raise Your Boy to Be a Soldier."

Long before America entered the war, many citizens were already thinking the country's entry was inevitable. Beginning in 1915, a preparedness movement, led by prominent Americans such as former president Teddy Roosevelt, had been growing, especially after the sinking of the *Lusitania*. The movement began to fund and to operate privately run camps in Plattsburgh, New York, and in other locations. These camps trained young men in marching, shooting, and general military procedures. The goal was to ultimately provide a huge pool of potential wartime officers. Tens of thousands of American men enrolled in these "Plattsburgh camps."

When America finally did enter the war on April 6, 1917, many people around the world, including the Germans, did not think the United States could mobilize fast enough to have a significant impact on the war before German U-boats forced the Allies to the peace table.

America surprised everyone, organizing faster than most would have guessed. Everything went into high gear, from a military draft to boot camps to the manufacturing of war materiel to the preservation of homeland food in the Hoover-directed US Food Administration.

The American Expeditionary Forces (AEF) were established on July 5, 1917, in France under the command of General John J. "Black Jack" Pershing. American forces fought alongside the British, French, Canadian, and Australian armies on the Western Front. The most notable campaigns in which Americans fought included the Aisne campaign at the July 18, 1918, Battle of Chateau-Thierry; the Battle of Belleau Wood in the summer of 1918; and the Battle of Saint-Mihiel and the Meuse-Argonne Offensive toward the end of 1918.

The Great War—also known as the "war to end all wars" from an expression coined by British writer H. G. Wells—concluded when the guns finally fell silent on the eleventh hour of the eleventh day of the eleventh month of 1918. Estimates vary, but the total casualty count from all sides is that there were approximately nine million soldiers killed and twenty-one million wounded. Civilian deaths during the war and in its immediate aftermath likely exceeded ten million. American casualties were approximately 320,000, of which 53,000 died in battle. An additional 204,000 were wounded.

No accurate death toll was ever made of how many Belgians and northern French civilians died behind German lines during the war.

FOOD RELIEF CONTINUES

When Prentiss Gray, his family, and the remaining American delegates took a train out of Belgium on May 1, 1917, three major food-relief problems still remained—securing ships for the CRB, getting the Germans to guarantee the 1917 harvest would go to the Belgians and northern French, and financing.

Regarding shipping, by May the CRB was able to ship approximately sixty thousand tons of foodstuffs a month but needed ships to handle an additional forty thousand tons. Even with the renewed unrestricted German U-boat campaign, available worldwide shipping from neutral countries was still substantial. According to Hoover, besides the neutrals' own shipping needs and their charters to the Allies, there were approximately four million tons of shipping available for commercial use all over the world. The CRB needed only a fraction of that to fulfill its needs, but because of U-boats torpedoing CRB ships, "the neutrals avoided charters with us."

Hoover provided the answer. In his new position as US food administrator, he had problems at home—most notably a drought that had impacted the 1917 harvest and decreased food supplies—but was determined to put pressure on the neutrals to provide the small amount of shipping the CRB needed.

On May 26, 1917, Hoover wrote to Secretary of State Lansing about the problem. He proposed an idea: "It seems to me the time has arrived when we might consider some definite service from these . . . [neutrals] of a character which does not jeopardize their ships but which leads them into the path of a little humanity. . . . That we should say to them that they should undertake to provide the transport of 100,000 tons of foodstuffs for the Belgian Relief . . . and that unless they are prepared to enter upon this path of decent dealing we shall reserve the questions of the export of foodstuffs from this country to . . . [them] until further notice."

Hoover continued, "It seems to me that if this hint were given at the present moment it probably would be as effective as direct action under embargo legislation."

The "hint" seemed to be a downright threat: provide shipping, and we'll provide food; don't provide shipping, and we'll withhold food.

It wasn't long before Hoover followed through on the threat. "As soon as we received the embargo powers from the Congress, we halted the shipment of this food [to the neutrals]. As Food Administrator, I notified the neutrals that I was prepared to obtain export permits for them, provided that they delivered part of their accumulated food to Rotterdam for the Relief and provided also that they chartered us additional ships."

By August, with a bit of prompting and negotiating, the neutral countries of Norway, Sweden, and the Netherlands had agreed.

By 1918, however, another shipping crisis arose. On March 3, 1918, the new Russian Bolshevik government signed the Treaty of Brest-Litovsk with Germany and the other Central Powers, which ended its participation in World War I. That freed up German soldiers to join the Western Front. As a result, Germany staged multiple attacks on the Western Front from March to July. While those attacks were ultimately checked by the Allies, they did speed up the demand for shipping to carry huge amounts of war materiel and troops from America to the Allies.

Between that increased need for ships and the Germans' continued U-boat success at sinking or damaging transports, the CRB's ability to charter ships was severely cut. But the Allied increased requisition of neutral ships for its purposes actually worked to the advantage of the CRB. According to Hoover, the Allied requisition program "drove the neutrals to charter to the C.R.B. as a lesser of perils." That secured adequate shipping for the CRB through the remainder of the war.

Regarding the 1917 harvest, it took a bit of time to resolve, as each previous harvest negotiation had. In the end, the Dutch and Spanish, along with the CRB Brussels office director, Belgian Fernand Baetens, were able to secure a guarantee from the Germans regarding the Occupation Zone, and they were able to secure an agreement that was similar to the 1916 harvest agreement arranged by Dr. Vernon Kellogg and Major von Kessler for northern France. In 1918, Villalobar and his Dutch counterpart in Brussels were once again able to secure the same arrangement for the 1918 harvest.

Continued financing would be much more of a struggle since the British and French had hoped that America's entry into the war would decrease their financial commitments to the CRB. America and Hoover did step up. Hoover explained, "I obtained an allotment of American 'loans' to Belgium and France for the C.R.B. amounting to $75,000,000." But there was an important requirement: "By Congressional stipulation, all American loans had to be spent in the United States." Hoover was able to increase congressional appropriations in November 1917, but the spending stipulation remained.

That still left money needed to handle the CRB's sterling and franc expenditures outside the United States. With some prodding, the British and French continued their subsidies to cover those expenses but at a reduced rate.

When it came to operations within Belgium and northern France, from the founding of the new Spanish-Dutch committee through to the German surrender on November 11, 1918, the group did the best they could. The Dutch and Spanish committee "performed with devotion and skill the duties which devolved upon it in respect to belligerent guarantees and negotiations with the Germans," according to an early history of the CRB.

Outside of Belgium, the CRB continued as it always had with financing, purchasing, and shipping, with the only difference being that its chairman was in Washington, D.C. This was, in fact, fortuitous for the relief because "in the face of a world shortage of ships and food and the increasing demands growing out of America's military effort, there were repeated insistent suggestions that in order to save the cause of the Allies from disaster the program of relief should be curtailed. Thanks to Hoover's position and influence in the councils of the Allies and the American Government these suggestions were never carried out, and Belgian and French relief received equal priority with war requirements."

An added benefit of the relief organization—one Hoover never would have mentioned before America entered the war but was one he stated clearly in a later book—was behind-the-lines intelligence. In his book *An American Epic*, he wrote, "We had constant insight into what was going on in Belgium and Northern France from our staff in Belgium through our Rotterdam office. That information was of daily value to us in Washington because it revealed the increasing failure of German food and raw-materials supplies." Luckily for the Belgians and northern French, the Germans, Hoover continued, "held fairly well to their guarantees concerning the native food supplies and our imports."

Germany's honoring of its agreements did not lessen the fact that Hoover, and by extension the American government and military, was receiving important intelligence regarding Germany's ability to continue waging war.

After the war, Belgium and many other countries received massive food relief as part of the American Relief Administration (ARA) until internal conditions were stabilized (see this chapter's section on Herbert Hoover).

THE SITUATION IN BELGIUM AND NORTHERN FRANCE

With the American entry into the war, the civilians in occupied territories had a cause for celebration, but they also faced the possibility that relief might end altogether or continue in some abbreviated form. As the months progressed, those who were fed and clothed by the CRB and CN came to be painfully aware that relief was decreasing, as overall living conditions were getting worse.

The average daily caloric intake per capita for the Belgians and northern French was a meager 1,522, which was less than half the prewar normal. And for many, according to Hoover, that average fell far short because "those who did heavy work had to have a minimum of 2,500 calories a day or there would have been no economic life; thus the rations for others fell far below 1,500 calories." Additionally, the calorie average was "totally inadequate in fats and proteins."

In October 1917, Belgian King Albert wrote to President Wilson outlining what was happening to his people and asked for renewed help and support of the relief efforts. Alluding to the big impact the German U-boat campaign was having on food reaching his country, he stated, "Since several months the imports of foodstuffs have been inadequate. . . . The Belgian population is confronted not only with hardship and suffering but with actual famine, the death rate is steadily increasing. Infantile mortality is appalling. Tuberculosis is spreading and threatening the future of the race."

Prior to King Albert's plea, Francqui wrote to Hoover from Brussels on July 2, telling him, "Since your departure, the situation has grown increasingly worse. The winter [1916–1917] was exceptionally long and severe and exhausted our last reserves in indigenous products. In the spring, the production of indigenous foods of general consumption was very restricted; for this reason and also because of the diminution in the importations, the demand made by the well-to-do classes was so heavy that the prices far surpassed the resources of the rest of the population."

He outlined in detail the changes, stating that 45 percent of the people were currently living "exclusively on the food imported by the C.R.B." and that the soup kitchens had gone from serving 2,100,000 at the end of 1916 to feeding 2,687,000. An additional 30 percent of civilians lived "*almost* [Francqui's emphasis] exclusively on the imported foodstuffs, being still in a position to procure for themselves a small addition in the foodstuffs sold by the communal or intercommunal stores, or on the open market."

"The remainder," Francqui continued, "that is about 25%, live on their own produce; this is the case with farmers living on their farms (20%) or for a great part depending on purchases in the open market, these are the rich classes (5%)."

Such conditions, Francqui contended, had led to an increase in mortality, and "in certain comparative graphs, the curve of mortality rises on the same proportion as the curve of the importations descends!"

Figure 18.1. The destitute, who had little before the war, had practically nothing during the German occupation, and their ranks grew every day with others who could no longer pay for their food.

Public domain; Herbert Hoover Presidential Library Archives, West Branch, Iowa.

Medical reports were coming in from all parts of the country, Francqui wrote, that showed "the terrifying progress of morbidity; principally through tuberculosis and various diseases caused by mal-nutrition."

What this was doing to the general population was significant. The people were "beginning to lose the patience and proud stoicism which you at one time so much admired. They send us petitions, sometimes imploring, sometimes threatening. In between times, they give most disquieting demonstrations at the markets and before the foodshops. We are perhaps on the eve of more serious outbreaks."

A month later, on August 6, 1917, Francqui wrote again, using stronger language. "The situation is becoming more alarming. The last vital resources of the great majority of the population—reduced for over seven months to scarcely half a food ration capable of sustaining life—are on the eve of becoming exhausted. For many, life is nothing but slow death; now already many people are commencing to die of inanition.

"We look with terror," Francqui continued, "upon what the approaching winter will be if a sufficient ravitaillement is not assured, owing to lack of ships."

Hoover felt the Belgian's frustration but could not return the communication with encouraging words or explanations of how many CRB ships had been sunk with full cargo holds of food for fear it might provide a wartime advantage to the Germans. "The distracted Francqui could not know of the shortage of food faced by all of the Allied world or of the lack of transportation as a consequence of the unlimited submarine war. And I could not advise him of all this lest this revelation of trying times among the Allies fall into German hands."

By November and December of 1917, the CRB was able to get the minimum monthly needs to Rotterdam, but then things got worse again. Francqui's letters and the reports out of Belgium and northern France continued in their desperate tone through the early part of 1918.

Francqui informed Hoover in early April 1918 that the bread ration had been reduced from 330 grams to 250 grams. "This is all the more painful because this reduction of the ration had to be made at a period of the year when resources of native foodstuffs are at their lowest."

But when shipping became plentiful in mid-1918 and with the bountiful American harvest that year, Hoover wrote that "Francqui's anguish was soon to be relieved. With our greatly increased fleet and our abundant harvest, I was able, in July, to transmit cheer and assurance that ample supplies were at last assured."

As the war wound down in October 1918, a potential final crisis to relief efforts developed when the German Army began retreating back through northern France and southern Belgium. Hoover explained, "There now arose the problem of how to provision the population of Northern France and that of Southern Belgium behind the retreating Germans, since transport of supplies from Rotterdam was cut off."

William Poland, director of the CRB's London office, came up with a creative solution. He bought twenty million military rations from the British Army that were valued at approximately $4.5 million and distributed those to the civilians cut off from Rotterdam supplies.

And with that, Hoover wrote, "The Germans made speedy retreat under President Wilson's ultimatums, and the C.R.B.'s troubles with them were over."

THE FLEMISH–FRENCH ISSUE

When Baron von Bissing died on April 18, 1917, it had been less than a month since he had issued a bold *affiche* declaring the country would be divided into two administrations: the Flemish headquartered out of Brussels and the French from Namur. Baron von Falkenhausen was appointed to succeed von Bissing as governor general in Belgium and continued the effort to separate the country into two.

Shortly after von Bissing's *affiche* was posted, Belgian government officials across the country met secretly to discuss what could be done passively to resist the new edict. Cardinal Mercier, the spiritual conscience of the country, wrote that in the end it was unanimously agreed that only the "highest officials of the central administration should resign and that lower officials should be free either to resign or remain at their posts."

The German response was in typical rigid fashion so that it would adhere to the perception that it was following the law. Before the Germans could take direct action against those who had resigned, the Germans had to correct something that had been done two years before. At that time, the Germans had issued an order allowing Belgian functionaries to resign without repercussions, regardless of the reason. That meant that those in 1917 who had just resigned over the Flemish separatist issue were within their legal rights. So, on May 19, 1917, von Falkenhausen issued an order to revoke that promise. With the past reconciled with current German needs, the Germans immediately arrested all those who had resigned over the Flemish issue. Those who did not agree to return to work were shipped off to German prisons.

Cardinal Mercier protested those arrests in a strongly worded letter to von Falkenhausen on June 6, 1917. The missive defended the rights of the men to refuse to work under international law and The Hague Conventions. He ended with a declaration of the Belgian spirit: "I beg of you to hearken to the voice of those who know intimately the Belgian people and their history, when they affirm that no violence will ever triumph over their patriotism."

The new governor general replied by stating he refused to discuss with the cardinal any questions that were not religious in nature.

It would be only after the end of the war that Belgium would return to being ruled by one administrative, governing body.

CRB CLOTHING AND THE BELGIAN LACE INDUSTRY

Milton Brown labored in London for months. Finally, on August 6, 1917, he turned in his 190-page clothing report and a $12 million purchase order. Working with

CRB London director Poland, Brown presented it to the British Foreign Office. His "biggest ambition," as Brown described it, was completed.

In the covering memorandum to the Foreign Office, Brown was brutally honest about what the Germans were doing in Belgium. "The present situation is that unhappily we must admit very extensive seizures of goods within Belgium." That did not matter, as far as Brown was concerned, because "the fact remains, that the country suffered greatly last winter, is suffering now, and will suffer very much more severely in the future, until the end of the occupation, if large stocks of raw materials are not imported at once to be made up within the country."

Brown wanted the British to understand that the benefits of approving his huge clothing order were not only to provide Belgians and northern French with much-needed clothes. "It must be realized," he wrote, "that the benefits of this work are not only the provision of clothing for the destitute but that they include, as well, a very valuable employment for from 60,000 to 75,000 unemployed, the moral and economic results of which cannot be too highly appreciated."

He also acknowledged that the British had never known the details of the Belgian clothing system, which he was explaining for the first time in his report. "The very efficient system of control set up within Belgium to ensure such supplies reaching their proper destination has not been known." The Belgian system, Brown assured the British, "guarantees practically every single unit going to its proper destination."

Not long after submission, the report and purchase order were approved by the British. Hoover explained that Brown's report, along with a report by Belgian doctors on the need for children to have adequate clothing, was enough for the British. "These reports and our own urgings finally secured approval of the Foreign Office for one of the largest single textile orders in the world up to that time."

In the end, the statistics on the clothing department were impressive, as related by Hoover: "Of the 24,384 tons of clothing that we handled, 10,571 tons were gifts and 13,313 tons were purchased. Of this total, 15,870 tons went to Belgium and 6,639 tons to Northern France. After the Armistice, we sold 1,375 tons of second-hand clothing to the American Relief Administration for its use in other parts of Europe."

Regarding the lace industry, by the end of the war, a substantial amount of lace that had been produced with CRB-provided thread was warehoused. Such overstock was not left to waste, however. Hoover proudly reported, "Mrs. Hoover organized committees of American women in England and the United States who promoted the sales during and after the war. In the end, these indefatigable women sold all the lace, and the Belgian women's committee divided more than $1,000,000 net proceeds among the individual producers, each according to the value of her product."

HERBERT C. HOOVER

As director of the US Food Administration from August 10, 1917, until July 1, 1919, Hoover was America's "food czar" and instituted a voluntary program of food conservation that became known as "Hooverizing." Homemakers across America embraced the austerity measures to show support for the war and for the man known to many as the Great Humanitarian.

After the war, he led the American Relief Administration (ARA), which provided food and relief supplies to much of Central and Eastern Europe. The ARA had been formed on February 24, 1919, by an act of Congress and was funded by $100 million in federal funds and $100 million in donations. In the immediate aftermath of the war, the ARA provided more than four million tons of relief supplies to more than twenty countries, including Russia during its famine in 1921, when more than ten million people were fed daily. The ARA ended operations outside Russia in 1922 and inside Russia a year later. The ARA played a critical role in the postwar survival and rebounding of Europe and could be seen as the precursor of the Marshall Plan after World War II.

On the American political scene, Hoover was considered by many a progressive and went through a short-lived candidacy for president in 1920. When Republican Warren G. Harding won the 1920 presidential election, he appointed Hoover secretary of commerce. Hoover served in that position from 1921 to 1928.

In 1928, Hoover—having never held elective office—was elected president in a landslide over Democrat Al Smith. Considered by many to be the most qualified individual who had ever held that office, Hoover took numerous and varied steps, both legislatively and executively, to halt the progression of what would later become known as the Great Depression. Some of what he tried did mitigate the situation, but he would ultimately fail to turn what was an unstoppable tide that would not fully recede until America entered World War II.

After his presidency, he and his wife, Lou Henry Hoover, lived in northern California until 1940. In December 1940, they moved into New York City's Waldorf Astoria Towers, which was their home for the rest of their lives. After Lou's death in 1944, Hoover gave their California home to Stanford University, and it became the official residence of the university's president.

After World War II, on March 1, 1946, President Harry S. Truman established the Famine Emergency Committee to aid in the fight against worldwide famine. Hoover was named honorary chairman, with St. Louis banker Chester Davis named chairman.

When announcing the committee's formation during a radio broadcast, Truman stated, "It is my duty to join my voice with the voices of humanity everywhere in behalf of the starving millions of human beings all over the world. We have a high responsibility, as Americans, to go to their rescue. . . . We would not be Americans if we did not wish to share our comparative plenty with suffering people. I am sure I speak for every American when I say that the United States is determined to do everything in its power to relieve the famine of half the world."

In combination with the Department of Agriculture, the committee sponsored worldwide food missions that sent Hoover to thirty-eight countries around the world. Hoover met with heads of state and government officials to enlist and coordinate their help in a global approach to fighting famine. Traveling with Hoover on these missions were numerous people, including many from the CRB days: Hugh Gibson, Perrin Galpin, Maurice Pate, and William Hallam Tuck.

From Hoover's reports, other findings of the committee, and work by other governmental agencies, America ended up exporting millions of tons of food to Asia and Europe, depleting its own reserves but helping a starving world.

In 1947, Truman appointed Hoover to be chairman of the Commission on Organization of the Executive Branch of Government—unofficially known as the Hoover Commission—to recommend administrative changes to improve the efficiency of the federal government. The Commission provided Congress with 273 recommendations, and the result was the Reorganization Act of 1949, which was passed by Congress in June 1949.

In 1953, when Hoover was nearly eighty years old, he was once again appointed, this time by President Dwight D. Eisenhower, to chair the Second Hoover Commission. The Commission's final report was sent to Congress in 1955.

Another lasting impact Hoover had on the world came from the official financial wrap-up of the CRB in August 1919. Hoover explained in a speech delivered in Belgium in July 1958, "At that time [1919] we found ourselves with about $39,000,000 in a special fund built up from the residues of world charity and from our trading with other nations." Hoover stated that $5 million, which was the French side of the money, was given to various charities in northern France.

Hoover and Émile Francqui worked together to determine what to do with the remaining $34 million. A large part of it, according to Hoover, "replenished the endowments of the Belgian universities. And, in 1920, with . . . large sums remaining in the Belgian fund we established in Belgium the *Fondation Universitaire*, a center of academic and scientific cooperation, and in the United States the Belgian American Educational Foundation, to carry on intellectual exchanges between our two countries. We later established the Foundation Francqui. The C.R.B. and C.N. survivors still participate in the management of these foundations. These organizations have contributed greatly to the advancement of science, education and public welfare."

In 2020, the Belgian American Educational Foundation (BAEF) is the leading independent philanthropic organization in the support of exchanging university students, scientists, and scholars between the United States and Belgium. Headed since 1977 by Belgian (and Yale professor) Emile Boulpaep, the BAEF has provided more than three thousand Belgians and more than nine hundred Americans with the opportunity for a period of advanced study or research in the partner country.

Hoover would be proud of how the CRB's residue funds from 1919 have kept working through the generations. Hoover died on October 20, 1964, at the age of ninety.

Notes

ABBREVIATIONS

HIA Hoover Institution Archives, Stanford University, Stanford, California.
HHPLA Herbert Hoover Presidential Library Archives, West Branch, Iowa.
NARA National Archives and Records Administration, Washington, D.C., and College Park, MD.
RG 59 Record Group 59: General Records of the State Department.
RG 84 Record Group 84: Records of the Foreign Service Posts of the State Department.

Note: I use the first three words of a quote, a sentence, or a paragraph to identify what my attribution is referring to.

READER AIDS

xxv "His fine idealism": Herbert Hoover, *An American Epic, Introduction, The Relief of Belgium and Northern France, 1914–1930*, vol. 1 (Chicago: Henry Regnery Co., 1959), 46.

PREFACE

xxviii The statistics are: George I. Gay, *The Commission for Relief in Belgium: Statistical Review of Relief Operations: Five Years, November 1, 1914, to August 31, 1919, and to Final Liquidation* (Stanford, CA: Stanford University Press, n.d.), 2–5.

xxviii "He didn't want": John L. Simpson, "Activities in a Troubled World: War Relief, Banking, and Business," an interview conducted by Suzanne B. Riess, 1978, Regional Oral History Office, The Bancroft Library, University of California, Berkeley, California.

xxix "When this war": Ben Allen, "Feeding Seven Million Belgians: The Work of the American Commission for Relief," *The World's Work*, April 1915, Ben Allen papers, HIA.

CHAPTER 1: 1914, SETTING THE STAGE

1 "To understand Germany": Unnamed German officer in Arthur Bartlett Maurice, *Bottled Up in Belgium, The Last Delegate's Informal Story* (New York: Moffat, Yard & Co., 1917), 96.

4 That assumption was; Belgian nationalism and quotes in section not otherwise noted: Hugh Gibson, "German Rule in Belgium" speech, Gibson papers, box 73, HIA.

4 Reflective of this; "When and how"; "One Belgian story": Émile Cammaerts, *Through the Iron Bars (Two Years of German Occupation in Belgium)* (London: The Bodley Head, 1917), 65–66.

4 People per square mile and population densities: Tracy B. Kittredge, *The History of the Commission for Relief in Belgium, 1914–1917* (Unpublished, n.d.), 8.

4 "To the Belgian": Arthur Humphreys, four articles in the *London Times* later compiled into a forty-six-page pamphlet, *The Heart of Belgium.*

4 "Famine sweeps over": Robinson Smith, "Hoover—The Man in Action," Robinson Smith papers, HIA.

5 "The whole machinery"; quotes in section not otherwise noted: Kittredge, *History of CRB*, 10, 11, 17, 13, 34.

8 The Comité Central gave: Ibid., 12.

8 The reason was: Ibid., 35.

9 "his dress never": Robinson Smith, "Hoover," Robinson Smith papers, HIA.

10 "in a wholesale": John L. Simpson, "Activities in a Troubled World: War Relief, Banking, and Business," an interview conducted by Suzanne B. Riess, 1978, Regional Oral History Office, The Bancroft Library, University of California, Berkeley, California.

11 Hoover was instantly: George I. Gay and H. H. Fisher, *Public Relations of the Commission for Relief in Belgium: Documents*, 2 vols. (Stanford, CA: Stanford University of Press, 1929), vol. I, 3; Kittredge, *History of CRB*, 37.

11 "At this point": George H. Nash, *The Life of Herbert Hoover, The Humanitarian, 1914–1917* (New York: W. W. Norton and Co., 1988), 19.

11 "It was an": Ibid., 19.

11 "the idea of": Kittredge, *History of CRB*, 37–38.

11 "approved heartily of": Ibid., 38.

12 "let the fortune": Will Irwin, *Herbert Hoover, A Reminiscent Biography* (New York: The Century Co., 1928), 135.

12 Heineman offered vice chairman: Kittredge, *History of CRB*, 38.

13 "The greatest hope": Edward Eyre Hunt, *War Bread: A Personal Narrative of the War and Relief in Belgium* (New York: Holt and Co., 1916), 319–320.

13 "a comprehensive scheme": *New York Times*, Oct. 18, 1914; Kittredge, *History of CRB*, 40–41.

13 Brussels food relief; expansion of program: Kittredge, *History of CRB*, 43.

13 On October 15: Nash, *The Life of Herbert Hoover*, 23.

14 "What! That man": Joe Green, "Some Portraits: Emile Francqui," Feb. 15, 1917, Green papers, Princeton Mudd Library.

14 Whitlock, who was: Brand Whitlock, *Belgium: A Personal Narrative*, 2 vols. (New York: D. Appleton and Co. 1919), vol. I, 398–399.

15 Details of early delegates: multiple sources including multiple CRB lists; Kittredge, *History of CRB*; Gay and Fisher, *Public Relations*, vols. I and II; delegate work list, Robert Arrowsmith papers, HIA.

16 One student, twenty-; Galpin as student organizer: Letters between Galpin and the CRB, starting Nov. 23, 1914, in the Executive Alphabetical Files, 1912–1942, Perrin Galpin papers, box 15, Galpin, HIA.
16 "You must forget": Ibid.

CHAPTER 2: FIRST CHALLENGES, FIRST STEPS

17 Within the first: Tracy B. Kittredge, *The History of the Commission for Relief in Belgium, 1914–1917* (Unpublished, n.d.), 100.
17 "The supreme test": Robinson Smith, "Hoover—The Man in Action," Robinson Smith papers, HIA.
17 "You will be": Brigadier General S. L. A. Marshall, *American Heritage History of World War I* (New York: American Heritage Publishing Co./Bonanza Books, 1982), 41.
18 "piratical state organized": George I. Gay and H. H. Fisher, *Public Relations of the Commission for Relief in Belgium: Documents*, vol. I (Stanford, CA: Stanford University Press), v (preface).
18 "The chief significance": Kittredge, *History of CRB*, 105.
19 "In carrying on": Ibid., 106.
20 "was an example": Tracy Kittredge, "Californians with Hoover in Europe," *The California Alumni Fortnightly*, part I, Kittredge papers, Box 7, HIA.
20 "a high conception": Ibid, part II.
21 "Starving Belgium was": Richard Norton Smith, *An Uncommon Man, The Triumph of Herbert Hoover* (New York: Simon and Schuster, 1984), 81.
21 "I employed myself": Letter from Hoover to Oscar T. Crosby, June 30, 1915, Gilchrist Stockton papers, HIA.
21 "the British posture": George H. Nash, *The Life of Herbert Hoover, The Humanitarian, 1914–1917* (New York, W. W. Norton and Co., 1988), 71.
22 "Kitchener had made": Allan Nevins, ed., *The Letters and Journal of Brand Whitlock*, 2 vols. (*The Letters* and *The Journal*) (New York: D. Appleton-Century Co., 1936); *The Letters*, letter to Rutger B. Jewett, April 9, 1914, 77.
22 Hoover and Asquith meeting: Nash, *The Life of Herbert Hoover*, 69.
22 "Hold this until": Nevins, *The Journal*, 77–78.
22 "You have America's"; "I will send": Ibid.
22 "You told me": Ibid.
23 The key to: Gay and Fisher, *Public Relations*, vol. I, doc. 119, 222.
24 The biggest hurdle: Ibid., 227–228.
24 "contribution of war": Brand Whitlock, *Belgium: A Personal Narrative*, vol. I (New York: D. Appleton and Co., 1919), 395–396.
24 "was to be"; remaining quotes in section: Kittredge, *History of CRB*, 110.
25 On January 13; quotes about Grey meeting: Ibid., 111–113.
26 "the question of ": Gay and Fisher, *Public Relations*, vol. I, doc. 129, 232–235.
26 "A routine appointment": Nash, *The Life of Herbert Hoover*, 84.
26 Hoover, not knowing; remaining quotes in section not otherwise noted: Gay and Fisher, *Public Relations*, vol. I, doc. 129, 232–235.
27 "Hoover scored the": Kittredge, *History of CRB*, 112.
27 "From this time": Ibid.
28 From the beginning: Kittredge, *History of CRB*, 56.

28 "He knew all": Herbert Hoover, *An American Epic, Introduction, The Relief of Belgium and Northern France, 1914–1930*, vol. 1 (Chicago: Henry Regnery Co., 1959), 46.
28 Percy was able: Kittredge, *History of CRB*, 56.
28 The number of: Ibid.
28 As the CRB: Ibid.
28 Procedures for each: Ibid., 57.
29 On board, each: Ibid.
29 "I told him": Hoover, *American Epic*, 130–131.

CHAPTER 3: HOOVER AND OTHER RELIEF EFFORTS

31 Branden Little's 120 relief committees and quotes; John Branden Little, *Band of Crusaders: American Humanitarians, the Great War, and the Remaking of the World*, PhD dissertation, University of California, Berkeley, Spring 2009, 105–107.
31 "All these efforts": Tracy B. Kittredge, *The History of the Commission for Relief in Belgium, 1914–1917* (Unpublished, n.d.), 61.
32 "During the first few": Ibid.
32 "few modest Belgians": Edward T. Devine, "Belgian Relief Efforts," *The American Review of Reviews*, vol. L, no. 6, Dec. 1914, 689–693.
32 de Forest in the committee: Ibid.
33 $50,000 sent to Page: *New York Times*, Oct. 23, 1914.
33 first grant of $100,000: The Rockefeller Foundation's history, on its website.
33 "give millions of dollars": "Plan Co-Operation in Belgian Relief," *New York Times*, Nov. 3, 1914.
33 All *Times* quotes on this story: Ibid.
34 "arranged to provide": "Rockefeller Pier for Relief Ships," *New York Times*, Nov. 9, 1914.
34 "In these arrangements": Kittredge, *History of CRB*, 62.
34 "War Relief Commission": "Rockefeller Pier for Relief Ships," *New York Times*, Nov. 9, 1914.
34 "The arrangements for": Ibid.
34 "the committee in": Devine, "Belgian Relief Efforts," 689–693.
34 "The impression prevailed": Kittredge, *History of CRB*, 62.
35 "To the embarrassment": Ibid.
35 $150,00 from CRB: "$300,000 Quick Help to Hungry Belgians," *New York Times*, Oct. 31, 1914.
35 "It's a fine idea": Kittredge, *History of CRB*, 62.
35 "We are asking": Ibid.
36 "arranged to have": Ibid.
36 "The Commission for": Ibid., 63.
36 "Mr. Hoover never": Robinson Smith, "Hoover—The Man in Action," Robinson Smith papers, HIA.
36 "The Commission for": Kittredge, *History of CRB*, 63.
37 "central committee": *Washington Post*, Nov. 12, 1914.
37 "Nobody it seemed": George H. Nash, *The Life of Herbert Hoover, The Humanitarian, 1914–1917* (New York: W. W. Norton and Co., 1988), 58.
37 died a quick death: Ibid., 58–59.

38 There was also: Kittredge, *History of CRB*, 57.
38 "Hoover informed Francqui": Nash, *The Life of Herbert Hoover*, 50.
39 "The New York": Kittredge, *History of CRB*, 64.
39 "the Commission would": Ibid.
39 "With the securing": Nash, *The Life of Herbert Hoover*, 62.
39 "I do not wonder": Hoover to Bates, Feb. 19, 1915, CRB Correspondence, box 2, HIA.
39 "You can always": Ibid.

CHAPTER 4: ROTTERDAM

42 two shipments: George I. Gay and H. H. Fisher, *Public Relations of the Commission for Relief in Belgium: Documents* (Stanford, CA: Stanford University Press, 1929), chapter II, First Measures, November 1914.
42 Hoover sent Millard: Vernon Kellogg, *Fighting Starvation in Belgium* (New York: Doubleday, Page and Co., 1918), 27; Gay and Fisher, *Public Relations*, chapter 11, 2.
42 Lucey details: Biographical sketch, *Mining and Oil Bulletin*, 7, July 1921.
42 temporary office setup: Tracy B. Kittredge, *The History of the Commission for Relief in Belgium, 1914–1917* (Unpublished, n.d.), 68.
42 two-day trip: "Distress in Belgium," British *The Morning Post*, Oct. 28, 1914.
43 150 safe-conduct: Kittredge, *History of CRB*, 70, 72.
43 Lucey and Shaler: Ibid., 68.
43 After Lucey and: Ibid., 69.
43 "neither definite information"; "Appeals, rumors": Gay and Fisher, *Public Relations*, chapter II, First Measures, November 1914.
43 Shaler car companions: British *Daily Telegraph*, Nov. 7, 1914, clip books, HHPLA.
43 "he brought no": Kittredge, *History of CRB*, 70.
44 The Dutch government: Ibid.; Britain's *Daily Citizen* newspaper, Nov. 14, 1914, clip books, HHPLA.
45 "Consigned to": British *Daily Citizen*, Nov. 14, 1914, clip books, HHPLA.
45 Members of canal trip: Ibid.; Kittredge, *History of CRB*, 70.
45 Belgium, like Holland; all canal details: Kittredge, *History of CRB*, 69–70; Karl Baedeker, *Baedeker's Belgium and Holland* (Leipzig, Germany: Karl Baedeker, 1910).
46 "As for the"; all quotes in section: Edward Eyre Hunt, *War Bread: A Personal Narrative of the War and Relief in Belgium* (New York: Holt and Co., 1916), 220–223.
48 Approximately three weeks: Kittredge, *History of CRB*, 73.
48 By the end: Ibid.
48 However, after the; following statistics: Kittredge, *History of CRB*, 235–236; Gay and Fisher, *Public Relations*, vol. I, 119–127.
48 As for the: Kittredge, *History of CRB*, 235–236; Gay and Fisher, *Public Relations*, vol. I, 119–127.

CHAPTER 5: LIFE IN GERMAN-OCCUPIED BELGIUM

49 Belgian atrocity stories: John Horne and Alan Kramer, *German Atrocities, 1914, A History of Denial* (New Haven, CT: Yale University Press, 2001).

50 "ring of steel": Britain's *Daily News & Ledger*, Dec. 7, 1914, clip books, HHPLA.
50 "The Flemings are": Edward Eyre Hunt, *War Bread: A Personal Narrative of the War and Relief in Belgium* (New York: Holt and Co., 1916), 337.
50 The Germans—and; "Among the German": a memorandum from von Bissing in *General von Bissing's Testament: A Study in German Ideals* (London: T. Fisher Unwin Ltd, n.d.).
51 Émile Cammaerts quotes in section: Cammaerts, *Through the Iron Bars (Two Years of German Occupation in Belgium)* (London: The Bodley Head. 1917), 50, 8–9.
51 "It takes quite": Earl Osborn journal, Jan. 27, 1916, Osborn and Dodge Family papers, Princeton Mudd Library.
53 After the border; von Bissing *affiche*: Commandant A. (Adrien) de Gerlache de Gomery, *Belgium in War Time*, translated from the French edition by Bernard Miall (New York: George H. Doran Co., 1915), 178–179.
53 All details, statistics, and quotes in section not otherwise noted: Roger Van den Bleeken, *Cappellen in den Grooten Oorlog* (*Cappellen in the Great War*) (Kapellen, Belgium: Heemkring Hoghescote, 2014); hereinafter: Van den Bleeken, *Cappellen.*
54 An idea to; "enthusiastically received by": Translation by Roger Van den Bleeken of the chapter by Jan Ingelbrecht, "Elektrische draadversperring te Putte," 213–232, in Van den Bleeken, *Capellen.*
56 "Belgium needed far"; all quotes in section: Hunt, *War Bread*, 296–298.
57 Four typhoid shots: Milton Brown letter to his mother, April 19, 1916, author's archives.
57 On April 1; Dr. Lucas report: Tracy B. Kittredge, *The History of the Commission for Relief in Belgium, 1914–1917* (Unpublished, n.d.), 292–296; Herbert Hoover, *An American Epic, Introduction, The Relief of Belgium and Northern France, 1914–1930*, vol. 1 (Chicago: Henry Regnery Co., 1959), 28–29.
58 "proud Paris of ": Hunt, *War Bread*, 164.
58 "one of the finest"; city description: Karl Baedeker, *Baedeker's Belgium and Holland* (Leipzig, Germany: Karl Baedeker, 1910), 89–144, 128.
59 By the winter: Hugh Gibson, "German Rule in Belgium" speech, Gibson papers, box 73, HIA.
59 "We were thus": Ibid.
59 "We began to"; "besieged the [German] Pass": Brand Whitlock, "Before the Storm," *Everybody's Magazine,* Feb. 1918.
60 Adding to the: Brand Whitlock, "Under the German Heel," *Everybody's Magazine*, issue #6, June 1918, Fifth installment.
60 "Resistance and disobedience": Gibson, "German Rule in Belgium" speech.
60 Quotes from von der Goltz's *affiche*: Hugh Gibson, *A Journal from Our Legation in Belgium* (New York: Doubleday, Page and Co., 1917), 188.
61 The impact of: Whitlock, "Under the German Heel."
61 "proudly turned their"; "rather than sip": Hunt, *War Bread*, 166.
61 "regarded as a": Gibson, *A Journal*, 241.
61 "since von Bissing's": Oscar E. Millard, *Underground News: The Complete Story of the Secret Newspaper that Made War History* (New York: Robert M. McBride and Co., 1938), 37.
62 This meant that: Hunt, *War Bread,* 37–38.
62 "The hum and" and Hunt's quotes on Antwerp: Ibid., 202, 203.
63 "as an outlet": Baedeker, *Belgium*, 169.
63 In the northern: Map of Antwerp, Baedeker, *Belgium*; Prentiss Gray, *Fifteen Months in Belgium: A CRB Diary* (edited and complied by son Sherman Gray, grandson Prentiss S.

Gray, and great-grandson Zachary S. Gray, Nov. 19, 2009; given to the author to use by Sherman and Prentiss Gray in Princeton, NJ, in 2013).

63 In early 1916; Gray's quotes and remaining information in section: Gray, *Fifteen Months*, 103–104, 99.

64 By May 1917; calorie details: Hoover, *America Epic*, 346–347.

CHAPTER 6: THE CRB DELEGATES

65 "What we were": Emil Holmann papers, folder 1, HIA.

65 They had more: Galpin to CRB, Nov. 29, 1914, Galpin papers, box 1, HIA.

65 The ten newly: Ibid.

66 "We propose to": Hoover to Galpin, Nov. 30, 1914, Galpin papers, box 1, HIA.

66 Each of the; "We had been": George F. Spaulding, "The CRB and the Chateau de Mariemont," (unpublished), in the Alan Hoover papers, box 8, topical files, HHPLA.

67 Nelson's entry into Belgium: John P. Nelson, ed. *Letters and Diaries of David T. Nelson, 1914–1919* (Decorah, IA: The Anundsen Publishing Co., 1996), 43–44.

68 All quotes in section: Tracy B. Kittredge, *The History of the Commission for Relief in Belgium, 1914–1917* (Unpublished, n.d.), 93.

70 Stratton letter to Hunt, dated Feb. 3, 1915: Gilchrist Stockton's papers, HIA.

71 All Hunt quotes in section: Edward Eyre Hunt, *War Bread: A Personal Narrative of the War and Relief in Belgium* (New York: Holt and Co., 1916), 243–252, 261.

73 All quotes in section: Kittredge, *History of CRB*, 196–197, 94, 96–97, 104.

75 The Americans were; all related quotes: Gibson to mother, Jan. 26, 1915, box 31, HIA; Hugh Gibson, speech "German Rule in Belgium," Gibson papers, box 73, HIA.

77 CRB passport: Herbert Hoover, *An American Epic, Introduction, The Relief of Belgium and Northern France, 1914–1930*, vol. 1 (Chicago: Henry Regnery Co., 1959), 26.

78 "We are badly"; "We want people": Hoover to Galpin, Nov. 24, 1914, Galpin papers, box 1, HIA.

78 At least six: The six recorded by Galpin as having gone into Belgium in the second wave of Oxford students but who are not listed on any official CRB lists are George B. Noble, Francis L. Patton, William H. Mechling, Clyde Eagleton, Alexander R. Wheeler, and Clarence A. Castle; Galpin to CRB London office, Dec. 4, 1914, Galpin papers, box 1, HIA.

78 "You know, this": John Simpson, oral history, Sept. 20, 1967, HHPLA.

78 "The requirements were": Ibid.

78 CRB membership lists: All lists made by official CRB sources have numerous errors and/or omissions; my list, which includes names and photos, can be found at www.jbmwriter.com/CRB-Delegates-Names-and-Photos.html.

78 "We don't need": Hoover cable to New York office, Nov. 22, 1916, John Simpson papers, box 317, HIA.

79 "I am full": Hoover to Gibson, Jan. 11, 1916, RG 84, correspondence, American Legation Brussels, 1916, vol. 181, file 848, Relief, NARA.

80 "She has done": Charlotte Kellogg, *Women of Belgium: Turning Tragedy to Triumph* (New York: Funk and Wagnalls Company, 1917), xvi.

80 "Everyone is crazy": Brown to mother, Sept. 25, 1916, author's archives.

81 "It gives me": NYC Office files, Box 323, folder 1, HIA.

81 "the most effective": Alexander Leitch, *A Princeton Companion* (Princeton, NJ: Princeton University Press, 1978).

CHAPTER 7: THE MECHANICS OF RELIEF

83 The importation goal: George I. Gay and H. H. Fisher, *Public Relations of the Commission for Relief in Belgium: Documents* (Stanford, CA: Stanford University Press, 1929), vol. I, doc. 20.

83 Wheat was the: The wheat process from ship to breadline consumer was detailed by Robinson Smith in a series of articles he wrote that were compiled into a document titled "The Feeding of Belgium," Maurice Pate collection, box 13, folder 11, Princeton Mudd Library.

84 "Two weeks ago"; "Three months ago"; all quotes by Smith in section: Smith, "The Feeding of Belgium," Princeton Mudd Library.

86 "Thefts by the"; "Lightermen were also": Joe Green, Dock Office, Green papers, Princeton Mudd Library.

87 The flour was; all details about bakers: Smith, "The Feeding of Belgium," Princeton Mudd Library.

88 CRB delegate Robinson; all Smith quotes: Ibid.

90 "At the Central": British *Morning Post*, Nov. 9, 1914, clip books, HHPLA.

90 "dismal rain": Brand Whitlock, *Belgium: A Personal Narrative* (New York: D. Appleton and Co., 1919), vol. 1: 402.

90 It was a bustle: British *Daily Graphic*, Nov. 9, 1914, clip books, HHPLA.

90 "They stood with": Whitlock, *Belgium*, vol. 1: 403.

91 Expansion of the Little Bees: Tracy B. Kittredge, *The History of the Commission for Relief in Belgium, 1914–1917* (Unpublished, n.d.), 16.

91 "German soldiers stood": Herbert Hoover, *The Memoirs of Herbert Hoover: Years of Adventure, 1874–1920* (New York: MacMillan and Co., 1951), 159.

91 "Relief means the"; all Smith quotes: Smith, "The Feeding of Belgium," Princeton Mudd Library.

CHAPTER 8: THE BELGIAN SIDE OF FOOD RELIEF

93 "should be impartially": Tracy B. Kittredge, *The History of the Commission for Relief in Belgium, 1914–1917* (Unpublished, n.d.), 77.

94 "enjoy entire": Ibid.

94 The CN itself: Edward Eyre Hunt, *War Bread: A Personal Narrative of the War and Relief in Belgium* (New York: Holt and Co, 1916), 348–349.

94 "main rival in": Francqui Foundation on its website.

94 "the iron man": John Hamill, *The Strange Career of Mr. Hoover under Two Flags* (New York: Faro, Inc., 1931), 316.

94 "a big-businessman": Hunt, *War Bread*, 272–273.

95 "extraordinarily low"; bread totals: Ibid., 280.

95 As for the; food totals: George I. Gay and H. H. Fisher, *Public Relations of the Commission for Relief in Belgium: Documents* (Stanford, CA: Stanford University Press, 1929), vol. I, 119, 20.

95 "The Commission": Kittredge, *History of CRB*, 77.
96 "this attitude of": Ibid., 86.
96 Francqui financial arrangements: Ibid., 75–76.
96 Each week a: Hunt, *War Bread*, 269–271; Robinson Smith papers, Article 7, HIA.
97 All quotes and details in section not otherwise noted: Kittredge, *History of CRB*, 78–79.
98 *Times* article interviewing two Germans: Kittredge, *History of CRB*, 82; *The New York Times Current History: The European War*, vol. 2 (New York: New York Times, 1917), 785, although this source says the article ran Nov. 6, 1914, but the dates of the responses to this article fit better with a Nov. 22 published date than a Nov. 6 published date.
98 "If America had": Kittredge, *History of CRB*, 82; *The New York Times Current History: The European War*, vol. 2: 785.
98 "If it is": Kittredge, *History of CRB*, 82.
98 "It seems that": Ibid.
99 Long before the; statistics: Milton Brown, *Clothing the Destitute*, author's archives.
99 To handle the: Ibid.
100 "turned to imports": Herbert Hoover, *An American Epic, Introduction, The Relief of Belgium and Northern France, 1914–1930*, vol. 1 (Chicago: Henry Regnery Co., 1959), 407.
100 "forwarded as fast": Brown, *Clothing the Destitute*, author's archives.
100 "Useful as these": Hoover, *American Epic*, 409.
100 "distributed under the": Gay and Fisher, *Public Relations*, vol. I, doc. 86, 160.
100 Emmanuel Janssen anti-American: Allan Nevins, ed., *The Letters and Journal of Brand Whitlock*, 2 vols. (*The Letters* and *The Journal*) (New York: D. Appleton-Century Co., 1936), *The Journal*, 262.
101 Four major components; all details and quotes in section: Brown, *Clothing the Destitute*, author's archives.
101 "pieces, yards and pairs"; hundreds of thousands: Charlotte Kellogg, *Women of Belgium: Turning Tragedy to Triumph* (New York: Funk and Wagnalls Co., 1917), 138.
102 "So efficient were": Hoover, *American Epic*, 408.
102 When the relief: Hunt, *War Bread*, 364.
102 For generations before; Approximately fifty thousand; (and some men): Hunt, *War Bread*, 364; Kellogg, *Women of Belgium*, 159.
103 A few years: Ibid., 158–159.
103 Its honorary president: Ibid., 17.
103 In early 1915: Hoover, *American Epic*, 410.
103 The simple, direct; Brown quotes: Milton Brown, "A Final Word to My Family," March 16, 1917, author's archives.
103 As for the; Each lace worker: Kellogg, *Women of Belgium*, 164, 160.
105 The Bunges during the invasion: Edouard Bunge, "What I Saw of the Bombardment and Surrender of Antwerp," Oct. 1914, unpublished document, author's archives.
105 After the city's: Erica Bunge's diary, Jan. 3, 1915, author's archives and oral history of the Bunge, Brown, and Miller families.
105 A plan for a dairy farm: Oral history and a large three-panel presentation that was awarded to Edward Bunge, Erica Bunge, George Born, and Hélène Born after the war for providing one million liters of milk to the children of Antwerp; Robert Withington, *In Occupied Belgium* (Boston: Cornhill Co., 1921), 34; Raymond Roelands, *Geschiedenis van Kasteeldomein "Oude Gracht" in Hoogboom* (Kapellen, Belgium: Culturele Heemkring Hobonia v.z.w., 2016); Roger Van den Bleeken, *Cappellen in*

den Grooten Oorlog (*Cappellen in the Great War*) (Kapellen, Belgium: Heemkring Hoghescote, 2014).

105 On Wednesday, March; remaining details in section: Van den Bleeken, *Cappellen*.

106 Erica was more: Author's family oral history.

CHAPTER 9: FOOD RELIEF IN NORTHERN FRANCE

109 Details and quotes from Gerard cable: George I. Gay and H. H. Fisher, *Public Relations of the Commission for Relief in Belgium: Documents*, 2 vols. (Stanford, CA: Stanford University Press, 1929), vol. I, doc. 263, 394–395.

109 For the previous: Gay and Fisher, *Public Relations*, vol. I, 393–394; Tracy B. Kittredge, *The History of the Commission for Relief in Belgium, 1914–1917* (Unpublished, n.d.), 136–137.

109 Francqui's objection to feeding Givet-Fumay: Kittredge, *History of CRB*, 137.

110 In December 1916: Ibid., asterisked footnote.

110 "We have had"; "make a substantial"; "we are already": Gay and Fisher, *Public Relations*, vol. I, 395–396.

110 By mid-February: Ibid., 397.

110 Gifford Pinchot well-known in France: Kittredge, *History of CRB*, 142.

110 On February 17; Hoover letter to Poincaré and related details and quotes: Gay and Fisher, *Public Relations*, vol. I, doc. 266, 397–399.

111 Hoover telegram to Pinchot and related details and quotes: Ibid., doc. 267, 399–400.

111 Pinchot memorandum and related details and quotes: Ibid., doc. 268, 400–401.

111 Hoover—probably frustrated: Ibid., 403.

112 "charitable institutions which"; "fiction": Ibid., doc. 271, 403.

112 "Major von Kessler": Kittredge, *History of CRB*, 158.

112 In dramatic and; "perched on the": Ibid., 141–142.

113 northern France statistics: Ibid., 154.

113 a minimum ration: Gay and Fisher, *Public Relations*, vol. I, doc. 287, 421–426.

113 Even with the: Ibid.

113 Details of the northern France organization: Ibid., 411–412.

113 Another major difference: Ibid.

115 A group photo; Another photo was: HHPLA, box 13, 1916: 26–50, 1917: 76–99.

116 The process to: Kittredge, *History of CRB*, 329.

116 "These [accompanying officers]": Allan Nevins, ed., *The Letters and Journal of Brand Whitlock*, 2 vols. (*The Letters* and *The Journal*) (New York: D. Appleton-Century Co., 1936), *The Journal*, 245.

117 "In general it": Kittredge, *History of CRB*, 152.

117 "nurses"; "my man Friday": told by a purposefully misnamed delegate to Madame Saint-Rene Taillandier in her book, *The Soul of the 'C.R.B.' A French View of the Hoover Relief Work* (New York: Charles Scribner's Sons, 1919), 145–146.

117 "we could have": Ibid.

117 These meetings became; "The nervous strain": Kittredge, *History of CRB*, 153.

117 Change in German officer name: Gay and Fisher, *Public Relations*, vol. I, doc. 315, 502.

118 The reality had: Joe Green, German "Belgeittsoffiziere" essay, Green Papers, Princeton, Mudd Library.

118 The changing role of officer and CRB delegate: Kittredge, *History of CRB*, 152.
118 "took very seriously": Ibid., 153.
118 This left the; "the [Brussels CRB]"; "supreme insult": Gay and Fisher, *Public Relations*, vol. I, doc. 315, 497–498.
118 "really did most": Green, German "Belgeittsoffiziere" essay, Green Papers, Princeton Mudd Library.
118 "Effort and accomplishment": Gay and Fisher, *Public Relations*, vol. I, doc. 315, 497–498.
119 "realized that American": Kittredge, *History of CRB*, 326.
119 "the most violent": Ibid.
119 "It's trench warfare": Gay and Fisher, *Public Relations*, vol. I, doc. 315, 502.
119 Nickname Pink: John L. Simpson, oral history, Sept. 20, 1967, HHPLA.
119 A 1913 graduate: Clare Torrey, oral history, author's archives.
119 FTC position: John L. Simpson papers, box 317, folder 9, HIA.
119 "the vistas of"; remaining quotes in section: Gay and Fisher, *Public Relations*, vol. I, doc. 315, 492–507.
122 With their great: Kittredge, *History of CRB*, 329.
123 "Many of the": Ibid.

CHAPTER 10: PRESSURES FROM VON BISSING

125 "Bissing's prime objective": Johan den Hertog, "The Commission for Relief in Belgium and the Political Diplomatic History of the First World War," *Diplomacy & Statescraft* 21, no. 4 (2010): 593–613. His source for this: "Bissing to Bethmann-Hollweg Letters & Journals of Whitlock Vol. 2, p. 165," but actually it's on page 173 and it is not that strongly stated.
125 During the first: George I. Gay and H. H. Fisher, *Public Relations of the Commission for Relief in Belgium: Documents*, 2 vols. (Stanford, CA: Stanford University Press, 1929), vol. I, 46–47.
125 "The Germans naturally": Tracy B. Kittredge, *The History of the Commission for Relief in Belgium, 1914–1917* (Unpublished, n.d.), 128.
125 What made it; "It was undoubtedly": Ibid.
126 To most Belgians: Ibid.
126 "came to express": Whitlock, sixteen-page memorandum to the State Dept., Aug. 10, 1917, RG 84, Diplomatic Posts, Belgium, Legation correspondence, Belgium, 1917, vol. 191, file 703.
126 Eight thousand American flags: Whitlock to Connett, April 3, 1915, in Gilchrist Stockton papers, HIA.
127 "there was but": Edward Eyre Hunt, *War Bread: A Personal Narrative of the War and Relief in Belgium (*New York: Holt and Co., 1916), 310.
127 In meetings with: Ibid., 311.
128 Whitlock letter to Connett and related quotes: letter dated April 3, 1915, Gilchrist Stockton papers, HIA.
128 "discharge its obligations": Kittredge, *History of CRB,*128.
128 Whitlock to von Bissing meeting: Herbert Hoover, *An American Epic, Introduction, The Relief of Belgium and Northern France, 1914–1930*, vol. 1 (Chicago: Henry Regnery Co., 1959), 141.

128 Whitlock not at meeting; brother's death: Allan Nevins, ed., *The Letters and Journal of Brand Whitlock*, 2 vols. (*The Letters* and *The Journal*) (New York: D. Appleton-Century Co., 1936) *The Journal*, 97–99.

128 "Von Bissing was": Hoover, *American Epic*, 141.

129 "I fully trusted": Victoria Allen, *The Outside Man*, unpublished, 144, HIA.

129 Hoover meeting with von Bissing; von Bissing's replies: Kittredge, *History of CRB*, 130.

129 "We did not": Hoover, *American Epic*, 141.

129 "boiling with rage"; "What do you": Nevins, *The Journal*, 98–99.

129 Hoover was furious: Ibid.

129 "It is absolutely": Ibid.

130 Hoover's next move; "we shall be": Gay and Fisher, *Public Relations*, vol. I, doc. 31.

130 Von Bissing's letter and Heineman: Kittredge, *History of CRB*, 131; Gay and Fisher, *Public Relations*, vol. I, doc. 32, 50–51.

130 "reiterating a number": Hoover, *American Epic*, 143.

130 He and the rest: Kittredge, *History of CRB*, 131.

131 British military and government attitudes toward CRB: Hoover letter to Whitlock, March 6, 1915; Hoover, *American Epic*, 143–144; Gay and Fisher, *Public Relations*, vol. I, doc. 35, 54–55.

131 "The British Foreign": Hoover, *American Epic*, 143.

131 "I have had": Gay and Fisher, *Public Relations*, vol. I, doc. 33, 52–53.

131 Connett position; "unfavorably impressed with": Kittredge, *History of CRB*, 175–176.

131 When Hoover wrote; Connett's letter; "However," he then: Ibid.

131 "Do not believe": Gay and Fisher, *Public Relations*, vol. I, doc. 34, 53–54.

132 "Fundamental fact is": Ibid.

132 "Von Bissing is": Nevins, *The Journal*, 107.

132 Germàn Bulle and the pass department: Kittredge, *History of CRB*, 132–133.

132 While passes would: Ibid.

133 Von Bissing letter to Whitlock; related quotes: Gay and Fisher, *Public Relations*, vol. I, doc. 36, 56, 40, 64.

CHAPTER 11: INTERNAL STRIFE AND BATTLE FOR CONTROL

135 "the first phase": George I. Gay and H. H. Fisher, *Public Relations of the Commission for Relief in Belgium: Documents*, 2 vols. (Stanford, CA: Stanford University Press, 1929), vol. I, 55.

136 "Many important decisions": Tracy B. Kittredge, *The History of the Commission for Relief in Belgium, 1914–1917* (Unpublished, n.d.), 199–200.

136 When the Chief; "Francqui's attitude was": Ibid.

136 "Adjustment of Functions": Gay and Fisher, *Public Relations*, vol. II, 65.

136 In this case; "if the time"; list of four items and quotes: Ibid., vol. I, doc. 41, 66–69.

137 Certainly none of: Ibid.

138 "the whole question": Kittredge, *History of CRB*, 202.

138 "We are here": Gay and Fisher, *Public Relations*, vol. I, doc., 42, 70–71.

138 "The view of ": Kittredge, *History of CRB*, 204.

138 The delegates were: Gay and Fisher, *Public Relations*, vol. I, doc. 42, 70–71.
138 "the attitude of "; "The relation of ": Ibid.
138 "This memorandum did": Kittredge, *History of CRB*, 204.
139 By July 1916, all bullet points: Ibid., 371.
140 "naturally very indignant": Ibid.
140 "rather inconclusive meetings"; "The difficulties with": Ibid., 371, 370.
140 After Hoover returned: Hoover letter to Percy, Oct. 18, 1916, RG 84, American Embassy, Relief, 848, 1916, vol. 805, NARA.
140 Hoover was incensed: Ibid.
140 Lord Grey's Oct. 20, 1916, letter and related quotes: Kittredge, *History of CRB*, 372–374.
140 "Hoover comes tomorrow"; "full of fight": Allan Nevins, ed., *The Letters and Journal of Brand Whitlock*, 2 vols. (*The Letters* and *The Journal*) (New York: D. Appleton-Century Co., 1936), *The Journal*, 310–311.
141 "defiant and unyielding"; Francqui was taking: Kittredge, *History of CRB*, 375.
141 "with a black"; "It is Hoover": Nevins, *The Journal*, 314–315.
141 "The more one": Ibid., 322.
141 "As to that": Ibid., 335.
141 When the Belgian: Kittredge, *History of CRB*, 376.
141 Hoover's gambit once: Ibid.
142 Back in Belgium: Ibid.
142 "made a secret": Nevins, *Journal*, 341.
142 Kittredge, in his: Kittredge, *History of CRB*, 376–378.
142 Hoover added his: Hoover to Whitlock, Dec. 29, 1916, RG 84, American Legation, Brussels Correspondence, 1917, vol. 70, file 848, NARA; copy correspondence box 7, HIA. I would like to thank Hoover biographer George H. Nash for helping me locate a copy of the Hoover-Whitlock letter.
142 "the neutral and"; "changes in form"; "Hoover immediately accepted": Kittredge, *History of CRB*, 377.
142 Francqui said he: Ibid., 376.
142 "If this contract": Hoover to Whitlock, Dec. 29, 1916, copy correspondence box 7, HIA.
142 Hoover was taken; "attitude in Brussels": Kittredge, *History of CRB*, 376; Hoover to Whitlock, Dec. 29, 1916, copy correspondence box 7, HIA.
143 "I did not wish"; To Francqui it: Hoover to Whitlock, Dec. 29. 1916, copy correspondence box 7, HIA.
143 Hoover—finding himself; "protested vigorously to": Kittredge, *History of CRB*, 376–377.
143 "The reason was": Hoover to Whitlock, Dec. 29, 1916, copy correspondence box 7, HIA.
143 Not to be; "made my own": Hoover to Whitlock, Dec. 29, 1916, copy correspondence box 7, HIA; Kittredge, *History of CRB*, 376–377.
143 "sledge hammer to"; all other quotes in scene: Hoover to Whitlock, Dec. 29, 1916, copy correspondence box 7, HIA.
143 Hoover and Francqui signings: Gay and Fisher, *Public Relations*, vol. I, footnote 16, 115.
144 document-heavy *Public Relations*: Gay and Fisher, *Public Relations*, 2 volumes (Stanford University Press, Stanford University, California, 1929).
144 "It was, of ": Kittredge, *History of CRB*, 378.

CHAPTER 12: CRITICAL CROP NEGOTIATIONS

145 Initially, Governor General: George I. Gay and H. H. Fisher, *Public Relations of the Commission for Relief in Belgium: Documents*, 2 vols. (Stanford, CA: Stanford University Press, 1929), vol. I, 55, and "The Belgian Harvest of 1915: March–July 1915," 522–550.

145 Hoover, working through: Ibid.

145 Francqui weighed in: Ibid., doc. 331, 531–532; Tracy B. Kittredge, *The History of the Commission for Relief in Belgium, 1914–1917* (Unpublished, n.d.), 198–199.

145 "had no right": Kittredge, *History of CRB*, 199.

146 Hoover told Francqui; "At first in": Ibid.

146 June conferences: Ibid.; Whitlock to von der Lancken: Gay and Fisher, *Public Relations*, vol. I, doc. 344, 546.

146 July 7, 1915, letter from Marquis of Crewe to Page: Gay and Fisher, *Public Relations*, vol. I, doc. 341, 539–542.

146 That stipulation was: Ibid., vol. I, doc. 38, 61–62; Herbert Hoover, *An American Epic, Introduction, The Relief of Belgium and Northern France, 1914–1930*, vol. 1 (Chicago: Henry Regnery Co., 1959), 147.

146 "I assign to": Gay and Fisher, *Public Relations*, vol. I, doc. 343, 544.

146 "sole right to": Hoover, *American Epic*, 148.

147 A direct benefit; fifty-four thousand tons: Gay and Fisher, *Public Relations*, vol. I, 549.

146 In spring 1916; details to end of section: Hoover, *American Epic*, 205, 216–219, 222–225, 230–232.

148 In Lille, for; "Salvation can only": Kittredge, *History of CRB*, 315.

148 April 1, Hoover; "degenerating into a"; bullet points: Ibid., 314–317.

148 The situation was; the four "classes": Hoover, *American Epic*, 227–228.

149 By early August; von Sauberzweig signed Cavell execution orders: Ibid., 238–239.

149 "was obstinate, arrogant"; details and quotes not otherwise noted: Ibid., 193, 238–239, 240.

149 Unfortunately, von Sauberzweig: Ibid., 238-241; Vernon Kellogg, *Fighting Starvation in Belgium* (New York: Doubleday, Page and Co., 1918), 58–65.

149 When the group: Hoover, *American Epic*, 238–241.

149 At 4:00 p.m.: Ibid.

149 "Extremely violent speeches"; "no worse for": Ibid.

150 Kellogg's account, which; "just one ray"; "if the request": Kellogg, *Fighting Starvation*, 58–65.

150 "This was our": Ibid.

150 "there came one": Hoover, *American Epic*, 241.

150 "apologetically mentioned that": Ibid.

150 Taking another drink; all quotes by Hoover in section: Ibid.

152 Kellogg's account explains; Kellogg, *Fighting Starvation*, 58–65.

152 "hasten the formulation": Ibid.

152 "The crisis was": Ibid.

152 By the end; "as the year": Kittredge, *History of CRB*, 338.

152 By September, the: Gay and Fisher, *Public Relations*, vol. I, 590–605; Hoover, *American Epic*, 227–25.

152 One critical behind-; "One important condition": Gay and Fisher, *Public Relations*, vol. I, doc. 379, 596.

153 A sad footnote; "consequently the Commission": Kittredge, *History of CRB*, 342.
153 With von Hindenburg; "The Commission made": Ibid., 342–343.

CHAPTER 13: ACCUSATIONS

156 But the schism: Tracy B. Kittredge, *The History of the Commission for Relief in Belgium, 1914–1917* (Unpublished, n.d.), 210; Herbert Hoover, "The Episode of Mr. Lindon Bates," CRB Executive Chronological File, 1912–1919, Bates, Lindon W., box 9, folder 6, HIA (hereinafter: Hoover, "Bates Episode," HIA).
156 To resolve those; "encountered difficulty through": Kittredge, *History of CRB*, 211; Hoover, "Bates Episode," HIA.
156 By the end: Cablegram to Hoover, Oct. 24, 1915, Hunt papers, box 15, HIA; Hoover, "Bates Episode," HIA.
156 Hoover cabled back; "many reasons why": George I. Gay and H. H. Fisher, *Public Relations of the Commission for Relief in Belgium: Documents*, 2 vols. (Stanford, CA: Stanford University Press, 1929), vol. II, doc. 575, 267.
157 Initially, the PR: Ibid., doc. 576, 267–268.
157 On August 28; "one of the": *Saturday Evening Post*, August 1915.
157 "For political reasons": Hoover cable 212 to Bates, Sept. 22, 1915, CRB correspondence, box 4, HIA.
157 On October 1: CRB–New York office cable 198 to Hoover, Oct. 1, 1915, CRB correspondence, box 4, HIA.
157 Cablegram from eight advisers: Copy in Hunt papers, box 15, HIA; the eight were Hunsiker, Connett, Sengier, Young, Shaler, Rickard, Honnold, and Kellogg.
157 Bates had taken; details and quotes in Bates story not otherwise identified: Hoover, "Bates Episode," HIA.
158 On October 28: Ibid.; Herbert Hoover, *An American Epic, Introduction, The Relief of Belgium and Northern France, 1914–1930*, vol. 1 (Chicago: Henry Regnery Co., 1959), 162.
158 Senator Lodge had: Henry Cabot Lodge to William Phillips, Oct. 22, 1915, RG 59, 55.48/389, NARA.
158 "because our negotiations": Hoover, *American Epic*, 161.
158 He responded with: Hoover to William Phillips, Oct. 30, 1915, RG 59, 855.48/395, NARA; copies in CRB correspondence, box 4, HIA.
158 "extraordinary esteem and"; "atom of moral": CRB correspondence, box 4, HIA.
159 "The Commission for": Page cable to secretary of State Lansing, Nov. 2, 1915, London American Embassy, 848 Belgium, Great Britain, RG 84, vol. 700, NARA.
159 Wilson CRB press release: Ibid.; CRB news clippings (New York office), vol. 10, 42, HHPLA.
159 Senator Lodge letter to the State Dept.: RG 59, Microfilm 675, roll 52, NARA.
160 "an energetic campaign": Kittredge, *History of CRB*, 211.
160 "a tense demand": Hoover, *American Epic*, 162, 169, 148–149.
162 Villalobar helped Gibson: Gibson to State Dept., Jan. 3, 1916, and Jan. 7, 1916, RG 84, correspondence, American Legation Brussels, 1916, vol. 181, file 848, Relief, NARA; Hoover, *American Epic*, 148–149.

162 Hoover arrived in: Letter from Gibson to Whitlock, Dec. 1, 1915, Gibson papers, box 65, HIA.

162 "There have been": Letter from Gibson to his mother, Dec. 1, 1915, Gibson papers, box 31, HIA.

162 Gibson's memorandum; all dialogue in the Dec. 1 meeting was created using the exact words attributed to each speaker in Gibson's memorandum: Hugh Gibson's six-page memorandum, dated Dec. 1, 1915, Gibson papers, box 72, HIA. This memorandum is not mentioned nor listed in Gay and Fisher's *Public Relations*. Listed in that book are three documents pertinent to the spy charges: doc. 43, 44, and 45. The event was also covered by two dispatches by Gibson to the State Dept., dated Jan. 3, 1916, and Jan. 7, 1916, which are found in RG 84, correspondence, American Legation Brussels, 1916, vol. 181, file 848, Relief, NARA.

164 Regarding the long-; "he was a": Vernon Kellogg memorandum of the meeting, Dec. 2, 1915, in Hoover, *American Epic*, 152; Captain Uhl from America is also described in Gibson's letter to his mother, Dec. 1, 1915, Gibson papers, box 31, HIA.

164 Hoover to Rotterdam; Gibson to mother, Dec. 9, 1915, Gibson papers, box 31, HIA.

164 "set up an": Hoover, *American Epic*, 149.

164 "for their opinions": Ibid.

164 What happened to the delegates: Delegates work list, Arrowsmith papers, HIA; Erica Bunge's diary entry, Dec. 1915, "Van Schaick had to leave on account of Boches in December," author's archives.

CHAPTER 14: A BREAKING POINT

165 The major concern; statistics: Herbert Hoover, *An American Epic, Introduction, The Relief of Belgium and Northern France, 1914–1930*, vol. 1 (Chicago: Henry Regnery Co., 1959), 179, 182.

165 With Francqui repeatedly: George I. Gay and H. H. Fisher, *Public Relations of the Commission for Relief in Belgium: Documents*, 2 vols. (Stanford, CA: Stanford University Press, 1929), vol. I, doc. 66, 121–122.

165 126,400 tons and 48,000 tons: Hoover, *American Epic*, 179–180, 182.

166 Hoover would not: Gay and Fisher, *Public Relations*, vol. I, doc. 76, 140–141.

166 "pressure from the": Hoover, *American Epic*, 186.

166 "It was a"; "We had no": Ibid.

166 As this critical: Allan Nevins, ed., *The Letters and Journal of Brand Whitlock*, 2 vols. (*The Letters* and *The Journal*) (New York: D. Appleton-Century Co., 1936), *The Journal*, 244.

166 The second was: Green memorandum, May 21, 1917, Green papers, Princeton Mudd Library.

166 Hoover illness: Gibson to mother, Jan. 14, 1916, Gibson papers, box 1, HHPLA; Hoover letter to Gibson, Jan. 18, 1916, RG 84, American Legation in Brussels, vol. 181, NARA.

166 "By the end"; "required working twelve": Hoover, *American Epic*, 198.

166 The nine points and all related quotes: Ibid., 198–202.

167 This issue would: Ibid., 206–213, 221–222.

168 He wrote a; "interested governments and": Ibid., 198–202.

168 "You know . . .": Ibid., 203; Gay and Fisher, *Public Relations*, vol. I, doc. 54, 92–93.

168 "The harmony which"; related quotes: Gay and Fisher, *Public Relations*, vol. I, docs. 54–57, 92–95.

169 The Germans were: Hoover, *American Epic*, 204–205.

170 As Ambassador Gerard; related details and quotes: Hoover, *American Epic*, 205, 216–219, 222–225, 230–232.

CHAPTER 15: THE GERMAN DEPORTATIONS

171 Belgium prewar statistics: Edward Eyre Hunt, *War Bread: A Personal Narrative of the War and Relief in Belgium* (New York: Holt and Co., 1916), 304–305.

172 In fact, one: Herbert Hoover, *An American Epic, Introduction, The Relief of Belgium and Northern France, 1914–1930*, vol. 1 (Chicago: Henry Regnery Co., 1959), 255.

172 They also issued: Léon Van der Essen, "Germany's Latest Crime," *Fortnightly Review*, no. 602 New Series, Feb. 1, 1917, 202.

173 Some skilled workmen: Tracy B. Kittredge, *The History of the Commission for Relief in Belgium, 1914–1917* (Unpublished, n.d.), 318.

173 "strike of folded": Émile Cammaerts, *Through the Iron Bars(Two Years of German Occupation in Belgium)* (London: The Bodley Head, 1917), 44.

173 "It became more": Ibid.

173 Hoover knew that: George I. Gay and H. H. Fisher, *Public Relations of the Commission for Relief in Belgium: Documents*, 2 vols. (Stanford, CA: Stanford University Press, 1929), vol. II, doc. 407, 34–35, 44–45.

173 They chose the: Ibid., 76.

174 The food supplied; Roubaix riot: Ibid.

174 And the sentiment: Kittredge, *History of CRB*, 317.

174 The German military: Gay and Fisher, *Public Relations*, vol. II, doc. 433, 73.

174 "saw-mills, roadways": Kittredge, *History of CRB*, 318.

174 "evacuate"; "volunteers would be": Gay and Fisher, *Public Relations*, vol. II, doc. 433, 73.

174 "while in principle": Ibid.

174 The Germans first: Ibid.

174 On April 22: Ibid.

175 "candles or other": Kittredge, *History of CRB*, 318.

175 Eyewitnesses to the; "machine guns were": Gay and Fisher, *Public Relations*, vol. II, doc. 434, 77.

175 "had orders to": Ibid.

175 While the stated: Kittredge, *History of CRB*, 321–322.

175 "Girls of good": Gay and Fisher, *Public Relations*, vol. II, doc. 434, 78.

175 Poland was horrified: Kittredge, *History of CRB*, 319.

175 "in the maelstrom": Ibid., 317.

175 In an incredible: Ibid., 317–319.

175 Major-General Zoellner: Erich von Falkenhayn, *The German General Staff and Its Decisions, 1914–1916* (Dodd, Mead and Company, 1920), 9.

175 "ornaments"; "in connection with": Kittredge, *History of CRB*, 319.

176 In attendance: Gay and Fisher, *Public Relations*, vol. II, doc. 433, 74.

176 "sympathetic nature, revolting": Kittredge, *History of CRB*, 319.

176 "The proper opportunity": Gay and Fisher, *Public Relations*, vol. II, doc. 433, 74.

176 "A bombshell bursting": Kittredge, *History of CRB*, 319.
176 Poland then turned: Gay and Fisher, *Public Relations*, vol. II, doc. 433, 74–75.
176 "proper and satisfactory": Ibid.
176 "the French people": Kittredge, *History of CRB*, 319.
176 "expressed himself as": Gay and Fisher, *Public Relations*, vol. II, doc. 433, 75.
176 "proved himself . . .": Kittredge, *History of CRB*, 319.
176 "was much affected": Gay and Fisher, *Public Relations*, vol. II, doc. 433, 75.
176 Major-General Zoellner: Kittredge, *History of CRB*, 320.
176 After the tea: Gay and Fisher, *Public Relations*, vol. II, doc. 433, 75.
176 Nonetheless, in the; Ibid., doc. 434, 76–80.
176 Most deportees did: Kittredge, *History of CRB*, 323.
176 The story of: Gay and Fisher, *Public Relations*, vol. II, footnote 27, 73.
177 In May 1916: Cammaerts, *Through the Iron Bars*, 49.
177 Then in early: Gay and Fisher, *Public Relations*, vol. II, doc. 407, 34–35., 44–46.
177 October 3, 1916, decree: Arnold Joseph Toynbee, *The Belgian Deportations* (London: T. Fisher Unwin, Ltd., n.d.), 41; "Belgian Note to Neutral Powers," *London Times*, Nov. 16, 1916.
177 the German plan and statistics: J. van den Heuvel, *Slave Raids in Belgium: Facts About the Deportations* (London: T. Fisher Unwin, Ltd., 1917), 2; Dr. Jens Thiel, in a speech Mar. 24, 2014, " 'Slave Raids' during the First World War? Deportation and Forced Labor in Occupied Belgium," said the figure was 500,000.
177 During the 1914: 218 killed; John Horne and Alan Kramer, *German Atrocities 1914, A History of Denial* (New Haven, CT: Yale University Press, 2001), appendix 1, 437; Joseph Green essay, no title, Jan. 10, 1917, Joseph C. Green papers, box 19, Princeton Mudd Library.
178 "slave raids": Term used to describe the forced deportations from 1916 to 1917. Multiple sources; one example, "Slave Raids in Belgium," *London Times*, Nov. 8, 1916.
178 Virton, its *affiche*, details and quotes not otherwise attributed: Joseph Green essay, no title, Jan. 10, 1917, and in letter to his parents, Jan. 14, 1917, Green papers, box 19, 37, Princeton Mudd Library.
178 Those who did: Toynbee, *The Belgian Deportations*.
178 "left" or "right": Left-to-freedom, right-to-deportation in accounts of Joe Green; Robert Jackson, handwritten relief memoir, part 3, pp. 4–5, HIA; Prentiss Gray's diary, 208, author's archives. Right-to-freedom, Left-to-deportation in the account at Wavre in Britain's *Daily Telegraph*, (Dec. 1916); Toynbee, *The Belgian Deportations*; Brand Whitlock's *Belgium: A Personal Narrative* (New York: D. Appleton and Co., 1919), vol. II, 628 and 645.
179 Capacity of cattle cars: "The Agony of Belgium," *London Times*, Nov. 21, 1916.
179 Singing Belgian and French national anthems: Toynbee, *The Belgian Deportations*, 14, 95; Robert Withington, *In Occupied Belgium* (Boston: Cornhill Co., 1921), 111; "Slave Raids in Belgium," *London Times*, Nov. 8, 1916.
179 "They are carried": Green, letter to parents, Green papers, box 37, Princeton Mudd Library.
179 "The delegates were": Whitlock, *Belgium*, vol. II, 628.
179 "Appalling stories have": Brand Whitlock's official report recorded in "One of the Foulest Deeds in History," *London Times*, May 18, 1919.
179 In total, more: Gay and Fisher, *Public Relations*, vol. II, doc. 427, 63–66.

180 In America, organized: *New York Times*, Dec. 16, 1916.
180 On December 5: Hoover, *American Epic*, 278–279.
180 "Should we risk": Ibid., 283.
180 This time, Hoover : Ibid., 278–279, 283–284.
180 Hoover finally made: Gay and Fisher, *Public Relations*, vol. II, 45–46.
181 Hallam Tuck's departure: Whitlock, *Belgium*, vol. II, 628; Charlotte Kellogg, *Mercier, The Fighting Cardinal of Belgium* (New York: D. Appleton and Co., 1920), 158; Pate, daily journal, 39, HHPLA.
181 Despite the international; Dec. 2, 1916; "very childish judgment": Gay and Fisher, *Public Relations*, vol. II, footnote no. 15, 45.
183 On January 24: Cardinal D. J. Mercier, *Cardinal Mercier's Own Story* (New York: George H. Doran Co., 1920), 336–337.
183 von Bissing had: Whitlock, *Belgium*, vol. II, 686.
183 As the cardinal; letter to Kaiser and quotes: Mercier, *Cardinal Mercier's Own Story*, 344–348.
183 On Friday, March: Ibid.
183 Nothing was said; 10,000 to 13,000: Jens Thiel, "'Slave Raids' during the First World War? Deportation and Forced Labor in Occupied Belgium"; Britain's *Daily Telegraph*, on Feb. 6, 1917.
183 58,500 and 62,155 deportees: Official Belgian figures, Fernand Passelecq, *Déportation et Travail Forcé* (Paris: Les Presses Universitaires de France, n.d.), 398.
185 "I saw trainloads"; "This was only": William Alexander Percy, *Lanterns on the Levee, Recollections of a Planter's Son* (New York: Alfred A. Knopf, 1941), 166.
185 "They had been": Prentiss Gray; Sherman Gray (son) and Prentiss Gray (grandson), eds., *Fifteen Months in Belgium: A CRB Diary* (Princeton, NJ: Self-published, 2009), 246–247.

CHAPTER 16: THE HUMAN TOLL

187 Smith article details and quotes: Robinson Smith, article 5, "How Does It Feel?" of "The Feeding of Belgium," (no publisher), in Maurice Pate papers, box 13, folder 11, Princeton Mudd Library.
188 "It is not"; "No, we have": Ibid.
188 By autumn 1916: Pate to father, Aug. 24, 1916; to mother, Sept. 1916; to Ann, Sept. 14, 1916; Pate papers, Princeton Mudd Library.
188 In late February; the family description: Pate report, Mons, Feb. 28, 1917, Pate papers, HHPLA.
190 "The conditions of"; "Belgium was like": Edward Eyre Hunt, *War Bread: A Personal Narrative of the War and Relief in Belgium* (New York: Holt and Co., 1916), 262.
190 "quite a number": Tracy B. Kittredge, *The History of the Commission for Relief in Belgium, 1914–1917* (Unpublished, n.d.), 153.
191 "Until late in": Hunt, *War Bread*, 262.
191 "breathing spells were": Ibid., 263.
191 "When we spent": Ibid., 264–265.
191 "soon grew impatient": Kittredge, *History of CRB*, 176.
191 Tempering the February; "it soon became"; "It was there": Ibid., 178.
192 "in a companionship": Ibid.

192 "arranged a series"; remaining quotes in section: Hunt, *War Bread*, 263, 265, 267–268.
192 Warren story; related quotes: Robert Warren, "A Statement of Circumstances Leading Up to and Attending My Arrest at Esschen on Saturday, April 24th, 1915," Stockton papers, box 9, HIA.

CHAPTER 17: THE LAST DAYS OF AMERICANS IN BELGIUM

199 By late December; "On account of": Maurice Pate diary, Pate papers, Princeton Mudd Library.
199 "The most important": Ibid.
199 On February 4: Ibid.
199 "shipping organization, which": Prentiss Gray; Sherman Gray (son) and Prentiss Gray (grandson), eds., *Fifteen Months in Belgium: A CRB Diary* (Princeton, NJ: Self-published, 2009), 227–228.
200 By late February: Ibid.
201 Von der Lancken: Brand Whitlock, *Belgium: A Personal Narrative*, 2 vols. (New York: D. Appleton and Co., 1919), vol. II, 701–704.
201 "the Imperial Government": Ibid.
201 Returning to the: Ibid.
201 At the same; "expressed his great": Herbert Hoover, *An American Epic, Introduction, The Relief of Belgium and Northern France, 1914–1930*, vol. 1 (Chicago: Henry Regnery Co., 1959), 284–285.
202 Eleven ships damaged or sunk in 1916: George I. Gay and H. H. Fisher, *Public Relations of the Commission for Relief in Belgium: Documents*, 2 vols. (Stanford, CA: Stanford University Press, 1929), vol. I, 343.
202 As Hoover had; bullet points: Ibid., 344.
202 Initially, Hoover quickly; "conclusions reached": Ibid., 287–288.
203 On February 3; "the Secretary's view"; other cable quotes: Ibid., 290.
203 Hoover's replacement plan: Gay and Fisher, *Public Relations*, vol. II, doc. 465, 128–130.
203 It also stated; "Think it extremely"; all details and quotes in section not otherwise noted: Hoover, *American Epic*, 290, 287–288, 292, 293, 296.
203 In a few; new route: Gay and Fisher, *Public Relations*, vol. I, 344.
203 Overall, the result: Hoover, *American Epic*, 296.
204 It was only: Ibid., 296–297.
206 "The country is": Allan Nevins, ed., *The Letters and Journal of Brand Whitlock*, 2 vols. (*The Letters* and *The Journal*) (New York: D. Appleton-Century Co., 1936), *The Journal*, 364.
206 "Everybody laughing at": Ibid., 364–365.
207 "I gave this": Ibid., 368.
207 Outside Belgium, events: Tracy B. Kittredge, *The History of the Commission for Relief in Belgium, 1914–1917* (Unpublished, n.d.), 418.
207 "to leave Belgium": Nevins, *The Journal*, 371–372.
207 The direct, explicit; "distinct relief": Ibid., 372.
207 On the evening: Kittredge, *History of CRB*, 422; Arthur Bartlett Maurice, *Bottled Up in Belgium, The Last Delegate's Informal Story* (New York: Moffat, Yard & Co., 1917), 177.
207 On Saturday morning: Whitlock, *Belgium*, vol. II, 795, 736–738, 779–805, 795.

208 "pale, melancholy days"; "The shops were": Ibid.
208 Brown's departure and quotes: Brown to Erica Bunge, April 21, 1917, author's archives.
208 He received a: Whitlock, *Belgium,* vol. II, 810; Nevins, *The Journal*, 372.
209 Whitlock sped back: Nevins, *The Journal*, 374.
209 According to Whitlock: Whitlock, *Belgium*, vol. II, 808.
209 Staying behind with: Nevins, *The Journal*, 376.
210 All tons imported to Belgium and northern France: George I. Gay, *The Commission for Relief in Belgium: Statistical Review of Relief Operations: Five Years, November 1, 1914, to August 31, 1919, and to Final Liquidation* (Stanford, CA: Stanford University Press, n.d.), 192–193, 196–197.
210 Promotion of Poland: Kittredge, *History of CRB*, 442.
210 Fernand Baetens's position; "had been far": Ibid., 440.
210 Two other non-Americans: Ibid., 423–424, 440–442.
210 On April 23: Ibid., 440–441.
211 By May 1; "Delegates had gone": Ibid.
211 "And so we": Gray, *Fifteen Months*, 271–280.
211 Tracy Kittredge, the; "So came to": Kittredge, *History of CRB*, 424.
211 "the greatest thing": Brown to Junior, April 29, 1917, author's archives.
211 "tremendous privilege rather": Brown to Erica Bunge, April 21, 1917, author's archives.

EPILOGUE

215 When Prentiss Gray; all details and quotes in section not otherwise noted: Herbert Hoover, *An American Epic, Introduction, The Relief of Belgium and Northern France, 1914–1930*, vol. 1 (Chicago: Henry Regnery Co., 1959), 329–333, 355–356, 376, 380.
216 "performed with devotion": George I. Gay and H. H. Fisher, *Public Relations of the Commission for Relief in Belgium: Documents*, 2 vols. (Stanford, CA: Stanford University Press, 1929), vol. II, 174.
217 "in the face": Ibid.
217 The average daily; all details and quotes in section not otherwise noted: Hoover, *American Epic*, 346–347, 340, 350, 351, 356, 381, 383, 376.
220 Baron von Falkenhausen: Brand Whitlock, *Belgium: A Personal Narrative*, 2 vols. (New York: D. Appleton and Co., 1919), vol. II, 777.
220 Shortly after von; "highest officials of": Ibid.; Cardinal D. J. Mercier, *Cardinal Mercier's Own Story* (New York: George H. Doran Co., 1920), 386.
220 The new governor: Mercier, *Cardinal Mercier's Own Story*, 389.
220 Brown's activities, clothing report, and quotes in section not otherwise noted: Brown's papers, including his final report, author's archives.
221 "These reports and": Hoover, *American Epic*, 409.
221 "Of the 24,384": Ibid.
221 Warehoused lace, "Mrs. Hoover organized": Ibid., 411.
223 Hoover's quotes from the July 1958 speech: Ibid., 450–454.
223 In 2020, the: The website for the Belgian American Educational Foundation.

Sources

CRB OFFICIAL REPORTS AND BOOKS

"Balance Sheet and Accounts, French Government Accounts, Belgian Government Accounts, Supporting Schedules, Covering Six Years from Commencement of Operations, October, 1914, to 30th September, 1920." No location: CRB, 1921.

Gay, George I. *The Commission for Relief in Belgium: Statistical Review of Relief Operations: Five Years, November 1, 1914, to August 31, 1919, and to Final Liquidation.* Stanford, CA: Stanford University Press, n.d.

Gay, George I., and H. H. Fisher. *Public Relations of the Commission for Relief in Belgium: Documents,* 2 vols. Stanford, CA: Stanford University Press, 1929.

INSTITUTIONAL COLLECTIONS

I studied the papers of more than fifty CRB delegates that I found in numerous research libraries and institutions. Three critical archives and the primary papers I read within them are:

Herbert Hoover Presidential Library Archives (HHPLA), West Branch, Iowa

Ben S. Allen, Hugh Gibson, Prentiss Gray, Joseph Green, Herbert C. Hoover, Edward Eyre Hunt, Maurice Pate, George Spaulding (found in the Alan Hoover papers), and Brand Whitlock. Also extremely useful were the comprehensive clip books, which contained hundreds of CRB-related newspaper clippings from the United Kingdom, and the oral history interviews.

Hoover Institution Archives (HIA), Stanford University, Stanford, California

Ben S. Allen, Robert Arrowsmith, Perrin C. Galpin, Hugh Gibson, Emil Holman (original spelling Hollmann), Edward Eyre Hunt, Robert A. Jackson, Tracy B. Kittredge, David T. Nelson, Maurice Pate, Robinson Smith, Gilchrist B. Stockton, and Robert Withington. Also extremely useful were the oral history interviews and the more than five hundred boxes of files under the Commission for Relief in Belgium.

National Archives and Records Administration (NARA), College Park, Maryland

Extremely helpful were the General Records of the State Department (RG 59) and the Records of the Foreign Service Posts of the State Department (RG 84), particularly the files of the American Embassy in London and the US Legation in Brussels.

AUTHOR'S ARCHIVES

My archives are open to any legitimate researcher. They include hundreds of letters and a diary written by my grandfather, Milton M. Brown, while he was a CRB delegate (January 1916 to April 1917), as well as an extensive final report he wrote on the clothing department. From my grandmother, Erica Bunge Brown, I have a small diary (edited by my mother) and numerous photos she took during the war. In addition, I have from my great-grandfather, Edouard Bunge, his extensive personal account, "What I Saw of the Bombardment and Surrender of Antwerp," which details his participation in the surrender of the city to the Germans. For more information about my archives or to obtain access, contact Jeff Miller at jbmwriter@aol.com or 303-503-1739.

PRIMARY AND SECONDARY BOOKS

After decades of research, a comprehensive list of sources would be excessively long. I have chosen the following as the most appropriate sources.

Ackerman, Carl W. *Germany, The Next Republic?* New York: Grosset & Dunlap, 1917.

Allen, Victoria F. *The Outside Man.* Unpublished.

Baedeker, Karl. *Baedeker's Belgium and Holland.* Leipzig, Germany: Karl Baedeker, 1910.

Beatty, Jack. *The Lost History of 1914, Reconsidering the Year the Great War Began.* New York: Walker and Co., 2012.

Beck, James M. *The War and Humanity: A Further Discussion of the Ethics of the World War and the Attitude and Duty of the United States.* New York: G.P. Putnam's Sons, 1916.

Bissing, Mortiz Ferdinand von. *General von Bissing's Testament, A Study in German Ideals.* London: T. Fisher Unwin, Ltd, no date.

Bland, J. O. P., translator. *Germany's Violations of the Laws of War, 1914–1915: Compiled under the auspices of the French Ministry of Foreign Affairs.* London: William Heinemann, 1915.

Cammaerts, Émile. *Through the Iron Bars (Two Years of German Occupation in Belgium).* London: The Bodley Head, 1917.

Collier, Price. *Germany and the Germans from an American Point of View.* London: Duckworth and Co., 1914.

Cruden, Robert M. *A Hero in Spite of Himself: Brand Whitlock in Art, Politics, and War.* New York: Alfred A. Knopf, Inc., 1969.

Danielson, Elena S. "Herbert Hoover." *The United States in the First World War: An Encyclopedia,* Anne Cipriano Benzon, ed. New York: Garland Press, 1995.

Davis, Arthur N. *The Kaiser as I Know Him.* New York: Harper and Brothers, 1918.

Dawson, Coningsby. *The Glory of the Trenches, An Interpretation*. New York: John Lane Co., 1918.

De Croÿ, Marie. *War Memories*. London: MacMillan and Co. Limited, 1932.

Domelier, Henri. *Behind the Scenes at German Headquarters*. London: Hurst and Blackett, Ltd., 1919.

Doren, Eugene van. *Les Tribulations du Manager de La Libre Belgique Clandestine 1914–1918*. Brussels: L'edition Universelle, 1947.

Druelle, Clotilde. *Feeding Occupied France during World War I: Herbert Hoover and the Blockade*. Cham, Switzerland: Palgrave MacMillan, 2019.

Fuehr, Alexander. *The Neutrality of Belgium: A Study of the Belgian Case Under its Aspects in Political History and International Law*. New York: Funk and Wagnalls Co., 1915.

Galpin, Perrin C., ed. *Hugh Gibson, 1883–1954, Extracts from His Letters and Anecdotes from His Friends*. New York: Belgian American Educational Foundation, 1956.

Gay, George I., and H. H. Fisher. *Public Relations of the Commission for Relief in Belgium: Documents*, 2 vols. Stanford, CA: Stanford University Press, 1929.

Gerald, James W. *My Four Years in Germany*. New York: Grosset & Dunlap, 1917.

Gibson, Hugh. *A Journal from Our Legation in Belgium*. New York: Doubleday, Page and Co., 1917.

Gomery, Gerlache de. *Belgium in War Time*. Nancy, France: Berger-Levrault; translation by Bernard Miall, New York: George H. Doran Co., 1915.

Graves, Dr. Armgaard Karl, with collaboration of Edward Lyell Fox. *The Secrets of the German War Office*. New York: McBride, Nast and Co., 1914.

Gray, Prentiss; Sherman Gray (son) and Prentiss Gray (grandson), eds. *Fifteen Months in Belgium: A CRB Diary*. Princeton, NJ: Self-published, 2009.

Green, Horace. *The Log of a Noncombatant*. New York: Houghton Mifflin, 1915.

Hendrick, Burton J., ed. *The Life and Letters of Walter H. Page*, 4 vols. New York: Doubleday, Page and Co., 1924.

Henry, Albert (directeur general au Ministere de l'Agriculture Secretaire general du Comité National de Secours et d'Alimentation). *Le Ravitaillement de la Belgique Pendant L'Occupation Allenmande*. Paris: Les Presses Universitairies de France, 1924.

Heuvel, J. van den. *Slave Raids in Belgium: Facts About the Deportations*. London: T. Fisher Unwin, Ltd., 1917.

Hoover, Herbert. *An American Epic, Introduction, The Relief of Belgium and Northern France, 1914–1930*, vol. 1. Chicago: Henry Regnery Co., 1959.

———. *The Memoirs of Herbert Hoover: Years of Adventure, 1874–1920*. New York: MacMillan and Co., 1951.

Horne, John, and Alan Kramer. *German Atrocities, 1914, A History of Denial*. New Haven, CT: Yale University Press, 2001.

Humphreys, Arthur L. "The Heart of Belgium." A collection of four articles that appeared earlier in the *London Times*. London: Arthur L. Humphreys, 1915.

Hunt, Edward Eyre. *War Bread: A Personal Narrative of the War and Relief in Belgium*. New York: Holt and Co., 1916.

Irwin, Will. *Herbert Hoover, A Reminiscent Biography*. New York: The Century Co., 1928.

Jeansonne, Glen, with David Luhrssen. *Herbert Hoover: A Life*. New York: New American Library, 2016.

Kellogg, Charlotte. *Bobbins of Belgium: A Book of Belgian Lace, Lace-workers, Lace-schools and Lace-villages*. New York: Funk and Wagnalls Co., 1920.

———. *Mercier, The Fighting Cardinal of Belgium.* New York: D. Appleton and Co., 1920.
———. *Women of Belgium: Turning Tragedy to Triumph.* New York: Funk and Wagnalls Co., 1917.
Kellogg, Vernon. *Fighting Starvation in Belgium.* New York: Doubleday, Page and Co., 1918.
———. *Headquarters Nights: A Record of Conversations and Experiences at the Headquarters of the German Army in France and Belgium.* Boston: Atlantic Monthly Press, 1917.
———. *Herbert Hoover, The Man and His Work.* New York: D. Appleton and Co., 1920.
Kittredge, Tracy B. *The History of the Commission for Relief in Belgium, 1914–1917.* Unpublished, n.d.
Klekowski, Ed and Libby. *Americans in Occupied Belgium, 1914–1918: Accounts of the War from Journalists, Tourists, Troops and Medical Staff.* Jefferson, NC: McFarland & Co., 2014.
———. *Eyewitnesses to the Great War: American Writers, Reporters, Volunteers and Soldiers in France, 1914–1918.* Jefferson, NC: McFarland & Co., 2014.
Lipkes, Jeff. *Rehearsals, The German Army in Belgium, August 1914.* Leuven, Belgium: Leuven University Press, 2007.
Little, John Branden. *Band of Crusaders: American Humanitarians, the Great War, and the Remaking of the World.* PhD dissertation. University of California, Berkeley, Spring 2009.
Lutz, Ralph Haswell, editor. *Fall of the German Empire, 1914–1918, Volume 1.* New York: Octagon Books, 1932; reprinted by Stanford University Press, 1969.
Massart, Jean. *Belgians Under the Eagle.* New York: E.P. Dutton and Co., 1916.
Maurice, Arthur Bartlett. *Bottled Up in Belgium, The Last Delegate's Informal Story.* New York: Moffat, Yard & Co., 1917.
Mercier, Cardinal D. J. *Cardinal Mercier's Own Story.* New York: George H. Doran Co., 1920.
Millard, Oscar E. *Underground News: The Complete Story of the Secret Newspaper that Made War History.* New York: Robert M. McBride and Co., 1938.
Miller, Jeffrey B. *Behind the Lines: WWI's little-known story of German occupation, Belgian resistance, and the band of Yanks who helped save millions from starvation. Beginnings, 1914.* Denver: Milbrown Press, 2014.
———. *WWI Crusaders: A band of Yanks in German-occupied Belgium help save millions from starvation as civilians resist the harsh German rule. August 1914 to May 1917.* Denver: Milbrown Press, 2018.
Morse, Edwin W. *The Vanguard of American Volunteers: In the Fighting Lines and in Humanitarian Service, August 1914–April 1917.* New York: Charles Scribner's Sons, 1919.
Nash, George H. *The Life of Herbert Hoover, The Humanitarian, 1914–1917.* New York: W. W. Norton and Co., 1988.
Nelson, John P., ed. *Letters and Diaries of David T. Nelson, 1914–1919.* Decorah, IA: The Anundsen Publishing Co., 1996.
Nevins, Allan, ed. *The Letters and Journal of Brand Whitlock*, 2 vols. (*The Letters* and *The Journal*). New York: D. Appleton-Century Co., 1936.
Patterson, David S. *The Search for Negotiated Peace: Women's Activism and Citizen Diplomacy in World War I.* New York: Routledge, 2008.
Proctor, Tammy M. *Civilians in a World at War, 1914–1918.* New York: New York University Press, 2010.
Roelands, Raymond. *Geschiedenis van Kasteeldomein "Oude Gracht" in Hoogboom.* Kapellen, Belgium: Culturele Heemkring Hobonia v.z.w., 2016.
Schaick, John van, Jr. *The Little Corner Never Conquered: The Story of the American Red Cross War Work for Belgium.* New York: The MacMillan Co., 1922.

Smith, Richard Norton. *An Uncommon Man, The Triumph of Herbert Hoover*. New York: Simon and Schuster, 1984.

Surface, Frank M., and Raymond L. Bland. *American Food in the World War and Reconstruction Period: Operations of the Organizations Under the Direction of Herbert Hoover, 1914–1924*. Stanford, CA: Stanford University Press, 1931.

Taillandier, Madame Saint-Rene. *The Soul of the 'C.R.B.' A French View of the Hoover Relief Work*. New York: Charles Scribner's Sons, 1919.

Toynbee, Arnold Joseph. *The Belgian Deportations*. London: T. Fisher Unwin, Ltd., no date.

———. *The German Terror in Belgium, An historical record*. London: George H. Doran, 1917.

———. *The German Terror in France*. London: George H. Doran, 1917.

Tuchman, Barbara M. *The Guns of August: The drama of August 1914, a month of battle in which war was waged on a scale unsurpassed and whose results determined the shape of the world in which we live today*. New York: Random House, 1962.

Van den Bleeken, Roger. *Cappellen in den Grooten Oorlog*. Kapellen, Belgium: Heemkring Hoghescote, 2014.

Vincent, C. Paul. *The Politics of Hunger: The Allied Blockade of Germany, 1915–1919*. Athens: Ohio University Press, 1985.

Whitlock, Brand. *Belgium: A Personal Narrative*, 2 vols. New York: D. Appleton and Co., 1919.

———. "Belgium, Before the Storm," "The Storm Breaks," and "Belgium, Under the German Heel." *Everyone's Magazine*, multiple issues, February 1918.

Whyte, Kenneth. *Hoover: An Extraordinary Life in Extraordinary Times*. New York: Vintage Books, 2017.

Wickes, Mariette, ed. *Love in the Time of War*. No location: self-published, no date.

Withington, Robert. *In Occupied Belgium*. Boston: Cornhill Co., 1921.

Zieger, Robert H. *America's Great War: World War I and the American Experience*. New York: Rowman & Littlefield Publishers Inc., 2000.

Zuckerman, Larry. *The Rape of Belgium, The Untold Story of World War I*. New York: New York University Press, 2004.

Index

About the Author

Jeffrey B. Miller has been a writer, magazine editor, and independent historian for more than forty years. In the 1980s, when his beloved grandparents died, Miller inherited their diaries, journals, correspondence, and photographs from World War I. His grandfather, Milton M. Brown, was a 1913 Princeton grad who joined the American-led, nongovernmental Commission for Relief in Belgium (CRB) and entered German-occupied Belgium in 1916 as a CRB delegate. Miller's grandmother, Erica Bunge, was a young Belgian woman who founded and ran a dairy farm during the war that provided milk to the children of Antwerp.

Inspired by his grandparents' stories, Miller collected and cataloged the papers of more than fifty CRB delegates, diplomats, and Belgians. After a decade of research, he wrote two critically acclaimed books on the subject. This book is the culmination and the distillation of his work into a concise history for readers interested in learning more about one of America's finest hours in humanitarian aid. It has become his life's goal to ensure that this little-known story is not forgotten. The men and women who worked so hard and sacrificed so much to help others in need deserve to be remembered.

His previous books include *Stapleton International Airport: The First Fifty Years* (1983); *Facing Your Fifties: A Man's Reference Guide to Mid-Life Health* (coauthor Gordon Ehlers; 2002), a *Publishers Weekly* Best Book of 2002; *Behind the Lines* (2014), a *Kirkus Reviews* Best Book of 2014; and *WWI Crusaders* (2018), a *Kirkus Reviews* Best Book of 2018.

He lives in Denver with his wife, Susan Burdick.